NUF..........

A Biography

Martin Adeney

ROBERT HALE · LONDON

Photoset in North Wales by
Derek Doyle & Associates, Mold, Clwyd.
Printed in Great Britain by
St Edmundsbury Press Ltd, Bury St Edmunds, Suffolk.
Bound by WBC Bookbinders Ltd, Bridgend, Mid-Glamorgan.

Contents

Illustrations

Between pages 128 and 129

PICTURE CREDITS

Nuffield College Archive: 1–3, 7–8, 12, 14. Centre for Oxfordshire Studies: 4. British Motor Industry Heritage/Rover Group: 5–6, 9, 13. *London Evening Standard*: 10. *Punch* magazine: 11. Nuffield Foundation: 15.

For Marius,
the businessman.

Introduction

There can be few people in Great Britain who do not stumble across the name of Nuffield at some time in their lives. Whether it is as part of a medical institution, an educational scheme or Nuffield College or the Nuffield Foundation itself, the name remains all pervasive.

But fewer and fewer can relate the name to the source whence it came – the self-made motor magnate who dominated public perception of modern British industry between the wars and who was largely responsible for enabling a British owned motor industry to survive at least until his successors threw it away. His original surname of Morris is now best-known in the context of a cult car still to be seen on the streets nearly fifty years after it was first designed – and which ironically he himself did not much like. For Nuffield like Rockefeller it is what he did with his money, not how he made it, which is remembered.

This book is an attempt to explain the man behind the name and to seek lessons his experience may still hold both for business and that difficult and poorly understood interface between business, society and politics.

But William Morris, Viscount Nuffield, has been dead for more than a quarter of a century; the industry he helped found is now largely in foreign hands; the value of the benefactions he made, though great at the time, has now been exceeded by other self-made men; his achievement in founding an Oxford college to bear his name is no longer unusual.

So why write about him now?

The answer falls into two parts. Firstly, Nuffield was a pioneer and what he did still has lessons for today. Secondly, a detailed 'warts and all' biography of Nuffield has not been available. The standard biography, Andrews and Brunner's *The Life of Lord Nuffield*, was commissioned quite deliberately to reconcile

Nuffield to the college he had founded. It was aptly reviewed by Guy Ramsey in the *Daily Telegraph* at the time as 'an official biography cast in officialese'. *The Times* called it 'more the story of the Nuffield Organisation and Lord Nuffield's benefactions than a personal biography.' The last major book on him, Richard Overy's brisk business biography, was published in 1976. It took the view that the shortage of primary sources meant 'there can be no definitive biography of Nuffield.'

That may be true, but there is certainly scope for a fuller study of Nuffield that does not simply concentrate on his business activity. And there is challenge too; Nuffield was a great man for trying to tell his story his own way and censor other people's versions. As he grew older so he embroidered more and the story changed. In his lifetime he tried to dictate to his friends as he did to his suppliers, warning them against talking to would-be biographers without his authorization and sometimes threatening legal actions against publication. He liked the bold sweeping statement that was often at odds with the facts. So the challenge is to strip away the layers of varnish applied as carefully as those on the veteran cars whom Nuffield's new techniques put out of business in the quest to discover the authentic Morris beneath.

And there is more evidence available since Overy wrote. I am most grateful to Dr Michael Brock and Sir David Cox, past and present wardens of Nuffield College for permission to consult and quote from the archive of Lord Nuffield's personal papers at the college, and also to see some of the papers of Sir Norman Chester who spent many hours in his ultimately successful attempt to reconcile Nuffield to the college he had founded. Chester's book on social studies at Oxford has cast further light while other published accounts include details of Nuffield's role in the founding of St Peter's College, and of his support of Sir Oswald Mosley when he first broke with the Labour Party. There is also illuminating work on industrial relations at Cowley by R.C. Whiting particularly in *The View from Cowley*.

Last but not least, this has been effectively the last possible moment to measure the written evidence against the judgement of those who knew Nuffield at anything like his prime. I was greatly assisted and charmed by the opportunity to discuss Nuffield frankly with one of his very few close friends Sir Robert Macintosh, who died in 1989. Sir Robert also supplied me with papers about his long controversy with the university about proper accommodation for the Department of Anaesthesia in which he was Nuffield's champion.

I have also benefited enormously from the very generous assistance of Mrs Dorothy Silberston who over the years has conducted a wide range of interviews with those who knew and worked with and for Nuffield. Mrs Silberston, who for a decade looked after Nuffield's old house, Nuffield Place, as keeper, is one of those who has done most to keep his memory green. So too have the members of the Friends of Nuffield Place who are dedicated to the preservation of his house in its original condition, under the benevolent ownership of the college. Mrs Silberston allowed me the use of the extensive material she had collected and provided very helpful guidance on sources.

But why bother to make the effort? The reason, I think, is that the Nuffield experience still has relevance. In some ways the Nuffield Story fits more easily into an American context than a British one. British industry, and British society for that matter, needs evidence and explanation of industrial success and the means by which it is achieved.

The relationship between business and Government; both industrialists' view of Government and politicians' view of industrialists is a source of much day-to-day comment but little analysis. Yet one has only to watch the short-lived progress of a string of industrial favourites through the doors of 10 Downing Street, under a succession of different administrations, to see the fascination and misunderstanding on both sides of the equation. In the event I am not sure how much the Nuffield experience tells us about that, except to urge caution and reinforce the view that the qualities for success in each discipline do not translate straightforwardly to the other; that time-scales are very different but that both sides depend on the other's performance more than they admit.

Lastly, perhaps the uneasy or downright suspicious relationship not just between business and academia but even more so between business and the intellectual establishment (the 'chattering classes' in a current phrase), is illuminated by the Nuffield experience. I am tempted to say that nothing has changed. The two seem to sit as uneasily together as they ever did; the divide curiously magnified by the increasing need for academic institutions and the arts to look for business sponsorship. Work for the BBC as I once did and broadcast about industry; that is acceptable. Work for industry and encourage it to explain itself, as I have done since; that is greeted with reserve sometimes bordering on the contemptuous.

So much for motivation. What of method?

The biggest problem in writing about someone at the end of their life is that your witnesses' views are coloured by their experience of the mature and elderly person. This is especially the case when writing of someone like Nuffield some time after their death when few who remember him at all are still alive. Almost by definition the man they knew was the man past his prime.

So when Sir Raymond Streat had lunch with the aging Nuffield at the college in 1957 he recorded, 'he really is the dumbest, dullest great man of all the dumb great men I have ever encountered.' Nuffield, if you please, was eighty at the time.

Miles Thomas, later Lord Thomas of Remenham, who worked with Nuffield from 1924 to 1947 was in some ways the person who knew him best. He neatly pointed up the contrast when he came to review the Andrews-Brunner biography. A dispassionate and objective study it might be but there was a lack of 'appreciation for the burning enthusiasm which made the young lad Morris outshine his contemporaries at skill in brazing metal' and 'whether it presents a living portrait of one of the most dynamic and colourful personalities of modern times, many who know Lord Nuffield will beg leave to doubt.'

Nuffield's desire for self-justification unfortunately encouraged him to try to disguise the memory of that enthusiastic young man in his various guises – the aggressive heckler at political meetings, the gambler, the hard drinker, the fast-moving entrepreneur always looking for new opportunities and putting sometimes ruthless pressure on his suppliers. It was a pity because it is both a more interesting and a more genuine story than the portrait of a peer of the realm, laden with honours and gravitas, which the self-conscious collection of Nuffield Place evokes.

Nuffield Place, his home from 1932, open to the public on weekend days during the summer, still has some clues to the enthusiastic Morris. There is the wide wrought iron gate once worked by remote control pads which were always having to be adjusted and there is the work cupboard built into his bedroom. There an apparently ordinary wardrobe opens to reveal a work-bench with vices and assorted tools. What is most striking is its small scale; it is not equipped for grand constructions, it is for small operations, primarily for repair. Nobody of the frequent visitors to the house remembers anything being made there; it was a place for tinkering, for setting to rights, for repairing clocks in particular. As Margaret Hawes, the wife of Lady Nuffield's nephew remembers, 'He used to do a lot of little jobs. He used to love it if anyone broke anything because my aunt used to say, "Your uncle will mend that" ... any china or things like that he was ambidextrous, very skilled with his hands.'

Nuffield was not a great original. He was a mechanic more than an engineer. Yet the rigorous development of the techniques of modern mass production and a grasp of what the ordinary motorist wanted taught his contemporaries and competitors an instructive lesson. It secured him a fortune, which he then made the seedcorn to shape initiatives and innovation in a bewildering range of activities. It was an achievement unmatched by his British contemporaries and by few since.

When a man changes his name part way through his life it presents a problem for a biographer about what to call him. Particularly when he has a claim to fame in both guises. No solution is perfect; I have chosen to refer to Lord Nuffield throughout by his original name of Morris, both because it was the name he used for most of his life and because I think it reflects the man better than the later encomia. I hope the usage is clear.

I have also deliberately tried to use as much first-person evidence and quotation as I can. The Nuffield story became so interwoven and reworked with gossip, good stories, hearsay and frank invention that I have endeavoured to source the information as much as possible, and either to steer clear of commonly told stories which I cannot confirm, or when they help to demonstrate an atmosphere, to make clear they are speculative.

The Nuffield papers in the college archive are a very mixed bag. Most of his papers went for salvage during the Second World War. What is left are the papers which came from two suitcases and a deed chest of Lord Nuffield which the archivist described as 'extremely miscellaneous and showing no sign of any original arrangement'. A further box of papers contained many of Lady Nuffield's papers and some of these came from Nuffield Place. Further material including the important personal and business cash books and various trust deeds were later deposited by Miss Ena Berry, Lord Nuffield's former secretary who was working for his private secretary, Carl Kingerlee.

The result is a strange collection which ranges from ephemera including prescriptions, visiting cards, skimpy notebooks from his early years, various personal letters, royal acknowledgements and invitations, to outline projects for wartime activities and immediate post-war operations in Australia. Amongst the most important items are detailed costings for various Cowley models during the First World War, the cash books and a typed biographical memoir of 129 pages with extensive pencil corrections and additions.

I refer to this as the 'biographical memoir' as opposed to the 'official biography', by which I mean the Andrews-Brunner published work. The document in the archives appears to be the manuscript to which Andrews and Brunner had access, compiled by Wilfred Hobbs, Nuffield's long-serving and influential private secretary. They say that it 'embodied his memories of the many conversations in which Lord Nuffield and he had reviewed the early days, together with Mr Hobbs's account of more recent history.' Its footprints are very visible throughout the Andrews-Brunner work. The extensive alterations, although not in Nuffield's hand, clearly reflect his own views and versions, and make it clear that it is his authorized view of events. I have used it, with care and critically, as such.

The best and most privileged witness to the second half of Nuffield's life is Miles Thomas, a journalist who joined him in the early twenties, became his Vice-Chairman in 1940 and remained a friend until the end. His wife, as Hylda Church, had been Nuffield's secretary after the First World War, and remained very close to Nuffield. Thomas tells a very good story. Unfortunately, shortly before he died, he went up to his room one afternoon and burnt all his papers. However, he left extensive reminiscences of Nuffield, in three principal forms; his own autobiography, *Out on a Wing*, published in 1964, his Nuffield Memorial Lecture for the Institution of Production Engineers in the same year, and a considerable number of newspaper articles and broadcast interviews subsequently. Although he occasionally contradicts himself, he is a generally reliable and uniquely informed source with a lively turn of phrase. I make no apology for using him extensively. I am also grateful for the assistance of his daughter, Dr Sheila von Bergen.

Compiling this account has led me into a variety of strange byways and I owe thanks to those who helped guide me through. I owe special thanks to Miss Christine Kennedy, the librarian of Nuffield College and Mrs Eleanor Vallis who looks after the Nuffield archive there for their guidance and patience. I am indebted to Malcolm Graham at the Centre for Oxfordshire Studies for assisting me with the variety of tapes and written material on the life of Nuffield which are lodged there, and to Christopher Leftley, the RAC librarian for permission to consult its collection and for seeking out further material for me.

I am grateful to friends and acquaintances of Lord Nuffield who found time to see me, and particularly to members of his family who retraced what were sometimes painful memories for my benefit.

My thanks too to the trustees of the Nuffield Foundation and its director, Robert Hazell, for support which made publication possible.

I am grateful to the BBC for permission to quote from a number of interviews, particularly those contained in the radio programme 'The Guv'nor', broadcast on 30 December 1955, and to Penguin Books for permission to quote from Miles Thomas's autobiography, *Out on a Wing*, originally published by Michael Joseph.

Above all, my family and particularly my wife, Ann, are owed my thanks for their forebearance in the months it took to write this manuscript during which a number of other responsibilities went by the board.

Finally a conceit. After living with the shade of Nuffield for so long I paid a last visit to Nuffield Place. As I left, my car, made abroad, temporarily failed to start. Was it, I wondered, the last tugging of the old patriot, who at the end of his years could still berate a BBC crew for arriving at Cowley in vehicles manufactured in Germany. Then another thought took its place. Could I but put the clock back to the times when he still lived in the house, as his friends had told me, I would not have had to worry. In a moment Milord's coat would have been off, the bonnet up, and I would soon have been on my way. Fortunately the car, containing some British components from firms he encouraged, started without him.

1 Early Years

At the very end of his life, Lord Nuffield complained to a visitor how much for the worse the world had changed in the past half century. When his caller ventured to suggest that he had himself been something to do with the change, Lord Nuffield agreed, adding however, that he had tried to do good with the money he had made.[1]

So throughout the progress of William Richard Morris, from the small boy on his grandfather's farm to the widely lauded Viscount Nuffield of Nuffield, Britain's most generous benefactor and its answer to Henry Ford, a question recurs. How much was he simply a child of his times; how much did he help to form them?

The answer is particularly difficult to unravel because his life reflected such huge social changes. When he was born, Britain was still a markedly agricultural country, but the huge flow from the countryside into the town (which his own factories would do much to encourage) was once more accelerating.

Morris himself was to be a creature of the process, just as surely as any of the agricultural workers he was to transform into car workers on assembly lines – words which were not yet in familiar usage – when he was born in Worcester on 10 October 1877.

It was a time hovering on the brink of momentous changes in lifestyles. Seven years before, the reforming Liberal Government had laid the foundations for modernizing Britain, universal education being one of its key measures. In nine years' time, in 1886, the German inventors, Daimler and Benz, each independently at opposite ends of the Neckar valley in Southern Germany would produce the world's first motor cars. The first cycle clubs were already forming, though for the next decade they would race cumbersome penny-farthings on roads which in England were worse than they had been earlier in the century – in the days before the triumph of the railways had relegated them to

17

increasing disuse and multiplying potholes.

In later years, Morris went to some pains, if not to rewrite history, then at least to put it in the most flattering light for himself and also for his father, Frederick Morris. His relations with his father were difficult. He ended by employing the older Morris himself, a situation fraught with contradictions, and the old man was clearly less than satisfactory to his son, though he was protective of him. His strong bond was with his mother. As Lord Nuffield Morris spent thousands of pounds to establish his family tree, tracing his ancestry back to a yeoman farmer in the thirteenth century in Oxfordshire, and he fiercely resisted attempts by would-be biographers to portray him as poor boy made good.

One replied in despairing self-justification, 'the fact of your mother's father sending all his girls to Miss Beaufoy's establishment for young ladies in Oxford is most valuable in ridiculing the "poor boy" bits.'[2] It was a measure of Morris's sensitivity about his beginnings.

In practice, the Morris background was no different from many of those who came from the villages and small towns around Oxford to work in his plants. The researches into his yeoman stock were mostly unspecific about what sort of farmworkers or farmers they were. His father's father had addresses at different times on High Street and Corn Street, Witney, the main streets of the town. His father, Frederick Morris, born at Witney in 1849, seems to have been quite a rolling stone, a description Nuffield himself applied to him in a frank moment.[3]

But the way he was described in later years by his son and by those who with his son's blessing wrote about him, tell us more about Nuffield's wish to be seen to have come from a respectable or middle-class background than about a colourful and enterprising man.

In later years the trowel was laid on thick. In 1937, Nuffield gave an interview which appeared in the *Sunday Express* on Boxing Day headed; 'My true story as told to Basil Cardew'.

Nuffield, it said, had spoken freely to stop misplaced 'human' stuff about him and to refute gross inaccuracies recently published about his early life.

In the safe in his office … lies the truth, the family tree I have been permitted to photograph … it shows that the first Baron Nuffield is not one of a line of nondescript working class people ... [he] is the last of a line of Oxfordshire gentry whose ancestry goes back seven centuries ... not a quarter of one percent of the population could trace their ancestry back this far.

It was, the article claimed, 'a grand contradictory broadside to the pious tales of "Bill Morris" rising from the gutter from unknown stock.'

It then described Frederick Morris.

A man of public school education, a stern disciplinarian, a kind father. Frederick Morris was a great accountant, had a financial brain ... the perfect business balance for the engineering genius of his son. [He] could write wonderful copper plate. His character was like that in effect, polished.

Nuffield's filial devotion or perhaps his need to make excuses for his father, led to further superlatives. Frederick was an expert horseman, and had a brave and romantic reason for crossing the Atlantic where he sought his fortune in Canada. At Hurst's Grammar School in Cowley, then just outside Oxford, in a building which would later become his son's first factory, he watched a master regularly, and, he believed, unjustly punishing another pupil. Finally he got up from his seat and knocked the master down. His parents then agreed that he should go to Canada.

But other members of the family knew a rather different story. Whether or not the school incident occurred, Frederick Morris and his brother were packed off to North America because their father, a widower, wished to marry again. His new wife, a lawyer's widow with children of her own, wanted the boys out of the way. In North America, the two boys went their separate ways; Frederick becoming a mail coach driver in Canada between Winnipeg and Toronto and then living with a Red Indian tribe for a time, before returning to England to find his father dead and his property in the hands of his stepmother.[4]

The Red Indian story was played down by his son in later years as the picture of the polished public school accounting genius grew, but in his brasher earlier years, Lord Nuffield made more of it. In 1928 he told one H. Massac Buist, who wrote a series of articles on 'W.R. Morris. The Man and the Romance' for *Autocar*, that after keeping his stagecoach job for eighteen months 'eventually he dropped off with the Indians' with whom Nuffield claimed he became an honorary chief and lived for ten years.

Then with a candour that was to be noticeably lacking in later years, Nuffield said, 'Although he was to me one of the best and most generous of men, by nature my father was a rolling stone. On this account, it was not surprising that when the time came for me to leave school, he had not gathered enough moss to do anything for me, and so I had to shift for myself.'[5]

Frederick Morris had left England when he was about seventeen. When he was twenty-seven, he married Emily Ann Pether whose father Richard, whose name he would give his son, farmed at Wood Farm at Headington, then on the outskirts of Oxford. From the dates it is clear he was in Canada a good deal less than ten years; perhaps much less. But his travels were not over. He moved to the Midlands from one job to another, managing a draper's shop and possibly a small brewery. It was in Worcester that his first child, William Richard, was born on 10 October 1877. He was to be the first of seven, but only two sisters lived to reach adulthood.

Three years after William was born, Frederick was on the move again. In Nuffield's bald account, he moved back to Wood Farm to take over as bailiff because his father-in-law's eyesight was failing. The family story is once again a good deal more interesting.[6]

Frederick Morris had taken a trip to London. While there he met with an accident, perhaps on the underground, and apparently lost his memory. His family in Worcester heard nothing, and after some weeks, the Pethers took their daughter and her family back to Wood Farm. Eventually Frederick returned home to find his family gone. He was then found the post of bailiff for his father-in-law until a dozen or so years later he had to give it up because of asthma.

The story begs many questions. Was it true? What was Frederick actually doing in London? It is clear that Frederick Morris was an erratic character, and much of the strength in the family, which was passed on to his children came from their mother, Emily. She lived on until 1934 always refusing to move out of her modest terrace house, in spite of her son's great wealth and his frequent offers to move her. It was to her more than his father that Morris looked and she who suggested the occupations the children should follow.

They were uncertain days and anxieties about money were a

part of them. They help to explain some of Nuffield's later extreme carefulness and his frequently penny-pinching concern to save money.

The Pether farm was at Headington Quarry, now in the outskirts of Oxford, but then separated from the comparatively small university town. It was here and in the neighbouring villages of Cowley that the young William Morris grew up, attending the village school, and occupying himself by fishing, rambling, and later cycling through the countryside.

There were two separate Cowley villages, Church Cowley and Temple Cowley, with the small hamlet of Hockmoor sandwiched between. They were largely rural with market gardens also growing food for Oxford, but one industrial employer, the Oxford Steam Plow company, which was established in Church Cowley, where William Morris went to school.

Morris stayed at school until he was over fifteen, at that period an unusually long time for someone with few academic pretensions. He only left when his father's health forced him to give up his bailiff's post.

He told few stories later of his schooldays and anyone who subsequently claimed to have known 'Bill Morris' at school was rapidly dismissed on the basis that he had never been known as 'Bill'.

Indeed, in the authorized biographical note in the Nuffield archive, almost the only reference to his schooldays is his dislike of being called Bill.

> This reminiscence, although quoted so often is entirely untrue, and he has always found justification in being intensely suspicious of those who claim past friendship with the words 'I well remember you in the days when you were Bill Morris'. Actually he was always known as William or Will, and his dislike of the abbreviation was only exceeded by a particular objection to being called Dick. In his schooldays any mention of the accepted shortening of his never used second Christian name could be depended upon to result in immediate and violent pugilistic protest.[7]

It was a convenient way of dismissing many who would claim acquaintance and there were plenty of impostors who did so. But there is some evidence that Morris, in the same way that he improved other parts of his story later, used the device to distance himself from his early acquaintances. Certainly it is true that the old friends he valued were those who had been with him in the early years of his business and had shown loyalty to him, and not his earlier friends. There are a number of witnesses who have insisted that he was known to some at least as Bill.

One of those who always claimed to have been an early friend and felt, with his wife, that Morris had to an extent cut deliberately away from his origins was Sidney Smith, whose descendants still live in Cowley. His son, Reg Smith, recalled him telling him how

> one day in the early 1890s, my father was attempting to build a greenhouse at his father's market garden in Temple Road when his closest friend, William Morris came along with an old bicycle.
>
> He asked my father to come and teach him to ride the bike. They went along to Garsington Road, then a rough road with high hedges and a wide grass verge on either side, and William soon mastered the machine.[8]

The year by Morris's reckoning was 1891. He was fourteen years old. The bicycle was a borrowed penny-farthing. It was a moment of great significance which was to shape Morris's life but for the time being it seemed just a part of adolescent progression, and an exciting experience being shared by thousands as the cycling craze began. Morris soon had his own bicycle, and together with Smith set out on increasingly ambitious cycling journeys.

Once they rode to London and left their bicycles with a shopkeeper on Oxford Street – but were unable to remember exactly where and had to get a policeman's help to find them.

On another occasion, in company with one Bill Simmonds, whose sister both men were to court, they set out to ride the dozen or so miles to Witney. Later Sidney Smith loved to tell the tale, as his son remembered:

> The other two knew that Billy Morris had no money so when approaching a tollbridge, they went on ahead. 'The chap behind will pay,' they shouted to the tollkeeper. When Billy Morris could not pay, the tollkeeper let the gate go. It hit Billy's back wheel, and he and his bicycle finished in a heap on the grass verge.

Smith told his family Morris was known for not carrying money.

Morris's enthusiasm for cycling had begun, an enthusiasm which was being shared by tens of thousands of others.

2   Cycle Maker

By the time William Morris and Sidney Smith were struggling to mount their first penny-farthings in the leafy lanes of Cowley, the bicycle in some form or other had been around for half a century. In about 1840, a Scottish blacksmith called Kirkpatrick Macmillan had produced an early example in Dumfriesshire. It was not until the 1860s however that anything like factory production started, and even then it was in France, where Pierre Michaux and his son Ernest converted a hobby-horse by the addition of pedals. By the mid sixties they were turning out about 400 a year in their workshop near Verdun.

It was from France that one Rowley Turner, whole uncle Josiah ran the Coventry Sewing Machine Company, brought back an example of the new velocipede in 1868. Trade in Coventry was depressed with both the ribbon and the watchmaking industries in difficulty, and the elder Turner was persuaded to make bicycles based on the French designs. He exported a batch to France, as well as selling in England, and when the Franco-Prussian War interrupted French production, business improved still further for what was now renamed the Coventry Machinists Company.

Coventry's light engineering skills were a fertile ground for the new industry. By 1879, there were about sixty firms making bicycles, most of them in Coventry and nearby Birmingham. But they were mostly small operations; in 1881 it is estimated that only 700 people were employed in the two cities in the trade.[1]

Running parallel with the growth in manufacture was the blossoming of cycling clubs for enthusiasts. In 1870 the Pickwick Cycling Club was formed and 1878 saw the start of both the Bicycle Touring Club and the Bicycle Union which would later become the National Cycling Union. By 1880, there were estimated to be about 230 clubs, but they were largely for the fit and athletic; it was no accident that one of the biggest was to be found among the young men of Cambridge where 280 had joined. It required physical agility to mount and control penny-farthing machines of assorted shapes and sizes with solid tyres, let alone to ride them any distance on the appalling roads of the time.

Bicycling was most decidedly an activity for sportsmen but one of the first targets for the new clubs was to lobby for improvement of the roads.

A textbook for riders written in 1874 set out details of various routes. Liverpool to Prescot was good but then, jumping somewhat, 'within six miles of Newcastle under Lyme a very bad bit, full of holes ... after leaving Lichfield a very trying road, short lengths being good and bad alternately ... from Mansfield to Doncaster ... very rutty and uneven. Tadcaster to York is quite impassable.'[2]

But by the end of the eighties, major developments began to put cycling within reach of all and led to boom time for manufacturers. The technical breakthroughs were the invention by James Starley, once a foreman at the Coventry Sewing Machine Company, of the safety bicycle with both wheels the same size and the sort of diamond shaped frame which would be recognizable today, plus the advent of the pneumatic tyre. This was patented in one version by Dunlop in 1888 and in another by Michelin four years later.

This, coupled with some improvement in roads and fuelled by rising affluence, brought an explosion of popularity for cycling and a huge expansion of the industry. With not a single motor car on the roads of Britain and the Red Flag Act which restricted cars not to be repealed until 1896, cycling became the modern craze as well as a highly convenient mode of urban transport.

The result was that by 1891 there were estimated to be 8,300 people directly employed in the cycle making industry; by 1896 some put the figure as high as 30,000.[3] This was the peak of the boom, the year when it was reported that agents hurried from factory to factory with cash in hand, pleased if they could secure even a couple of makes. Nor was it simply whole bicycles which were sought after; a huge business grew up supplying parts from which even smaller and more local makers could construct machines.

Companies like Chater-Lea, Abington and above all the Birmingham Small Arms Company (BSA) supplied hundreds of kits. In 1896 BSA was selling 2,000 a week; in 1899 it referred in its trade catalogue to 'numerous complaints from purchasers of machines' who had ordered fittings but received either incomplete or imitation sets. It listed what it provided – a bottom bracket, a head, two fork ends with parallel chain adjustment, a seat lug, two hubs and two pedals.[4]

One of the early motoring characters, Monty Tombs, described the 1890s like this;

> If you wanted to get from the outskirts of a town to the centre, then you either walked several miles there and back or to the nearest horsedrawn tram route or you hailed a horse-drawn cab or hansom. The safety bicycle was emerging from the penny farthing. Incidentally safety bikes were not by any means mass produced by big firms but the parts were made by Charter Lea or BSA and your local bike builder brazed the whole thing up to your taste at an overall price of about five pounds.[5]

At about the same time Rudge was selling a machine for £24 which it reduced to £13 in the face of competition from imported American cycles. When Raleigh produced one which sold at £10 in 1900 it was seen as bringing the bicycle in reach of the working classes.

From this ferment sprang some of the first names of the British motor industry as their experience in the cycle industry and the opportunities for greater profits in the latest emergent industry drew them. Morris was to be among them but not yet. But this time Starley, styled 'the father of the cycle industry', had formed his Rover company; Hillman and Singer having worked for him had founded their own firms, while Humber and Sunbeam were already household names.

The young William Morris was an eager participant in the cycling mania of the times. After learning to ride the penny-farthing he had managed to buy a second-hand cross-framed safety bicycle with solid tyres. It was not the most modern machine and he spent hours taking it to pieces to make improvements. Later he would claim that this was where his engineering ability first began to show.

So when in 1893 at the height of the bicycle boom Morris's father became unfit to work because of his asthma, the cycle industry seemed a sensible place for fifteen-and-a-half year old William to start work. It was an industry much in demand with a beckoning future and he had shown some aptitude. It is not clear whose idea it was but it seems certain that his mother had a major say. According to her granddaughter, Mrs Rawlence, 'She had this idea that all her children should have a trade.'

Morris had some reputation as a handyman; his sister remembered him constructing a model bicycle and making her a penknife out of discarded pieces of other knives. So Morris was apprenticed to a cycle agent called Parker in St Giles, in the centre of Oxford, where he was under a foreman called Dupper. His pay was five shillings a week and Morris began to learn his trade. There were hundreds like him and there was no indication that he was to be in any way remarkable.

But he was a determined character, prepared to trade punches at school if he thought he was being made fun of and quick to spot the opportunities in the fast-growing industry. After nine months he asked for a rise of a shilling a week and when it was refused he left to start on his own.

According to one account years after the event, he chose the worst possible moment to make his request – in the middle of a family row at his employer's home. Morris would insist later that regardless of what had happened, he had been determined to make his own way.

> My so-called apprenticeship was a complete myth because I was never taught to do anything. And for that reason in nine months I said to my employer, 'I wish to give you a week's notice and from then onwards I will pay my own wages.' At that time I was earning five shillings a week and I had asked for a rise to six shillings and he said I wasn't worth it and that's the reason I gave him notice. When I arrived home, my father called me the biggest fool he could possibly think of; but it wasn't so many years afterwards that he changed his mind.[6]

Morris established a repair shop at his parents' house. He used the garden shed as a workshop and when he progressed to finished machines he exhibited them in the window of a front room. A carpenter who lived opposite painted a sign which was placed in the front garden.

Soon after he had started, Morris had a lucky break. An Oxford vicar, the Revd Francis Pilcher of St Clements, was passing and noticed the new sign. He had met the boy before and asked if he could build him a bicycle. Morris quickly agreed even though the parson was six feet three inches tall. It needed a huge frame of twenty-nine inches but Morris successfully completed it and it served as a useful advertisement for the new business.

Morris continued to maintain it for years. An entry in his notebook for 1905, a dozen years later, records what was obviously a major overhaul: *'Rev Pilcher. Gear 85. 65. Bars raised. Frame 26. Cranks 7½. Brakes coaster and front. Bell challis. Tyres 1½. Saddle Brooks.'*[7] Years later, his fortune made, the bicycle turned up in a jumble sale and Morris took the opportunity of buying it back and keeping it next to his office at Cowley.

His own version was that he had been 'so surprised, I hardly knew what to say, but anyway I said, "Yes Sir I will build you a bicycle" '.[8]

According to Miles Thomas, Morris then had difficulty in finding the money to buy the parts. He asked an uncle who lived at Headington who refused the four pounds he wanted and borrowed instead from a Mrs Higgs who lived nearby and had saved the money for winter fuel.[9] To show his appreciation he had his shirts made by her daughter in later life. Morris hated to be called lucky, always insisting that he had worked hard and made his own luck. He did acknowledge however that it had been a lucky beginning. Yet the fact is that he was almost bound to make a success given the booming market even though there was a growing number of cycle makers in the city. Kelly's directory for Oxford for 1895–6 lists twelve; by the time Morris was listed in 1896–7, he was one of sixteen 'Cyclemakers and agents'.

The cycle-dealers sold machines made by the well-known makers as well as making their own from the kits supplied by BSA and others, as we have seen. But it was not simply a matter of fitting pieces together; brazing of the tubes was, for example, one skill required. Here Morris prided himself on his expertise and when a crucial slide on the only linotype machine possessed by the local weekly newspaper, the *Oxford Times* cracked and no spares were available, he presented himself to the office and offered to repair it. He had the greatest difficulty in persuading the foreman to take him seriously; beside the fact that cast iron was not thought suitable for brazing. The young Morris's persistence prevailed however and he was allowed to take the part back to his workshop. After four hours he returned with the job complete; he charged twelve shillings and sixpence and was delighted to find the machine still in use until 1937 when it was finally scrapped.

Morris had most of his parts supplied from Birmingham. On occasions he himself would cycle the 120 or so miles there and back in a day to collect parts and then work late into the night to complete the job; an almost unbelievable schedule. He also put his cycling to other business use; by taking up racing, he advertised his machines as well as his own sporting ability.

Throughout his life he was immensely proud of his cycle racing achievements and a case containing his medals was one of the features most prominently on display to visitors to his office at Cowley. There was no false modesty about it. The biographical note prepared with his blessing stated, 'Any detailed account of his cycle racing career would be tedious as it would largely be a repetitive record of ... unbroken success.'[10] It was a lesser Morris exaggeration.

Morris took up competitive cycling in 1894 at the age of seventeen. He claimed that he always raced his own make, although there is a suggestion that he started on an Osmond which was a type stocked by his old employer, Mr Parker. If so, it was not for long. Morris prided himself that one of his machines weighed only sixteen and a quarter pounds and was 'possibly the lightest in the world at the time'.[11]

A newspaper cutting in the Nuffield archive records Morris's arrival on the racing scene at the annual races of the Oxonian Bicycle and Tricycle Club held at the Iffley Road Running Ground. Dancing followed and the grounds were 'beautifully illuminated with Chinese lanterns and nightlights'. The Hungarian Band, it was noted, 'played a capital selection of music during the races'. In the One Mile Championship of Oxford for the Swinhoe Cup, 'the great attraction', Morris, won his heat 'by four lengths, looking round', to reach the final where he met the holder, one A.H. Beesley:

As the latter had only to win the cup this time to make the trophy his own, considerable interest was taken in the result. All the men were together at the sound of the bell but on entering the straight Morris and Beesley came away, the race ultimately going to the former by a few inches.[12]

The seventeen-year-old also announced his arrival by coming second in the half-mile handicap but Beesley got his revenge in the one mile handicap: '[he] got among his men at the last lap and won as he liked.'

Morris was equally successful at both long and short distances. He enjoyed breaking into sudden sprints in his longer races and burning off his competitors. It was, he claimed with satisfaction, an unorthodox style; a delight in doing things in his own idiosyncratic and unexpected way stayed with him for the rest of his life.

There is a striking picture of him taken at the time showing a powerful rider in black singlet and skull cap. It owes something however to art; apparently showing him powering down the track, it was in fact posed stationary with someone holding him upright who was subsequently painted out.

Morris won about a hundred championships over the next few years. In 1897 at the championship held by the Berks, Oxon and South Bucks Centre, he told a fellow competitor that he did not expect to do much because he had just had all his teeth out.[13] He was predictably unplaced, but the incident and the pain and suffering it had caused him led later to his pioneering decision to endow the first chair of anaesthesia in Britain, at Oxford.

His most successful year was in 1900 when he won seven championships in what he intended to be his final season. Some of the cycling enthusiasm was beginning to wane. Entries were down; in Oxford the East Oxford and the Oxonian Club were both wound up. Nationally the boom in cycle sales and manufacture was over; Morris himself was beginning to turn his attention to motor-powered machines.

The reports of that year's Berks, Oxon and South Bucks Centre Championships at Reading paid tribute to his success in winning both the one mile (by four yards) and the ten mile (by a bare half yard). In both cases he defeated an Oxford University student.

As the local press recorded:

Morris has had a remarkable season. He has won the whole of the championships promoted by the local centre, and a large number of other events including the One Mile Championship of Oxford, the Mile Championship of the Oxonian B and T.C. as well as winning the fifty mile race open to Oxfordshire and setting up first figures for the one hour unpaced ride ... Morris has stamped himself as one of the finest riders ever produced in Oxford, and there is no doubt that if he would stick to it he would be in the same class as Chim, Palmer, etc in a very short time.[14]

But it was time for more attention to be spent on the growing business, and the increasing hold on Morris's imagination which the rapidly growing and developing motor industry was beginning to exercise.

The Red Flag Act which had effectively stunted the growth of a British motor industry by insisting that a man with a red flag should walk in front of every horseless carriage had been repealed towards the end of 1896. This was a signal for every frustrated inventor to try his hand and for a series of speculators who had made fortunes out of the cycle boom to get in on elaborate schemes to corner the market in the new industry. It was a highly erratic start and some of the machines in whose production the public was led to invest were little more than imaginary. But there was no doubt about the enthusiasm of the public or of the engineers anxious to catch up on the ten year start which the Germans and the French had enjoyed.

Morris at nineteen was not yet of this number, probably fortunately for his long term success. He was still a small cycle assembler and only gradually learning the requisite engineering skills. He would always say proudly that he had never had an engineering lesson in his life while acknowledging that he lacked the inventiveness and engineering understanding of an Austin or a Lanchester, both of whom were now building their own original cars. But Morris was also learning something even more important for his eventual success; the careful control of cost which, in their enthusiasm, managed to escape most of the early car makers.

The excitement of the new motor age swept Morris up with it. Throughout his life he was a barometer of popular moods. Among his papers was found a copy of the first edition of the *Daily Mail* which was published for the first time on 4 May 1896, announcing its intention of 'issuing all the news of the penny press for a half-penny'.

Its front page provided a bridge between the waxing and waning enthusiasms. Amongst the advertisements was one from the king of the speculators, Ernest T. Hooley, advertising the opportunity to buy into his latest ramp, the Cycle Manufacturers Tube Company, a £250,000 company formed to manufacture the weldless steel tubes which were a key component of the modern bicycle and for which he claimed to have orders for millions of feet from 'important' cycle manufacturers. The coming age was foreshadowed in the paper's editorial columns; these echoed the soon to be successful campaign of Mr Hooley's close associate, Harry J. Lawson, to have the Red Flag Act repealed.

> Britannia's task of ruling the seas has left her a little careless of the rule of the road as applied to horseless vehicles ... the law of the red flag is exquisite nonsense as it operates for the regulation of motor carriages ... and has had the effect of making England lag far behind continental countries in the latest development of road traffics ... we have but six manufacturers of motorcars on this side of the channel when in France they are already reckoned by the hundred ... The motor car will never displace the smart trotting pony or the high stepping team but it will end the cruel labours of the poor equine drudges that strain before omnibuses and drays and save the broken-down favourite of the Turf from the bondage of the nocturnal cab.[15]

In 1900, Morris was in no position to make a motor car himself, or even to own one. But his business was expanding. In 1896 he had started to rent a shop in the very centre of Oxford at 48 High Street, an area thronged with undergraduates. His workshop at home had become too small; it was expand or turn work away. It was, said Morris, the first of many occasions when he was faced with the same choice; his decision, he claimed, never varied.[16] Still, it was a big step; one account says he was unable to find the full rent and used two of his new bicycles to pay for the deal. But it was a great success; the business expanded, Morris rented a workshop for repairs in nearby Queens Lane (which later was renamed Longwall Street), and amongst the jobs he secured was the contract to service the bicycles for the postmen employed at the Oxford Post Office.

A charming glimpse of Morris's relations with his customers comes in a letter to a young woman called Maude Marillier for whom Morris offered to build a bicycle in 1899. It seems that he may have hoped for rather more as he offered her a special price and Miss Marillier kept his letters as well as those from the man she subsequently married; they were sent in when the *Oxford Mail* held a competition for the best memories of Lord Nuffield on the centenary of his birth.

Written on paper with the original heading – 'From W.R. Morris, cycle maker, 16 James Street, Oxford; Repairs of all kinds on the shortest notice. Lamps, bells, bags, pumps, spanners, oilers, toe-clips and other accessories at moderate prices.

Enamelling and plating a speciality.' – it set out terms in a pleasant copper plate.

> *Madam.*
> *I have thoroughly examined your cycle and find that the tyres are in very bad condition and the machine requires a thorough overhauling generally, and the utmost I can allow you in part exchange is £4.15.0 which I think is a very fair price for it, but if you think you could do better by selling it yourself, I would much rather you did so – Trusting to receive your further orders.*
>   *Yours faithfully*
> *P.S. The machine I offer to build you will be equally as good as Miss Brock's*

A second letter, also dated 27 March, set out the price of a new bicycle.

> *Herewith I beg to quote you price for a 'Morris' Cycle built to following specifications for the sum of £12.10.0. net cash – I trust to be favoured with your esteemed order.*
> *A Lady's 'Morris' cycle fitted with Clipper tyres and rims – Tangent spokes – Leather Gear Case, Transparent front – Press Guard, Brake and Mudguards, fitted with 'First Grade' fittings throughout, and guaranteed for Two Years.*

Written up the side of the page was 'Please treat this quotation as strictly private as its much below my usual price'. A final letter dated at the end of May is a receipt for the new machine with the old one in part exchange.[17]

Altogether however, the last year of the old century was not a romantic success for Morris. An old girlfriend, Alice Simmonds, who apparently felt she was being taken too much for granted, preferred to marry Morris's old friend Sidney Smith instead. They had been a bit of a threesome, wandering through the Cowley meadows on Sunday afternoons when Alice had time off from her job as a lady's maid, with Morris often bringing a bag of love-heart sweets. The others would later delight in telling their children how they would give him the slip after the sweets were exhausted.[18]

Morris's ineffective romantic approaches contrasted with the vigorous muscularity of his cycling and working life which were to impress almost all who came in contact with him. After his triumphs on the cycle track in 1900 he was to have one more unlooked for moment of glory when he was suddenly challenged three years later to defend the cups he had won in the Oxfordshire championships for the one and fifty miles. The rule was that whoever won three years running could keep the trophy. As Morris had won in the previous years and the club was being wound up, he had not unreasonably clung onto the trophies.

Suddenly he was challenged by those seeking to establish a new club either to defend the trophies or to hand them back. It was the kind of challenge that the combative Morris refused to pass up even though he had not trained for two years; a sharp indication of the kind of man he was becoming.

In his own words; 'They had no claim on those cups for the reason they did not belong to them, but I wouldn't have it said that I had not won them. Anyway I did not answer the challenge. They only gave me fourteen days' notice, after being two years without riding, but to their great surprise I turned up.'[19]

The local paper recorded:

> He was more than a match for his rivals proving himself by far the best man in the district. He won the one mile championship with little effort ... Wenborne was runner-up, the rest of the field being many yards behind. Six faced the starter for the fifty miles championship and very early in the race Morris with H. Galpin in close attendance began lapping the others. When 11 miles had been completed Galpin retired from the race. The next man was Wenborne, about a mile in arrear and on his giving up a hopeless task after riding pluckily for sixteen miles, Morris was called off by the officials and proclaimed the winner.[20]

So unexpected had been the challenge that Morris no longer had a racing cycle of his own make on which to compete; instead, to his chagrin, he was forced to use one from a large manufacturer, a Rudge Whitworth.

The challenge had been a matter of pride, cycling was no longer central to the business. Soon after he had taken over the Longwall workshop, Morris took the major step of extending its use to cover the garaging and repair of cars. It was a good time for it; in 1904 there are estimated to have been only 8,465 motor cars on the roads of Britain; by 1910 the figure had gone up by more than six times. Once again, Morris was reflecting the popular movement, effectively reading the trends.

Morris was to claim later that he had purposely allowed the cycle business to dwindle and die but in reality it seems to have been a gradual process; he could not afford to. He was so short of capital that he had to take a partner when he made his first sortie into the motor business. There was no question of attempting to build a car; he had nothing like the resources. It had to be the motor cycle.

Here Morris had a headstart. According to Miles Thomas, the Morris bicycles had always had a reputation for solidity and had been particularly strongly made. They were a good test-bed for him to mount an engine and begin his motor manufacturing. His first design, registered on 4 March 1902, shows little more than an engine fixed to a bicycle frame and the completed machines exhibited at the Stanley Show in London later that year fit the same description.

For his first machine, he constructed his own engine, a single cyclinder 1¾ horsepower version which he machined from bought-in castings, and gave him, he said, most of the knowledge he needed about motor cycle engines. He formed a partnership with another Oxford cycle maker, one Joseph Cooper, to make motor cycles, but now took the commercial decision to buy in engines which were made by the prominent French firm of de Dion which supplied many of the early British manufacturers.

Morris, who seems to have used Cooper mainly for financial support, worked all hours of day and night to complete the machines for the Stanley Show which was the great showcase for the industry. Parts arrived late and for the four days before the show he went almost without sleep to complete the job. The day before the exhibition was due to open, he loaded two machines onto the train to London, accompanied them to Paddington station and made sure they were packed for transportation to Islington where the show was to be held. There was a deadline of 10 p.m. to be met.

Morris took the Underground and fell fast asleep. It was not until hours later that an alert porter shook him awake to ask him how many more times he would go round the circle. He completed his journey, standing to keep awake, and managed to get his cycles onto the stand with five minutes to spare. He never tired of telling the story.

The exhibition was a success. The design of the motor bicycles with an innovative countershaft chaindrive and three speeds with a clutch was admired. But the partnership with Cooper did not last. Encouraged by the reception at the show, Morris was anxious to order three more engines to build three more machines. Cooper, more cautious, wanted to buy the engines one by one. It was the climax of disagreements which had continued throughout their association. Morris saw his partner as the essence of caution and himself as a man who did not hesitate to take some risk. They dissolved the partnership but remained friends. Morris however, found himself once more without the extra capital he wanted.

Then began probably the most unhappy period of his career, scarring him for life and gouging deep the conviction that in business he must go it alone without trusting anyone else to take charge. The singlemindedness he developed carried him through the difficult days in the founding of his business; ultimately it helped to destroy the empire through its founder's reluctance to trust anyone else with it.

The Morris motor cycle had been a success but Morris was still short of capital for its production. At the same time others in Oxford were becoming aware of the business potential of the new industry and also of Morris's specialised knowledge of it. In 1903 an undergraduate at Christ Church, who had been left money, decided to invest in the motor trade. He approached an Oxford businessman, F.G. Barton, to see if he would join him. Barton advised him to bring in Morris because of his engineering skill.

A partnership was formed with its headquarters at Barton's showrooms at 16 George Street, Oxford, and subsidiary showrooms in his shops at Bicester and Abingdon. Barton became general manager; Morris was works manager, apparently giving up his own Oxford premises, while the undergraduate was supposedly a sleeping partner. In practice he bought a Serpollet steam car which he ran flamboyantly round the city earning the nickname of the 'Easter Egg' and spent a great deal of the partnership's money on his interpretation of salesmanship – entertainment for other undergraduates. It would be difficult to imagine a greater contrast with the style of Morris's previous business activity.

For a while, Morris was absorbed with the development of his motor cycle. He had patented the carburettor design and developed an early device for operating the clutch by cable from the handlebars. The 1904 catalogue of the Oxford Automobile and Cycle Agency contained testimonials for the Morris motor cycle which it advertised as usable in all weathers 'as side-slip is impossible'. One described it as 'a perfect revelation ... taking a really stiff hill on thick mud with the throttle half open' while another claimed to have ridden 3,800 miles with only one stop of over five minutes, punctures apart.

But within months the business was starting to go downhill. Morris prided himself on his head for drink, but unlike Barton, he rejected the undergraduate's approaches to join in entertaining the customers, preferring to concentrate on production. Except for one occasion that is, when he made a point of drinking his partners under the table.

In the smug prose of the biographical guide prepared with his approval, 'He purposely took an opportunity of demonstrating to his associates that their powers of absorption ... were not only far less than those of which he was capable when he chose, but totally inadequate to the type of life they were leading.'[21]

It would not be the last time that Morris used his strong constitution to put down a business associate but it had little practical effect. In the year after it had started, the business collapsed. Morris was left with less than nothing. His own version was that he had only his tools, some which he had constructed himself, and his share of the debts which came to £50. Miles Thomas told a more poignant version which we may presume he had at some time from Morris himself. That was that as the effects of the business were sold off, Morris had to stand in the rain to bid for his own tools.[22]

It was a dreadful moment made even more humiliating by the fact that 1904 was the year in which he got married. On 9 April he wed Elizabeth Maud Anstey, whom family friends were to know as Lilian. The new Mrs Morris was the daughter of a farrier who had left his wife and family to go and live in Leeds where he had a post with the university. His daughters worked to support themselves; the oldest and the youngest both became teachers; Elizabeth worked in the celebrated Oxford department store of Ellistons as a dressmaker; in the 1980s there were still people who could recall having their school uniforms made by Miss Anstey.

The two had met through cycling. All three of the Miss Ansteys had joined a cycling club where Morris was also a member and two of the three were to meet their husbands there. It was a touring club more sedate than the fierce racing in which Morris had been previously engaged and the members went on lengthy rides together. Elizabeth Anstey was a strong, tall, young woman and a useful partner to the athletic Morris on a tandem. Members of the club thought little of long trips even though the roads were still often in poor condition. Some would go as far as Brighton, over 100 miles away for the weekend. William Morris and Miss Anstey did better; they would sometimes go over the Welsh mountains and back to Aberystwyth for their weekends.

So in one respect Morris had found a partner with common interest and experience; in another too. Both came from somewhat similar backgrounds and both had had the same wrenching experience of having to support the family in their teens because of the inadequacies of their fathers. Morris had been fifteen when his father had become unable to work; Elizabeth Anstey's father had left the family when she was sixteen. It was an experience that those who knew her said had always marked her and when her life with Morris started as his business collapsed, it reinforced a belief in the fundamental uncertainty of life which helps to explain the reputation she later had of extreme carefulness with money which tipped over into meanness.

Her nephew's wife, Margaret Hawes, a close friend of hers in the last years of her life, says, 'She was always frightened it would happen again.'

The new Mrs Morris was to stay very much in the background of her husband's increasingly successful and public life. She was a quiet person, sometimes painfully shy, who would be perhaps happiest in her garden. Her husband was protective towards her. In the authorized Nuffield biography, she has a chapter to herself. It rates less than a single page. During their lives Nuffield declined to allow her to be interviewed. There were no children and Miles Thomas, one of a handful who knew them well, described them as not having a very happy home life.[23]

But Morris never forgot the way she supported him at the moment when his business was in ruins. It was said that she sold all her jewellery except her wedding ring to help keep them afloat. He told Dr Christopher Chavasse, the Bishop of Rochester who had pressed him successfully for funds for St Peter's Hall in Oxford, that 'nobody could have been a better wife to him when they were living in a small house and he was fighting for his life to build his business'.[24]

3   The First Car

The collapse of the Oxford Automobile and Cycle Agency had wiped out almost everything that Morris had built up over the thirteen years since his father's illness had caused him to leave school and set out to try to support his family. But he retained both the goodwill of his customers and suppliers and the reputation which had caused Barton to seek his partnership in the first place; that of the best technical man in Oxford.

So as he struggled to rebuild his business, he did not need the charity of a Pilcher; he was able to borrow money from suppliers to supplement a small bank loan to restart operations. He once more returned to the Longwall Street workshops and rented his old showrooms at 48 High Street.

He began again with a new determination and two resolutions; that he would put all his money into production, not promotion (which was simply a restatement of his practice anyway), and that he would never again entrust his business future to a partnership with anyone else. If from time to time he borrowed money it was on the basis that the lender had no say in the conduct of business; if that was attempted the Morris answer was to end the arrangement and return the money.

It is impossible to say how much the legendary care with which Morris calculated his profit margins owed to the shock of the collapse of the Automobile and Cycle Agency and how much his careful ways were already in evidence. But there can be little doubt that the episode reinforced the almost obsessive concern to count the pennies – a character trait of both Mr and Mrs William Morris.

It was fortunate for Morris that the collapse occurred when he was still part of a small enterprise. 1904 was a year of some of the grandest gestures in the emerging British motor industry. It was the year in which Henry Royce was building his first car, machining his parts to a standard of precision which would become a legend. It was also the year in which plans were laid for a factory for the Argyll motor company at Alexandria on the northern slopes of the Clyde which was intended to employ over 2,000 men to produce as many cars a year. The cost approached a quarter of a million pounds, an astonishing sum for those days, and the works was to boast golden domes, marble floors and 500 wash basins for the workers with clean towels provided.

It was in striking contrast to the old wooden shed shared with a potato merchant to which Morris now moved back in Longwall Street. But four years later Argyll was bankrupt and by 1914 Morris's first model was being made in almost as large numbers as those being assembled beneath Argyll's golden domes, so rapid had been the change in the Morris fortunes.

It is a suitable moment, as the twenty-seven year old Morris set out to re-establish himself in an enterprise which within eight years would allow him, as he claimed, to have retired and lived in comfort for the rest of his life, to draw together a picture of the man.

Lithe, well-muscled, of medium height, with fine brown hair on which he prided himself and which he would exercise his scalp to keep in good condition, the young Morris impressed those who met him with his nervous restless energy. Frank Lanchester, who knew him through the motor business, described him as 'agile, mentally very quick, dark in complexion and of distinctly athletic build'.[2] He spoke with a pronounced Oxfordshire burr which he retained all his life.

Pictures of him at this time show him almost always with a cigarette in his hand. He remained a heavy smoker. In Morris factories, unlike those of his rival Austin, smoking was permitted.

His work dominated, and he was proud of it. He always hated to be called lucky. 'When I look back on my early business career and think of the hundreds of times I have worked through a day and night and on through the next day, perhaps foolishly without sleep … the results can hardly be called luck.'[3]

His few diaries and notebooks of the time tell little. They are largely blank but have occasional lists of jobs to be done; some domestic, mostly work. They show him as meticulous but no great writer. It was the figures which mattered.

Outside business he seems to have had few special interests, though there were some of the enthusiasms of an Edwardian young man of no special pretensions. He retained a great liking for the cockney music hall singer Albert Chevalier (not to be confused with his French namesake), who offered songs like 'Boiled Beef and Carrots' and 'Any old Iron'. Morris had a party trick of dressing up in a flat cap and muffler to perform as Chevalier. Late in life he even bought Chevalier's own costume. He also knew many of the Gilbert and Sullivan comic opera songs by heart.

There exists in the Nuffield College Archive an old cricket scorecard for the match between Oxford University and the University Authentics on 7, 8 and 9 May 1906. It is a single piece of card of the type which had pre-printed advertisements on one side with details of the match on the other side in a form which could be updated on a simple printing machine at the cricket ground. Amongst the advertisements is one for '*W.R. Morris. Motor and Cycle Engineer. Showroom 48 High St. Cycle Store, Queens Lane, "Morris" Motor Garage 100 Holywell St. Oxford.*' Across it, written in capital letters in the pencil which Morris favoured for all his notes is doodled 'ROTTEN PLACE' in self-deprecating humour. The other side has details of the university's second innings added in pencil.[4] It conjures up a picture of Morris for once at rest, watching the game at the university ground in the Parks. He enjoyed playing football and cricket and later occasionally took part in works teams.

Morris had some trouble with his eyes at about this time. An appointment card which he retained records an appointment at the Oxford Eye Hospital on 28 September 1905, and his notebook at the time listed a 9.30 appointment.[5] Morris does not appear to have had eye troubles for most of his life and this may have been some acute incident, perhaps associated with machining metal. He was however, a notorious hypochondriac. He still retained a prescription from about this time, and until his old office at the Morris garage was finally cleared for demolition an ancient bottle of medicine still sat on the desk.

It is a striking fact that Morris seems to have retained no close friends from this time, either from his old Cowley acquaintances or from Oxford itself. The people he would value were those who had worked with him in the early days though they were never close friends but mostly favoured employees, prized for their loyalty, something by which Morris set enormous store.

One of these was Alfred Keen, one of three non-family members to have special bequests made to them in the Nuffield

will. Keen, who joined Morris first in 1903 at the age of fourteen
had had plans to be apprenticed in Reading, but it would have
meant a payment of £10 in order to be taken on. Instead an uncle
in the Oxford police force who lived in James Street suggested he
work for Morris who paid him two shillings and sixpence a week.

Keen described what he found when he started work at
Longwall doing cycle work. He was mainly taught by Morris
himself and there was only one other person working there. It was
a long wooden shed. 'We had one or two odd cars about, a 3½
horsepower Berzy and others. They used to come to Longwall and
were stored there. We used to use the downstairs and upstairs was
the workshop ... the left-hand side was used by a fruiterer as a
warehouse.'[6] The rest of the staff consisted of a man and a boy
who looked after undergraduates' bicycles in Queen's Lane and
Frederick Morris whom William had now employed to look after
the High Street showroom and to keep the books.

George Tobin who joined as a driver in 1906 when Morris
branched out into car hire (which in those days meant car and
driver) said, 'We called him among ourselves "Uncle". We didn't
call him that to his face. He worked there just the same with his old
blue smock on. Just a mechanic like ourselves and there was no
question of any position like he got now because he really was an
honest to goodness workman and he was a clever mechanic,
there's no question about it.'[8]

Robert Giles who was employed from an orphanage to look
after the undergraduate bicycles and later left because he could
make more money as a gas company labourer remembered the
way Morris always wore a cap.' We boys were sure he slept in it.'[9]
Early pictures of him do indeed almost always show him in a cap,
but then there was a significant change, as Giles noted. 'Later he
discarded the cap for a felt hat. I recall asking him if he had lost it.
"No", he said, "I have come up in the world." It puzzled me but I
never saw the cap again.'

It was still a very tight business. Tobin says, 'The wages were
very small. I got sixpence an hour, twenty-five shillings a week and
uncle was getting something like four pounds ten shillings and his
father certainly couldn't have had more than two pounds ten
shillings a week.'[9] Giles who was taken on later had to work six
and a half days and Morris insisted that he and the other boy
attended Sunday School.

A glimpse of Morris's daily routine is provided by a small

leather-backed notebook in the College archive which he used in 1905 and 1906.[10] It is largely a collection of lists. So Christmas Eve of 1905 finds a lengthy collection of tasks.

Lost ticket GWR
Steam Plow re cups (a reference to the Oxford Steam Plow Company, then the major employer in the Cowley villages)
Isons re tanks (holes for bolts)
Manders re varnish
Hall re photo hub (?)
Vulcaniser tyre repair
Copper tube for Juleton (?) car
Fit carburettor and governor
Look to gears and back axle
Send reps to United Motor Industries
Fit up radiator etc
Look to coil and contact breaker
Re brass edging for car
Go to bank
Boys notice shop
Get socks for Monday

Other references in the book gave the sums spent on the gas account in May (17s 2d), on insurance (10s 5d), and on income tax (8s 9d), and another note '*FM remind me re Pilcher in about 14 days time. Cycle.*' which was a reference to his father.

From the time he restarted his business it was clear that Morris's interest was now with the motor car. Although the cycle business brought in some steady cash and there was continuing business from old customers such as Mr Pilcher (whose bicycle repairs were still figuring in the business accounts for 1906), the interest in it was gone and the cycle boom as such was over.

Keen remembered,

Right in the early days he was always interested in any new car that came along, and he was the first to have a look at it. I can well remember him saying that he would like to substitute a four cylinder engine for the single cylinder engine in the car he was driving because he thought that was the proper thing for a small car even in those days, in 1902.[11]

Morris's motor business now grew rapidly. It was an ideal time. 1904 had seen over 8,000 cars on the road and by 1910 it was over 53,000. It was still primarily a rich man's pastime; the age of the cheap popular car in Britain would have to wait until after the First World War and the flowering of the Morris achievement. Oxford undergraduates were overwhelmingly the children of the better-off and the opportunities for Morris to garage and maintain the new vehicles multiplied.

In 1906 he was admitted as a Freemason which cannot have harmed his business opportunities, and the same year he started a hire car service. Soon he started to run taxis as well, rapidly identifying the new trend. In 1904 only a solitary motor-cab had been licensed to ply on the streets of London. So the 12 horsepower Siddeley-Wolseley employed by Morris in 1907 was one of the first in a provincial city.

In 1908 he formally left the cycle business, selling the enterprise to Mr E. Armistead who took over not just the High Street shop but also the rights to the motor cycle. It was technical difficulties which had partly persuaded him. The accumulator ignition then in general use was unreliable and could not stand up to the inevitably bumpy road conditions, for all the testimonials in the Morris catalogue. It was not until the magneto ignition was developed at about the time Morris sold out that the motor cycle became sufficiently reliable for a big increase in sales. The fact however was that Morris had become absorbed by the motor car and his rapidly growing business with it.

He had already sought more space at Longwall, taking over the yard from the potato merchant, Symonds, but by 1909 the new initiatives had brought in so much extra business that he took the decision to make a major rebuilding on the site. The result was 'The Morris Garage' which was promptly, to his glee, christened 'The Oxford Motor Palace' by a local newspaper.

The motor industry in Britain at this stage was extraordinarily fragmented. Every year a dozen or more brand new manufacturers would start up. They came in all shapes and sizes; offshoots of existing engineering undertakings like Napier or Wolseley, diversified cycle makers like Rover, licensees of foreign companies like Daimler, enthusiastic new inventors like Royce or Austin. One estimate is that by the time the First World War broke out in 1914 almost 400 British motor manufacturers had been founded but for many life had been all too short; something over 100 still remained in existence.[12]

Added to this was a range of imported vehicles which in some years almost equalled the number of home produced cars. Many of them came from France which until overtaken by the United States in 1906 had been the world's largest producer of cars. Similarly parts could come from a range of sources – from the manufacturers themselves, from their suppliers, many of whom were in the Midlands within easy reach of Oxford, or from abroad.

In such uncertain times dealers like Morris had to court manufacturers and take a range of dealerships and in return were sought out. The Morris quiver included the Scottish company Arrol-Johnston, Belsize, the American Hupmobile, as well as the nearer Midland firms of Humber, Singer and Standard, plus a number of motor cycles.

Just how much in demand early cars were can be illustrated by the Morris experience in finding a vehicle for a customer in election time in 1906. The request came from a candidate named Smeaton who had failed to find any car available in Stirlingshire in Scotland where he was standing and was then referred to Morris. Extraordinary as it now seems, Morris was unable to find a car for sale anywhere; instead he suggested that he go to Paris and bring back any suitable car he could get hold of.

Then began an astonishing journey for the young Oxford mechanic, equipped perhaps with the specimen copy of a dictionary of French and English terms from the Hugo Institute which his notebook of the time records. It was a route other British agents in search of cars had taken but there is no evidence of Morris ever having been to France before.

He set off immediately after Christmas 1905. In fact, the list of jobs to be completed in his pocket-book for Christmas Eve reflect not so much the unfinished business to be got out of the way by the Christmas break which would have been short anyway as what needed doing before what would be an extended absence in France. His 'socks for Monday' were to be sorely needed on a French journey in which the temperature throughout remained below freezing.

He arrived in Paris, then the hub of the world's motor manufacture, to find it almost impossible to find a car for sale even though he had cash with him. Eventually he discovered a Lacoste and Batman, a reputable make, handed over his money and paid a mechanic to oil and grease the car.

Throughout his life Morris was to have an unhappy relationship with the French and their motor industry. Now twenty-five miles after he had started on New Year's Day, the gearbox and axle seized up; there was no sign of any lubrication, and the parts were not repairable. He returned to Paris by train to purchase replacements and spent the night fitting them.

The following day he set out for the Channel ports and was still driving at midnight when an exhaust valve broke five miles before he reached Amiens. This was not such a serious matter as it was a frequent occurrence and Morris had brought spares with him. Unfortunately they turned out to be an eighth of an inch too long and he spent the next hour and a half grinding them down to size on the hard pavé road. It was, he reflected ruefully later, a rare circumstance of a French road user being pleased with the surface.[13]

Morris reached Oxford on 5 January and set Keen to drive the car to Scotland. But he was soon on his way to York to hunt for a blacksmith to repair a broken axle bevel. At Berwick the component fractured again and Morris and Keen spent twelve hours working through the night once more to repair it. Finally as it drew into the Smeaton drive the car broke down again, and embarrassingly Mr Smeaton was not far behind in a horse-drawn carriage demanding to know why the vehicle was a week late.

It was two more days before the parts were refitted after being repaired by an Edinburgh blacksmith and Morris was able to take his customer on a trial run around his election meetings. Once more the car seized up; once more Morris and Keen worked through the night to have it ready.

In the morning he offered Smeaton a straight choice; take the car and pay for it or he would take it off and find a buyer himself. It was a seller's market; the deal was closed and Morris was able to persuade himself that the absence of further news about the car was evidence that it thereafter performed satisfactorily.

He had spent almost all his liquid capital on the car and he had made a substantial loss because of the expense of buying spare parts. But he comforted himself with the thought that after such a journey he could be confident that he would always be able to bring any car to the end of any journey he undertook.

It also demonstrated clearly the level of skill and technical know-how which he had now garnered from his daily experience of dealing with the problems of Oxford motor cars. In the course of it he had come to know closely both the manufacturers and suppliers of the infant motor industry. He benefited of course from Oxford's proximity to the Midland towns which were becoming the centre of the new trade, Birmingham and particularly Coventry.

He was in the best possible position to compare their products and design. At the day to day practical level he was sufficiently impressed by the carburettors produced by the Coventry engineering firm of White and Poppe to insist on fitting them to any make of car which had carburettor difficulties. But in the longer term he was already tempted to try his own hand at producing a car, using the experience of ordinary motorists' requirements to construct something which would be generally popular.

Morris's memory was that his closest attention was always for the 'demerits' of cars; the challenge that fascinated was to design a car that would incorporate improvements to overcome what the biographical note called, with an echo of the exasperated mechanic, 'the recurring troubles so disheartening to those whose constant job it was to have them rectified.'[14]

But dramas were one thing and finding the finance was another. Business started to take off in 1910 when sales almost doubled from £8,500 to £16,000 and the profit of £1,500 was almost as much as he had achieved in the previous four years combined. In 1911 they were up by almost half as much again. By this time Morris's mind was made up; he would take the gamble; at the 1910 Motor Show he was already discussing who might supply the necessary components; in the following two years he would spend two or three days a week in Coventry.

John Conybeare was one of the wealthy undergraduates who had their cars garaged by Morris. He remembered finding Morris at work late one night.

> I came into the garage about 11 o'clock and Morris was there; and we got talking and he said 'Come into the office'. And I went in and he had a whole lot of blueprints which I knew nothing about, and it was just on the lines of the standard four cylinder car that was being sold in larger forms. I thought, it's going to be an expensive job to set up all the plant to make a thing of this kind; and I don't know whether I hinted that but ... he told me that he wasn't going to make a single part of it himself ... so it was only going to be a matter of assembly and therefore would need a very small amount of capital.[15]

It was still likely to be more money than Morris had available. In 1910 the business made £1,500 profit before tax – the equivalent of the purchase price of less than a dozen cars. But he gained the support of another former undergraduate who had made his acquaintance through the garage business but in a less friendly way.

This was the Earl of Macclesfield who had come to Morris to threaten proceedings after his car had been in collision with one of the Morris hire cars. Morris greeted him with some amusement, pointing out to him that the hire car had had three chief constables as its passengers and any claim was unlikely to succeed.

It was however the start of an enthusiastic relationship and when in August 1912 W.R.M. Motors was formed to undertake manufacture, Macclesfield took £4,000 of preference shares. The others were held by Morris with a few going briefly to a friend. With the Morris determination to do things his own way and unhappy experience of partnerships, it was inevitable that the relationship would end in tears but it lasted into the 1920s and Morris himself would take part in the cricket or football matches which garage teams, christened by Macclesfield 'The Sparking Plugs', would play at his estate near Oxford.

Morris made two key decisions as he planned his car. The first was to buy in the parts and not manufacture them himself, setting him apart from most British manufacturers of the time. It was a decision in principle; he had learnt from his days as a cycle maker, but economics also forced it upon him. It was, as it happened, exactly the same decision which Henry Ford had made in the United States, again for financial reasons.

It was regarded there as almost standard practice but as the magazine *Automobile Engineer* noted towards the end of 1911 in Britain, 'the manufacturer who buys finished parts and puts them together has been generally regarded rather contemptuously and it is usual to assume that cars made in this way cannot be really good.'[16] His low cost base was to be a key factor in his ability to ride the slump of the early 20s and emerge as the dominant British motor maker.

The second decision was where to pitch the new vehicle. Clearly a car built from other people's components could not give itself any tag of exclusivity. At the other end of the market some thought the future would lie with the so-called cycle-cars, adaptations of motor cycles to capture the market for low-priced transport. Morris would have none of it. He wanted a small car that had a powerful four cylinder engine and many of the characteristics of a larger model but at an affordable price.

'Outstanding reliability with low running expenses' is how the biographical note puts it.[17] In the process he and other manufacturers like Humber who were thinking on similar lines effectively created a new type of car, the light car, which would become the target for the middle classes as their incomes grew.

Just how sharp Morris's instincts were was indicated in 1913 when the oldest motor magazine, *Autocar*, founded seventeen years before to campaign for the repeal of the Red Flag Act, spun off an offshoot called 'The Light Car'.

Its first edition explained that, 'The smaller form of light car has been handicapped by its recent association with the cycle car as the cycle car is more or less in the experimental stage while the light car being in the main a big car in miniature has very little of the experimental element'. It went on, 'The British small car seems to be a separate "creation" of our engineers, where the French light car is more often an adaptation of old notions'. Amongst the vehicles picked out for special mention was the first Morris car.[18]

A dozen or so years later Morris would write;

> In 1911 I became convinced there was going to be a big demand for a popularly priced car. What had happened about bicycles I felt sure would happen with cars ... I became convinced that the best way for the small concern to manufacture was to get specialists on every separate unit of the job. The work is better and more cheaply done while the cost and worry of more plant is avoided. Money is conserved for better use in other directions.[19]

The key component for the new vehicle was, of course, the engine. Here Morris went no further than the firm of White and Poppe whose carburettors had so impressed him.

The company had been established in 1899 by Peter August Poppe, a Norwegian who had started by working on precision navigational instruments and was a friend of the explorer Nansen, and Alfred James White, a Coventry man who had been a director of the Swift company which manufactured bicycles, and later cars.

The new company was set up to make carburettors, engines and other components. The accuracy of their machining and their clever design work had enabled them to use parts which were interchangeable between their products and effectively resulted in the first British challenge to the domination of French engines in the proprietary market.

Morris knew Peter Poppe well and his dealings with the firm became a touchstone for other suppliers. Hans Landstad, another Norwegian, worked on the engine design at White and Poppe. Landstad would become one of the keys to Morris's success. He was a huge bear of a man who had run away to sea and become a ship's engineer. When he joined Morris later he found time to teach young workers to wrestle and box and would take them to sea on his boat. In rough weather he would delight in dangling lumps of bacon in front of the queasy while he roared with laughter.

He recalled;

It was in 1911 that he [Morris] came up and told us what he wanted. And that's when I started laying out various diagrams for the new engine. And in 1912 Morris started coming regularly up to us; some time it might be seven o'clock in the morning or ten o'clock at night, but of course he had also to go round firms in Birmingham. Then the manufacturers in Birmingham phoned through to us and said a man from Cowley had been writing them that he wanted to place an order for axles, various things. Was he safe because they couldn't imagine cars being manufactured in Oxford? And he had told them White and Poppe had accepted the order. Was it safe for them to do it?[20]

The firm which telephoned was almost certainly E.C. Wrigley of Soho in Birmingham who supplied Morris with axles. As for wheels, Morris was a pioneer, being the first car maker to use the newly patented process developed by the works manager of the Shropshire firm of Joseph Sankey. The wheels, in the familiar spoked artillery pattern, were made in two halves and welded together. Here Morris showed he was more than a collector of proven good ideas; he would back innovation that satisfied his technical judgement. And he wanted to be involved in the process.

When Buist wrote his articles for *Autocar* in 1928 he noted how in most components Morris had ordered for the first car, he had wanted alterations from standard.

I have talked over these beginnings with more than one of those with whom he dealt. All agree on one point. They never knew anybody who wanted so many alterations and yet they had to recognise the fact that each detail was dictated as the result of a practical user's and repairer's experience.[21]

Morris's diary for 1912 records some of his visits; an eleven shilling and sixpenny ticket from Birmingham on 19 March; White and Poppe drawings at Coventry on 15 July as well as jottings about the prices of components. A set of Powell and Hanmer lights were priced at £3 and 15 shillings with headlamps; two side lamps and a tail light on their own, apparently an option, came to twenty-eight shillings and sixpence. His first engine order was to be for 300 engines at a cost of £45 each. '£13,500.10 percent. £1,350 deposit for 300 engines.'[22]

In among the calculations he reminded himself to get some eye lotion; he was having trouble again, perhaps through overconcentration.

As the parts started to arrive, Tobin remembered;

The hours he put into that car, well nobody knows. I think he must have dreamt that car nearly but we all admired him. It was no good our saying we were tired. We never wanted to in those days ... the men worked for the love of the thing.[23]

Keen recalled the afternoon the first engine arrived from Coventry.

We worked through the night to put it together. In the morning it was ready, the Guv'nor had just had a short trial trip up the road and he said 'Now we'll put it down and we'll test it on Monday.'[24]

The excitement spread round Cowley. Mrs Elizabeth Tossel lived near Morris and used to keep Alfred Keen's wife company in the evening while he worked with Morris.

It was about one in the morning. I said I really must go but they came in and said 'Don't go for a moment. We want to show you something'. They took us out in the shed and said 'What do you think this is we have been working on every night, it is our first engine.' Of course we were very thrilled.

When they tested it, she remembered, 'they used to keep coming up and down on the thing for days and days ... have you seen children playing on a piece of board with four wheels; that's all it looked like.'[25]

Tobin was struck by the reaction of Frederick Morris.

When it came back it was passed as OK and his father was

very thrilled – there was nobody in the world like his son – his father comes running round and I remember the words to me 'I knew Willie could do it.' He always called him Willie. In his own family; not generally to us. But he did that day. He said 'I knew Willie could do it', and Willie did it.[26]

In fact the car was late. White and Poppe were behind with the engine, apparently because one of the extra draughtsmen they had employed had drawn a component to the wrong scale. Morris had planned to have the car ready for the Motor Show but had to attend the show with no more than the blueprints. The first pictures of the car were taken using a block of wood for the engine and a broomstick handle for the steering wheel. It was a bitter disappointment but such was the Morris reputation or powers of persuasion that he managed to secure an order for 400 cars from Gordon Stewart, a London car dealer who founded the firm of Stewart and Ardern and became Morris's first distributor. Crucially he also paid a deposit.

Morris's premises were quite inadequate for the construction of cars and so he looked for larger ones. He settled on the old Military Training College in Cowley which had been empty for twenty-one years and was available for a cheap rent. There was also a sentimental connection; part of it had been the old Hurst's Grammar School where his father had been educated.

Gordon Stewart came down to collect the first production car himself. But his triumphant send-off came to a grinding halt after only a few hundred yards when the universal joint broke. A new one was fitted but the car broke down again at High Wycombe, halfway back to London, when the replacement disintegrated as well. Behind the disappointment had been a disagreement between Morris and Poppe. The engine maker had insisted that the joint be made from cast iron because of its good wearing qualities. Morris had wanted phosphor bronze with apparently some support from Landstad but Poppe had remained adamant.

Now Morris lost his temper. He telephoned White and Poppe to demand, 'Are you all mad you Coventry engineers?'[27] Landstad was at the other end of the line.

I had of course to do what Poppe wanted. And we had some trouble with it because Poppe was very pig-headed – that universal joint, that was a great fiasco. Poppe wouldn't give in and he made it out of cast iron … And Morris phoned me up and I felt just as I would when I was a boy and had a birch rod ... Oh he gave me hell. I couldn't get a word in myself so I just had to take it.[27]

After that the joint was made from bronze although Poppe still argued that it was the quality of the steel which had been the problem. The early cars also found the clutch stuck when cold and a modified design was fitted free to customers while the car's steering was improved by slightly widening the track.

The car rapidly established itself. The pages of *Autocar* were soon full of the praise of satisfied owners. Looking back in 1919 it wrote,

Very few cars find a way straight to the heart of the motor user with the speed and completeness that attended the start of the original Morris Oxford ... cars ... The specification of the new car sounded well but the performance and quality of the vehicle itself were more than up to expectations. In fact there is little exaggeration in saying that the adequacy with which the car supplied a want, only half appreciated at the time, exercised a considerable influence on the creation of the modern light car market.[28]

Motorists liked the car for the performance of the engine, for its reliability, and for some of the features which Morris had adopted from cars for which he was agent. Its gearbox design owed something to the Belsize cars and from the American Hupmobile he took the idea of enclosing the transmission to protect it from mud and spray; something which few British cars at that time had adopted. Morris had not set out to produce the cheapest car. His aim was set out in a description in the 1914 catalogue of 'distinctive features'. 'To the purchaser of a small car who is most frequently his own driver the ability to start at any time at a moment's notice, simplicity of control when driving and absolute freedom from trouble are of the first importance.'

It was an aim which coincided with a shift in the market. The early British car makers had predominantly catered for the wealthy who would have chauffeurs or mechanics on hand. Now increasingly it was the middle classes who were seeing the possibilities of motor travel. Their standby had rapidly come to be the car produced for their counterparts in the United States, the utilitarian but utterly reliable Model T Ford.

The first Model Ts had been imported into Britain in 1909 and in 1911 the assembly of Fords from imported parts was started at Trafford Park in Manchester. By 1913 they were selling 3,000 a year more than any British manufacturer; in 1914 6,000 were sold, more than double the output of the largest home-grown producer, Wolseley. It was a basic car. It had no doors and was famously available only in the single colour, black. But it was dependable, simple to repair and its slow-revving American engine gave it plenty of power, which helped its reputation for coping with the difficult conditions experienced by farmers, armies or ordinary citizens on the poor road surfaces which still obtained.

Morris could not approach the low price its long production runs allowed; his first Oxford sold for £180; in the same year a Model T was being advertised at £135, and it had four seats as against the Oxford which *Autocar* described as a 'two seater torpedo'. Instead Morris had to rely on what came to be a particularly English preference, a range of extra features which made even small car drivers feel as if they were being looked after as well as those who could afford the luxury models. He was to be helped too by the new horsepower tax which penalised the larger engined cars and by the Oxford's fuel economy. But it was clear he would soon need a bigger car.

Morris's growing success was making him something of a figure in Oxford. In 1913 he forced himself onto the attention of the city in an episode which illustrated the dynamism and pent-up energy which seemed to burst out of him in his middle years. It was his first excursion into politics, if on a small scale, and demonstrated the style which would characterize much of his political dealing, a determination to act quickly and a singlemindedness which was blind to the difficulties and often to any other point of view. In enterprises in which he was involved Morris was not to be a cooperator; he would insist on running things his way or not at all.

At issue was Oxford's public transport. For the past decade, the city had been arguing about the introduction of an electric tram service to replace its long obsolete horse trams. In spite of negotiations with various companies, by 1913 nothing had happened and a new argument, that the tram wires and standards would be an unsightly intrusion into the mediaeval university city, was growing in force. Still the ancient horse trams clopped on. Then in November 1913 Morris and a group of supporters applied to the council for a licence to operate motor buses. They had been running on the streets of London for a dozen years already.

The council temporized and when Morris had heard nothing for three weeks he announced that he would put buses on the road within two weeks, setting up a company for the purpose. It would have been illegal to ply for hire without a licence but he took legal advice from a resourceful young lawyer called Frank Grey and procured six buses of the type used in London plus experienced drivers from the Daimler company.

With a flair for the dramatic, the buses were driven down from Coventry in the dark, garaged overnight and only in the morning did they become visible, waiting outside the horse tram depots.

Morris got round the law by selling no tickets on the buses. Instead coupons were available from shops at a price of a penny for each of six stages between Cowley, the station and the Parks. A notice on the coupon announced, 'Coupons cannot under any circumstances be obtained in the buses. W.R. Morris. Manager'.

The effect was explosive. The horse trams were emptied and as the city council pondered what to do, Oxford filled with letters to the newspapers and packed public meetings. Morris wrote to the *Oxford Times* that interested parties were circulating statements that he was acting in the interests of a big firm in London. 'My sole object is to provide the public with an up to date service for which they have vainly been asking for years.' He proposed to buy more buses and issue shares to Oxford people only. He offered to pay the council the same rent as the company which ran the horse bus service. Again it refused a licence.

On 30 December he made a rare entry into the generally blank pages of his dairy. 'Bus meeting Town Hall. About three thousand present, 3,000 for. One against.' On 6 January: 'Tradesmen's dinner to meet at George St re buses.' By then he was on the brink of victory. On 7 January the council capitulated. It had attempted to outflank Morris by allowing the horse bus company to operate its own Tilling-Stevens buses but it did little to reduce the trade for the Morris operation. Now it allowed both parties to operate. On 7 January Morris recorded in equally laconic style, 'Council Meeting. 12 licences to each'.

He was in reality greatly relieved. Money was still tight and his profit for 1913, though his largest so far, only came to £5,400. He confided later that if the confrontation had continued much longer, he would have run out of money. As it was, he rapidly arranged to sell his licences and hardware to the horse bus company. His diary entry for Saturday 24 January records, 'Bus licences. Contract signed and deposit paid to Grey'.

Grey, like Lord Macclesfield, was one of those to whom Morris had cause to be grateful but with whom Morris, after a long period of amity (in Grey's case even canvassing for him in the khaki election of 1919) would quarrel violently with and thenceforth never acknowledge again. But now he looked for his help and support on a new project.

Morris was relieved to conclude the bus controversy not just for financial reasons but because his brain was engrossed with the problems of expansion of his business. He was endlessly thinking of ways to improve his cars and to expand the range. Three days after settling the licences, he was noting, 'Poppe Play in cars at speed, roller too near centre'. But when he started to cost the ideas he was forming for a four seater car, he did not like what he saw. He would have difficulty in competing on price with American cars of similar specification.

His response was decisive. He would go to America himself and see how it was done. It was a bold step but Morris may have been less sure of himself than he seems subsequently. Certainly he asked Grey to go with him, as Grey would remind him at a bitter public meeting nearly ten years later, in 1923. 'When he was not so confident in his success as he is now ... he had a great belief in me because I had got him safely through the bus controversy.'[29]

Morris travelled to Liverpool and boarded a Cunard liner for the United States. In typical style, he kept a careful note of every penny he spent but managed to leave the ship richer than when he had embarked. His neatly pencilled notes record that on 15 February, a Sunday, he had cash in hand of £4-6-9 and £250 pounds in some form of notes. On 17 February he spent 3d on a paper and three shillings and fourpence on two lots of drinks. But by the end of the day he had amassed £264-3-2 as a result of what are referred to as 'Winnings £10'.[30]

It is a suspiciously round figure. It may have been a prize for a shipboard competition such as guessing the distance the ship had travelled in the day. But a more tempting explanation can be found in the 1928 *Autocar* articles. They tell a story, obviously related by Morris himself;

On a voyage to America some cardsharpers were always after him; but he told them the fact that he did not play.

Eventually they became so insistent that he offered to toss sovereigns with them for two hours. When this began everyone gathered round. After about one and a half hours. Morris was £150 out but at the end of the two hours he was £2 to the good and the sharper was in a perspiration. The fellow never worried him for the rest of the voyage. Nor thereafter did any of his fraternity, the pests of the Atlantic.[31]

It was the kind of story about himself Morris liked; taking on the self-confident and beating them at their own game. But it shows him once again prepared to take risks but only in a form in which he could have some influence on the outcome.

Winnings do not appear again in the diaries but a picture of Morris's life on board does. There is five shillings for an orchestra concert, numerous bills for drinks and wine and a tip for the tea steward and also for the staff of the engine room which the motor manufacturer inevitably went to inspect. In the United States, Morris would do some sight-seeing; a trip to the top of the Woolworth skyscraper, then the highest in the world, commemorated by a souvenir ticket, but his destination was the emerging motor capital of Detroit.

A clutch of business cards still kept together in a wallet record a wide range of contacts together with pencilled instructions about where to dismount from trams. There were bankers and a couple of journalists as well as a catholic selection of manufacturers, the Detroit Pressed Steel Company, Timken Detroit Axle, Zenith Carburettors, the National Spoke and Nipple Company, and fourteen others.[32]

The most significant card is that of Harry J. Warner, second Vice-President of the Continental Motor Manufacturing Corporation. Morris would say later that the American suppliers whom he had met had been unwilling to sell to him because of another English manufacturer who had been there shortly before and had let them down. Be that as it may, he returned with specifications for a Continental engine, and a price which at about £18 was less than half what he had paid White and Poppe for his original Oxford engines.

Poppe was not long left in ignorance. On his return Morris showed him the specifications and invited him to tender a price. In discussions with Landstad it became clear that the firm could do no better than £50 an engine and Landstad suggested that he should take leave of absence and spend six months working in the United

States to study the methods in use. Morris was quickly brought into the discussions and enthusiastically agreed. On 18 April Morris was once more on board a Cunarder, in the first class of the fastest of them all, the *Mauretania*, then current holder of the Blue Riband for the fastest crossing of the Atlantic. In the second class was Landstad, paying his own way and carrying with him, at Morris's suggestion, his drawing board.

Morris was soon down in Landstad's cabin as the two men set about the design of a new car which would rely heavily on the American parts that Morris had inspected on his previous visit to Detroit. Unfortunately for Landstad the *Mauretania* at full throttle was not a comfortable seaboat and the combination of rough weather and a cabin full of the smoke from Morris's chain smoking was too much even for him. The designing had to be left to Detroit where the two men shared a room in a much less pricey hotel than the Pontchartrain where Morris had put up before. Here, as the room filled up with sample parts, Landstad balanced his board first on the bed and then on some boxes he had acquired. Morris continued to smoke until they could scarcely see across the room.

The result would be the Morris Cowley. Its engines were to be supplied by the Continental company for a price that turned out to be even lower than first quoted – less than £18, and for good measure Morris also ordered axle, gearbox, steering gear and carburettor from the United States. Landstad went to work for Continental and also found ways to inspect the works of other major manufacturers including Ford.

It was an astonishing outcome. Here was the Oxfordshire garage owner, in many ways an archetypal little-Englander Edwardian patriot leading a British challenge to Henry Ford and crossing the Atlantic to find the weapons to do so in the American's own back yard. Ford would be challenged by a car which was half American.

It was a mark not just of the shrewdness of Morris but his willingness to back his own informed hunch against what had been the received wisdom. American parts and machines were well-known in Britain; many of those which had equipped the opulent Argyll works had come from Cincinatti, but British car makers, priding themselves on their craftsmanship and attention to detail, were apt to dismiss American worksmanship as rough and ready.

The success of Ford however was making them reconsider. Another dissenting voice was the correspondent of the *Automobile*

Engineer. He wrote from the USA in 1912 that the engine and transmission of the cheap American car were deliberately heavy and large and 'it was intended to keep the engine so inefficient that it can never overload itself or any portions of the vehicle.'

It was not by accident that the Cowley's engine was always thought to have plenty of power to spare. It was roughly half as big again as the engines fitted in British light cars.

The American manufacturers also had the benefit of the economies of long production runs. Since overtaking French production in 1906 the volume of vehicles pouring onto American roads had grown by leaps and bounds. In 1911 White and Poppe in Coventry, one of the most successful English engine makers, had produced less than 1,000 engines; by 1915 the Continental Motor Company in Detroit was turning out 46,000 in a year. Poppe's chances of competing on price, even given much cheaper transport costs and the famed advantages of his company's interchangeability, were negligible.

The result was that Morris left Detroit after placing an initial order for 1,500 engines. He left Landstad behind to supervise the first production numbers. It had been a successful visit and he had been amused and cheered by a visit to Niagara Falls where he and Landstad had tried a fortune-telling machine. 'Act on your first impression,' it said. 'It is always right.'

This time he had chosen to return by Canadian Pacific steamer, the *Empress of Ireland*. But a delayed train caused him to miss the sailing. It was a stroke of the luck Morris was always reluctant to acknowledge. In the early hours of 19 May as the liner steamed slowly down the St Lawrence river in thick fog she was rammed amidships by a Norwegian collier.

It was the worst disaster since the *Titanic*. She sank quickly taking with her 840 of the 1,050 passengers, most of whom had been asleep below decks. Had he caught the ship, Morris would almost certainly have been among them.

News of the disaster shocked Landstad. The name Morris did not appear on any list of survivors. It was some time before Morris, who had switched his journey to New York to return on the Cunard Line, heard of the disaster and was in touch.

Back in England he prepared for the building of the new car and the increasing sales of the Oxford, now further improved and a de luxe version with a wider track available. In 1913, Morris had produced 393 cars and his pre-tax profit had more than trebled to

£5,400.[33] In the first four months of 1914 he had already surpassed his production for the whole of the previous year. By the end of July the works had built 763 cars, figures which were only exceeded by the likes of Ford, Wolseley, Rover and Singer.

In the heady atmosphere of expansion W.R.M. Motors decided to place an advertisement on the front page of the *Daily Mail*, but within a few hours Morris knew he had wasted his money and his business was once more in the melting pot. It was August 1914 and Britain had declared war on Germany.

4   The Lessons of War

Uptil the outbreak of war in 1914, Morris had been essentially the master of his own fate. It was true that he had been swept along on a number of the tides of economic history – the cycle boom, the affluence of the Edwardian period which encouraged the rapid development of the motor industry, the shift of population from country to town and so on. But in practical terms he had chosen the direction in which he wanted to move and done so. Even after the disaster of the shared agency, business was generally sufficiently buoyant, and his own stock so good that for all the pain, his re-start was rapidly managed.

But the war brought an uncertainty which disrupted Morris's strategy and forced him to look for other unenvisaged means to keep his enterprise alive. There were many who failed as a result of the difficulties war brought, and others like Morris's great rival, Austin, who came within a hair's breadth of disaster.

That Morris not only survived but came through the war with his reputation and his ability enhanced was a tribute both to his capacity to deal with the unexpected and also to the practical mechanical and organizational skills of which he was the master in his generation. He learnt lessons from the war which some of his greater competitors totally failed to spot.

None the less the war could not help but be a traumatic time for Morris. It saw the deaths of his father and one of his two sisters; it brought to a halt his dreams of rising production. It left both him and his factory drained and exhausted. Yet it was the lessons learnt and confirmed in the war along with a momentous Government decision restricting foreign competition for more than half a century which, within a few years of the signing of the Armistice, would enable Morris to become the dominant force in the British motor industry.

The immediate impact of the declaration of war was seen in the production figures. After turning out over 100 cars a month for most of the year, the August figure (with some holiday impact) was as small as nine, and September twelve. But it was uncertain what the war regulations would mean and how long it would last.

So when the President of the Continental Motor Company in Detroit, Alfred Tobin, wired Morris to ask whether he still wanted the engines for the Cowley, Morris strongly insisted that he did. He went ahead with the construction of an extension of the Cowley works with a single storey steel workshop on the old parade ground, and by the end of 1914 production had been increased to over fifty a month.

Landstad had returned, to work full-time for Morris at the end of 1914, arriving with the first Continental engines, and in April 1915 the new Cowley was shown to the press. Its price, reflecting the benefits of American purchasing, was ten pounds less than the more elderly and lower-powered Oxford.

By then there were growing question marks about the continuation of car production in the increasingly serious war situation. Morris was already feeling the impact of shortage of materials and the disappearance of his workforce to the trenches.

One of the many Morris anecdotes[1] suggests that he did himself volunteer for the army but was turned down by the recruiting officer when he gave his occupation as motor manufacturer. It is a plausible tale but seems dubious. It is not a story that Morris himself told and does not appear in the biographical memoir prepared by Hobbs. Frank Grey taunted Morris with the fact that he had not joined up at one of the rowdy election meetings in 1924 after the break in their friendship.[2] He was in a position to have known if Morris had attempted to enlist.

But it seems intrinsically unlikely. Morris was dedicated to the success of his business; he had the Cowley engines on the way and to abandon it all to ruin would have been out of character. Besides, it did not need a recruiting sergeant to tell him that from the country's point of view he would be better employed running his factory. By the end of 1915 the connection was specific. Morris was manufacturing armaments alongside sharply reduced numbers of cars.

The attitude of the Government to the motor industry in the war was confused. While some production was seen as key to the war effort, much came to be regarded as frivolous. So whereas Daimler production was commandeered from the start, Rolls

Royce armoured vehicles became a sought after weapon, and the basic Model T Ford was a maid of all work for the forces on all fronts; most other manufacturers found their products increasingly regarded as a luxurious frippery. When the big drive to produce armaments under Lloyd George got under way, the production methods they were pioneering in Britain were seen as a vital assistance, but for turning out other products.

Morris's great rival Austin, who was making fewer cars but had a far larger establishment to keep employed because he manufactured most of his own parts, was reduced to making horse-drawn wooden limbers for the Imperial Russian Army to keep his enterprise in being; an ironic step for a motor manufacturer. By 1915 Morris was seeking armament work from the Government as it became apparent that in spite of the considerable interest the launch of the Cowley had aroused, the market for cars was diminishing. Indeed by 1916 public opinion had shifted to the point where the populist *Daily Mail* was calling for all private motoring to be banned.

The mixed attitudes to the car were demonstrated in the debates in the House of Commons in the autumn of 1915 on the Budget proposals of the Chancellor Reginald McKenna. These were to be momentous for the motor industry, imposing a huge tariff of 33 per cent on all motor imports as well as on such other luxury items as table glass, hats and musical instruments. McKenna justified the proposals on the grounds of saving foreign exchange and unnecessary luxury and the debate was full of complaint about the huge numbers of cars to be seen at still well-attended race meetings and other examples of ostentation. It was left for others to point out that most of the luxury vehicles were the products of British factories; many of the imported vehicles, more utilitarian, were for commercial use.

A few years later the McKenna duties were to seem to Morris as the key to his business, and would propel him briefly onto the centre of the political stage. They would have a momentous effect on the direction of the motor industry after the war. But initially for Morris the chief effect was to add a third to the price of the engines and other components he was importing from the USA, making the search for alternative work even more urgent.

He had started the search for Government orders within months of the outbreak of war. At first he discussed the manufacture of shell cases for 18 pounder field guns but instead he landed an order for hand grenades, and the first were delivered in July 1915 just after the launch of the Cowley.

At first however the successful organization of Morris's business worked against him. His was essentially an assembly operation. The reliance on suppliers to do the manufacture meant that Morris had little manufacturing machinery on which to carry out the essentially jobbing work which was available. The comparison may again be made with Austin. His works, with its facilities for parts and engine manufacture would be hugely extended in the war with hutted encampments being constructed for many of the 20,000 workers who would be taken on. Morris would finish the war with only a few hundred.

None the less the contract for grenades was followed by one for the cases of the bombs fired from Stokes trench howitzers and, more important, Morris found his expertise in demand on Ministry committees dealing with production.

Towards the end of 1916, after the battle of Jutland, one of these committees started to discuss the problems of production of a new device for naval mines, a complicated sinker which paid out the mine's cable until it locked at a predetermined distance from the bottom and then dragged the mine down with it.

It was being made in the naval dockyard at Portsmouth, a highly traditional operation based on entrenched methods used by skilled workers who were notoriously resistant to change. Production was running at forty a week; a frustrating exercise for an admiralty intent on laying a huge North Sea minefield to help blockade the German fleet after the Jutland stalemate.

Morris saw an opportunity. The assembly of complicated parts economically and rapidly into a whole was exactly what his motor manufacture was about, and his factory had available the large amount of space necessary for the operation. The committee did not believe his claim that he could boost production to 250 a week. But within three weeks Landstad had produced detailed drawings of the jigs needed for suppliers to machine the parts to the exact tolerances which were essential if parts would come from a range of different firms. Morris secured the contract and by the end of the war Cowley was despatching 1,200 a week by train to the northern ports.

The key once again was his precision and exact understanding of the control of suppliers. Just as the Ministry benefited from his pre-war experience, so the links forged and the lessons learned in the war would make him even more effective when it was over. In particular the personal contacts he had made would be of great benefit. Already Morris was beginning to gather round him some of the vital members of a team, mostly drawn from those he had worked with and evaluated as suppliers.

Landstad was one such. Another would be Arthur Rowse, a superintending engineer in the Ministry of Munitions in Birmingham, who worked with him in commissioning and inspecting suppliers and arranging for construction of the jigs.

Government work kept Morris solvent but it made him no fortune. The Ministry had taken over the major part of his factory for mine sinker production and paid him a salary of £1,200 a year as controller. W.R.M. Motors had actually made a loss of £1,700 in 1915, and although in 1916 it managed its best ever result, making over £20,000, its profits had fallen back to £8,700 in 1918, the last year of the war. Morris had to pay for and store his Cowley parts even if he could not use them.

When the war ended, the Ministry departed, taking with it the extra machinery it had provided. Morris was left with his pre-war equipment, much of it now worn out from four years of continuous production. He had some cash in hand, nearly £5,000, and enough parts to begin production again of some Cowleys; but his market was uncertain, many of his original labour force gone and his capital diminished. The OBE awarded by the Government was no recompense for its refusal to pay for dilapidations. Worse still, Morris's constitution which in spite of some minor ailments and what would become acute hypochondria was extremely tough, had been weakened by the pressures of wartime production.

Emotionally too it had been a hard few years. His father, Frederick Morris had died at the age of 66. In later years there had been little left of the dash of his youth. At the Morris garage he had been very much one of the hands, looking on at the jokes and horseplay, and there is something pathetic about the story of him running through Cowley exclaiming 'I knew Willie could do it'[3] when his son produced his first car. His grandchildren remembered him as a quiet man who said very little. Now he was weakening. He caught flu, returned to work, but jumped off a bus short of the stop and fell. On New Year's Day 1916, he died.

There was greater tragedy to follow. Morris's younger sister Alice had married a man called Percival Minns. Minns had worked for his brother-in-law as one of the hire car drivers for the garage, but he had then gone to Scotland as a chauffeur. In 1914, he contracted pneumonia and died. Alice Minns moved back to Oxford with her two small children to live with her parents. Two years later she too died, leaving her children as orphans.

John Minns, who was six, was then brought up by his father's family. But three year old Pansy Minns was left to be looked after by Emily Morris, assisted by Lilian Morris. There is some confusion in the family about who was actually responsible for Pansy Minns but it was not a happy story. According to her cousin, Mrs Rawlence, she was even fostered for a while with a foster mother who wanted to adopt her.

Then after a year or so she was withdrawn and sent to boarding school where she often stayed even in the holidays. Lilian Morris was responsible for her clothes and much of the arrangements. Later Pansy Minns was taken under the wing of the only surviving Morris sister, Mrs Yockney, who had moved to London. Regular entries in the Morris private cash book in the twenties and thirties record comparatively small but precise sums of, for example, £55-6-11 or £76-3-2 being sent to the Yockneys for Pansy Minns or 'Pansy's expenses'.[5]

It is a sad story, which does little to put the great philanthropist Nuffield or his wife in an encouraging light. They had no children, for reasons which were often speculated about later, though Lilian Morris as Lady Nuffield would be described as being very fond of children.[4] But now faced with close relations in difficulties, they seemed to have adopted an arm's length approach. Even John Minns says he was never invited to the Morris's home. Although his uncle gave him advice, and he remains fiercely loyal to him, it was at his office that he was expected to see him.

So as the war ended there were signs of coldness and strain in what little time Morris had left for personal life amongst his trafficking with suppliers and supervision of his busy works.

His health now started to fail. The symptoms resembled diabetes. He went for tests. His doctor told him he was exhausted, and needed immediate rest and treatment. He suggested a health spa in Germany and overrode Morris's patriotic protests that he could never go so soon after the war, by telling him it was the only place the treatment was available.

So Morris spent six weeks at the beginning of 1919 at a small spa called Bad Neuenahr, praised the friendliness he received and returned home, as he put it, with a touch of lingering hypochondria, after 'almost entire restoration of health'.[6]

5   Triumph

Morris returned to Cowley to face formidable problems. His factory was in disrepair, his suppliers in disarray, his markets in doubt and his carefully worked out strategy in pieces. He was left with his own grasp of the business, his determination and the reputation his cars had established. Yet it was enough. When tens of car companies failed to restart after the war and scores more collapsed within a few years of the armistice, it took William Morris a mere half dozen years to establish himself as the dominant force in the British motor industry, displacing even Henry Ford and all his works.

Once again he was riding a tide just as he had been after 1904. The huge rise in car ownership in Britain baffled the economists as it rose year after year from the early twenties through the thirties, less affected by slump and recession than either the United States or Germany. Every year more of the middle classes somehow found the money for the nice little car that became a trademark of the British industry with Morris almost their patron saint.

They were exactly the kind of customer for which his cars had been designed. His targets were ease of operation, simple maintenance, and a host of special features, many at no extra cost. Morris had made his point graphically in the 1914 London to Edinburgh run, insisting that his entrants wore straw hats and ordinary suits. No need for the special motoring clothing traditionally so necessary for repair and maintenance on the way.

As each new motor show brought out unexpected quantities of new buyers, so Morris would be there with new incentives. He would be the first to provide lights and spare wheel as standard, the first to guarantee money back for dissatisfied customers. He would attempt to standardize repair charges. He would offer hire purchase, free insurance, a 'motor house' to garage the car, the Morris owners' own magazine and club, and so on and so on.

Above all, in the Morris tradition, he would offer the keenest prices.

It was one of the greatest of the British motoring pioneers, S.F. Edge, who wrote of the days before the First World War:

> If one bought a car, it was always delivered minus lamps, horn, windscreen, hood, spare wheel, luggage grid and all the 1,001 refinements which are found on even the cheapest cars today. The purchaser discovered that even after he had put his cheque down for his car, he was very far from being out of the wood; he required all these accessories and they usually involved a further expenditure of the best part of £100.
>
> [Morris] was one of the first to appreciate the great drawback of this system. Shortly after the termination of the war, he began to equip his cars with all the necessary fitments; first one accessory and then another was included without additional cost; and to these he gradually added certain refinements which were not essential, but useful and much appreciated by every car owner. Year after year he made every effort to stop the purchaser having to buy something else after he had parted with this cheque and the success of the scheme is too well known to need comment.[1]

It was a shrewd assessment of the taste and temper of the English car buying public with whom Morris was closely in tune; what he offered was almost exactly the kind of thing which half a century later would commend Japanese cars so rapidly to British buyers. As a garage owner, Morris was in a position to understand, but then so were others. There was an empathy with his customers which marked him out.

But all this was still to come as Morris contemplated the rebuilding of his car business in 1919.

Strictly speaking, it had never stopped. Car production had continued on a small scale throughout the war in parts of the factory not employed for the assembly of mine-sinkers. In 1918 the factory turned out 198 Cowleys using the American engines. But it was clear that major decisions would have to be made about where to find reliable long-term suppliers to resume the progressive expansion on which the company had prided itself before the war.

But it was typical of Morris that he should first turn his attention to another problem, one which demonstrated the heat of his desire to keep the management of his business in his own hands alone. It also pointed to a gift of making strategic decisions about the long-term needs of the business in ways which meant that the short-term expedients did not stifle future expansion. It was a characteristic of Morris during this period that a range of decisions, particularly about suppliers, were made deliberately to prevent not immediate bottlenecks and difficulties but those which might arise from hugely increased production.

As striking was the way that he did not allow the grand visions (as they had with Argyll) to cloud and distort the ruthlessly practical control of costs. Otherwise Morris's still small enterprise would have foundered long before it sailed into the golden sunshine of his dreams.

His first initiative was to change the distributors of his cars. In order to get out of the contracts, he had to take the extreme step of liquidating his own company. It was an extraordinarily quixotic action, the only way his lawyers could recommend of escaping from the existing contracts, particularly the one which provided W.H.M. Burgess with the distribution rights for the whole of the South of England. When the advertisement appeared in the *Oxford Times* at the beginning of 1919 that the company was being 'voluntarily liquidated' it had to stipulate that creditors send in their claims to Morris's solicitors, Thorntons, before the due date of 1 February.[2]

It caused major difficulties for the business and Morris still had to pay compensation to Burgess after further legal wrangles. But he achieved the objective of maintaining tight control over his distributors and positioning them so that they could sell to best advantage the greatly increased numbers of cars he intended to produce.

Four years later Morris was to set out his ideas in coherent form in what would become a kind of standard text. In an article in the magazine *System* he wrote of 'Policies which have built the Morris Motor Business'.[3]

> The problem of our sales side is not so much finding the buyer as discovering means of educating the retailer to our point of view – which is expansion ... In this country the dealer has got into the habit of thinking of car sales in small numbers. Yet our whole aim is to sell cars in large numbers. We get our own profit; we keep the dealers' profit reasonable; simply in order that we may be able to sell cars in quantities. Having educated the dealer to this point of view,

the next trouble of the sales manager is to train him to the idea of personal expansion. For instance, if one of our dealers sold a hundred cars last year, he was probably extremely pleased with the result. He thinks his showrooms, his sales staff, and everything else is superb – and good for another ten years. What our sales department wants however is a sale of 200 cars next year.

Morris's ideas of how to achieve this by advising and insisting on the lay-out of premises, the training and organization of staff and so on, were well in advance of his time. They could almost have been the blueprint, for example, for the reorganization of Ford of Britain's franchises forty years later, a move which would help it to market leadership. Unfortunately by then Morris's successors in the British Motor Corporation would have long forgotten the lessons set out in *System*.

The same article set out his views on suppliers, the second pressing problem he was having to address.

So long ago as 1912 I became convinced that the best way for the small concern to manufacture was to get the specialists on every separate unit of the job. The work is better and more cheaply done, while the cost and worry of more plant is avoided. Money is conserved for better use in other directions. Even at the end of the war when we could have started to produce the Morris car very largely in our own works, I held to the other policy. There is no point in producing any article yourself which you can buy from a concern specialising in that work. I only buy a concern when they tell me they cannot produce enough of the article in question.

The outside firm that makes perhaps one only important part is probably making in even larger quantities than we should. It is interested in nothing else. Therefore it can keep its governing brains concentrated on the problems connected with that unit in a way impossible to a concern manufacturing a highly complicated article. Even the cost of transport is little increased.

These are perhaps the most quoted parts of the Morris philosophy but they need to be balanced by two observations about what Morris actually did in practice. He very soon bought up some of his key suppliers and was ruthless in attempting to direct the policies of others particularly when it affected supplies for his rivals in the industry. He also established his own production of certain key supplies if only to prevent the manufacturer thinking he would have a free ride.

The first problem he had to address was engines. His American supplies were out. It was more final than the McKenna duties; the Continental company were discontinuing the engine. Morris's small order was now irrelevant to such a hugely expanded company. But White and Poppe were also no longer available. During the war they had expanded hugely so that by the end of it they were employing 12,000 people. They had demand from other companies for their engines, particularly from the Dennis company for much larger engines for commercial vehicles. By the end of the year White, the controlling director, was to agree to take-over by Dennis.

Morris hawked round the design of the Continental engine which Landstad had reworked for English production but at first without success. Either companies were uninterested or their standard of workmanship was too low. Finally he was approached by the Hotchkiss company, a French armament manufacturer which had set up a wartime factory for making its machine-guns in Coventry after the German invasion of France. Now the wartime demand was over, the English factory with a workforce and management trained in precision engineering was hungry for work. It seemed to be suitable but Morris had a key question to ask, one vital for a man short of ready cash – would a deposit be required. The answer was no, and the deal was struck.

The supply of bodies was another problem. Pre-war, Raworths in Oxford had supplied them for the smaller Oxford, but Hollick and Pratt in Coventry had made them for the larger Cowley. With the smaller car discontinued, they would all now have to come from Coventry.

A pencilled alteration to the biographical note sets out the difficulty involved. It was not simply that numbers of chassis had actually to be driven to Coventry for their bodies to be fitted – a waste of time and money;

> It was regarded as a far less serious handicap than that threatened by the limitation of the production resources of the Hollick and Pratt factory. It was rapidly becoming apparent that these works, catering widely for many of the firms in the motor trade would be unable to cope with increasing orders with any degree of promptitude.[4]

Morris's answer was to set up his own body shop on an allotment across the road from the Cowley plant. Before 1919 was out it was joined by a foundry. He had been dissatisfied with both the price and quality of the cylinder blocks being made for the Hotchkiss engine and had decided to teach the foundry trade a lesson. Another supplier, Dohertys of Coventry, established a radiator factory, Osberton radiators, in an old ice-rink near the Woodstock road at the opposite end of Oxford from Cowley. But Morris was soon to find himself dissatisfied with its quality standards too. His solution this time was to help two of the firm's Coventry foremen to buy it.

To finance the rather unintended expansion, he was forced to risk his cherished total business control by raising £49,000 in the form of £20,000 of loans and £29,000 in 7 per cent preference shares. He liked to boast, inaccurately, that it was the first and last time that he went for working capital from outside sources.

Macclesfield took £25,000 worth of shares, which took account of £17,500 already invested, and an injection of a further £7,500. A Witney engineer, Mr W.H. Young, and the Oxford banker A.B. Gillett, took £2,000 each. Morris was issued with £75,000 of shares as governing director of what was now to be named Morris Motors Ltd, in consideration of the assets of the business and a further £16,185 of his own money which he had just paid in. Half a further loan of £20,000 came from Lancelot Pratt, the head of Hollick and Pratt who was a close friend of Morris, and the other half came from Gillett in 1920.

So Morris was now equipped to face the demands of a post-war market radically changed from what he had known in 1914.

The war had introduced thousands of members of the armed services to motor vehicles for the first time. They had seen their capabilities and learnt to drive and maintain them. With the coming of peace, it was no longer mainly the wealthy with chauffeurs among their household staffs who were looking to purchase motor cars. It was the middle classes, including some with service gratuities to spend. At the same time the decline in wealth among the upper classes meant that they too were more inclined to seek for an economic style of motor than the handbuilt carriages of pre-war days.

For a time it was a sellers' market. There were not enough cars to be had. The Cowley had been put on sale in 1915 for £158 guineas. In 1920 a second-hand Cowley could fetch double the price. Although huge numbers of commercial vehicles had been turned out during the war and army surplus lorries swamped the market, there was no such source for cars, and as most car makers, like Morris, had had to switch to alternative production, there were few new cars available.

It was not surprising that in the two years 1919 and 1920, forty-six new motor manufacturers were established and banks seemed willing to lend on the most flimsy prospectuses. But both new and more established firms like Austin and Napier began to suffer from what soon became a feature of post-war industrial life – skilled labour shortage, which pushed up prices, wages, and industrial unrest. The long moulders' strike of 1920 which affected the traditional industrial centres, including the Midlands and London, delayed Austin's return to production and destroyed Napier's intentions of resuming car production amongst others. Morris, in what was then an industrial backwater, escaped disruption.

The result was a field day for the Ford motor company. With its purpose-built mass production plant in Manchester, its 6,000 cars a year had been the most built by any manufacturer before the war. As its competitors bitterly complained, far from limiting manufacture during the war, the services had welcomed the contribution of the Model T in all kinds of roles, from scout-cars to ambulances.

With production geared up and the extra duties on imported cars and parts no barrier because of demand, Ford sold over 15,000 cars in Britain in 1920, compared with Austin's production of 4,319 and Morris's growing output of 1,932.

Challenging Ford was to become one of Morris's goals. Although he continued to acknowledge the superiority of American production methods in his repeated visits to the USA, he remained an Edwardian patriot. 'I find it difficult as a worker not to think of my country and the British Empire,'[5] he said. The success of American owned Ford had been seen as an affront by many British people. When Henry Ford had financed the sending of a 'peace ship' to Europe to try to halt the war in 1915 he and his company had particularly been attacked by the most powerful newspaper owner Lord Northcliffe in the pages of the *Daily Mail*.

Now Northcliffe was to give Morris a major boost; not the last time the establishment would give the Englishman an unashamed advantage against the American competition. Towards the end of

1921 he arranged for a crony, the paper's motoring correspondent, John Prioleau, to take a standard Morris car abroad to France, Italy, North Africa and Spain to demonstrate the ability of a British car to cope with the sort of rough conditions that the Model T Ford was built for. The car was nicknamed 'Imshi', the arabic for 'Get on', but the make was not revealed until the completion of an almost trouble-free journey – an enormous publicity coup for Morris.

But by then he and the British motor industry could do with any help going. The high hopes of post-war resurgence had collapsed in a classic slump in 1921. Manufacturers were squeezed between rising costs of labour and materials and a Government, anxious to deflate, which raised taxes. As a luxury item, car sales were among the first to suffer and the annual Motor Show was a disaster. As the biographical memoir put it, 'The many who had counted on it to bring them industrial resurrection returned disconsolate to their factories where they found order books as empty as stockrooms were full'.[6]

Morris was among them but his response to the problem would take him to a position of leadership with remarkable rapidity. His business had been growing quickly, which in the sudden downturn made him particularly vulnerable. His total sales of 1,932 in 1920 were more than he had managed in total before the war, but they told only half the story. Monthly production had been accelerating, reaching 276 in September just before the Motor Show. The crisis was rapid. Production was halved by November and then again by January, when only seventy-four cars were built.

His debts mounted correspondingly. His overdraft doubled to over £84,000 while he ran up debts to his suppliers of £50,000. All around, other manufacturers were facing similar problems. For Morris it must have seemed as if his world was destined always for collapse. After the failure of the agency, he had painstakingly rebuilt only to have the war halt the rapid ascent of his business. After finding war work to keep the business going, he had just surmounted the problems of peace only to find himself in the biggest financial crisis of his life.

His response now was a brave one, though others at the time saw it as desperate and reckless. Put simply, he made huge price cuts and re-established the market. By recovering a big volume of sales, he was able to make more money even though his margins appeared to be lower. It was to be a classic formula in the motor industry, where the importance of volume was to become paramount, but Morris was only to manage it by the skin of his teeth and a considerable amount of luck.

If there was one thing he hated throughout his life, it was to be called lucky. He told Massac Buist in 1928:

> It has been said on so many occasions that I have been abnormally lucky in my business career and I find generally by people who have taken life in a go-as-you-please manner. They in consequence have not succeeded in doing anything above normal and in some cases have utterly failed. I am of the opinion that no man should go into serious business unless he is prepared to work hard and do his utmost in directing others, in which case he will have little time for play. On the other hand, if he wishes to place pleasure before business, he should not accuse the successful man of luck, when generally it should be termed the result of hard work.[7]

There was a sense in which this was true of his escape from disaster. It was predicated on the very tight control of cost which was evident in his 1915 estimates for Cowley production where all the overheads – lighting, heating of the factory, insurance, telephone, travel and even 'customer satisfaction' are itemised and allocated to the costing of each car adding another thirty shillings to the price. He also benefited from the relatively small scale of his operation and the fact that his suppliers had to bear some of the pain from the sudden build-up in stocks, and had a common interest in his survival which made them receptive to the idea of cutting their own prices.

None the less he was lucky; assisted by Government action to change motor taxation which gave low-powered cars like his an advantage and an economic recovery which allowed him to clear his debts rapidly.

He was not the first or only manufacturer to make price cuts although he was often to claim it. The rival Bean company which had grown rapidly after the war had done so in October 1920, cutting £105 off its 11.9 horsepower four seater; at the same time Morris, who was more vulnerable to rising raw material prices with less integrated production, put £215 on the four seater Cowley's price. But as the Bean had been double the price, the Cowley was still cheaper. The Bean cuts did not have the same effect for various reasons; their early timing, the fact that they still did not make the cars obviously the cheapest in their class, plus Morris's reputation for value in the lower priced market which Bean had not yet entered and which was most sensitive to price.

So when Morris made what he called 'the biggest decision I ever made in my life'[8] it was by no means clear he would succeed.

> The slump found us with a factory full of cars from one end to the other and we were still looking for space to accommodate the output. I decided to reduce the price of all models by approximately £100 which meant that I was losing £80 on the sale of every car because I had bought the materials at the famine prices obtaining ... you see I felt like this at the time, 'If I am to go out, I may as well go out kicking.'

Later he described the moment;

> I sent for my manager [who was Hugh Wordsworth Grey] and suggested to him that the price should be dropped by a hundred pounds per model, and he said, 'How can you do that with the profit you are making today?' I said, 'Well, you are making no profit at all because you are selling no cars. I therefore give you instructions to go and do exactly what I've suggested and also to double up the supplies.' He went to the door, and stood in the door as much as to say, 'He's gone at last.' With that he slammed the door and went out.[9]

Others suggest however that once again Morris had gilded the tale. Miles Thomas, who joined the company in 1924 knew Grey, by now sales manager, well. 'There has always been a controversy about who suggested these dramatic price cuts. Morris claimed he thought up the idea himself ... Grey told me he himself put the idea to "the Boss".'[10]

Whatever the case, Morris had to approve the measure, and in February 1921 the prices of the Cowley were cut by a fifth. At the same time Morris persuaded his suppliers and backers to take their share of the burden. He increased his bank borrowing, helped by the continuing support of his bankers, Gilletts, who had been impressed by the way he had paid back creditors after his earlier bankruptcy as a matter of honour. He also persuaded some suppliers to allow delayed payment. Dunlop gave extended credit on tyres while the Lucas company, whose rapid expansion had been heavily dependant on Morris orders, agreed to give him two months' credit. Morris then persuaded other suppliers on the basis of their example.

His distributors were less happy. They were unconvinced by the price cut, and reluctantly accepted a cut in their commission rate from 17½ to 15 per cent. As Morris insisted that the cars only left the factory after being paid for in cash, he had won himself a new credit line. By contrast, his own suppliers were paid in arrears, and he arranged for firms like Dunlop and Lucas to extend the payment period.

He told his biographers that he had not expected to be back in the black for two years.[11] But business picked up so fast that by the end of May he had paid off the bank overdraft of £84,315 and met all his debts to suppliers. At the same time he had tightened up the organization of production with Landstad and Arthur Rowse reducing the inventory time for storing components to three weeks between delivery and assembly.

In February sales trebled after the price cut to 236 and rose to 400 in March, only falling back slightly in the summer. At the October Motor Show when other manufacturers started to cut their prices in earnest to try to compete, Morris made another cut reducing the price of the Cowley by another eighty pounds or so. So the four seater which had been priced at £525 in January now cost only £341; his strict economies and the benefits of larger production runs had meant that far from losing on his initial price reductions, he had increased his profits to around £50 a car.

The company had announced two slightly adapted de luxe models for the show and Morris's price cuts had made his stand the centre of attraction, after the latest news. George Tobin remembered;

> They thought the man was mad. The general crowd, they craned at the stand. At Olympia you couldn't get there. There was one thing about it; if you got down to look underneath, you couldn't get up. You stooped down to look underneath the car on the stand and you couldn't get up for the crowd. It was terrific; it really was a sensation. They predicted it was the finish. But it wasn't you know.[12]

Morris took his usual simple line.

> All our competitors called me a cut-throat and everything they could think of. But if I may say so, it was the salvation of the motor trade. At that time all the manufacturers in this

country were making very few cars at as high a price as they could possibly make. I had reversed that order to make as many cars as possible at as low a price as possible.[13]

Progress was swift and spectacular. In 1921 3,076 cars were sold; in 1922, 6,956. In 1923 the business took off with sales of 20,042 and profits which approached a million pounds (£927,000). In 1925 Morris was selling 53,582 cars as well as 6,256 commercial vehicles, 40 per cent of the production of the whole British car industry and his pre-tax profit was over £1.5 million.

Along the way he had hugely expanded his workforce and retreated somewhat from his policy of dependence on outside suppliers as it became obvious that some of the key component makers would be unable to meet his burgeoning requirements, for a variety of reasons.

The first to be swallowed was the Hotchkiss engine plant. When Morris suggested the company plan for production of 500 a week, he was told that the most the factory could accommodate would be half that number. Morris, who had for some years acted as his own chief buyer, knew the factory well and was convinced that it had a much greater capacity if organized properly. He offered to buy the plant and the French company, whose main operations had remained on the Continent, accepted. His experienced works managers lifted production from 250 to 420 a week within four months.

At about the same time, Morris took over the bodyworks at Hollick and Pratt, also in Coventry. Here it was at the suggestion of the managing director Lancelot Pratt, Morris's close friend and backer. Pratt argued that as the firm had largely ceased to do business with other motor firms because of the huge increase in Morris orders, it had effectively become a branch of Morris Motors. But there was more to the deal than that. The relationship between the two men on both a business and personal level had become increasingly close, and Pratt moved to join the Morris team which was now increasingly made up of men from supplying companies whom Morris had got to know and respect, and had then poached. Pratt took over as Morris's deputy with the title of Deputy Governing Director. The trust which Morris put in him was exceptional.

Much more typical of his behaviour was the way he had forced a breach with another man without whom the company could not have started, because – the fatal accusation – he had appeared to question the way the 'Governor' was running the company.

This was none other than the Earl of Macclesfield who had put up £4,000 in 1912 to found W.R.M. Motors and had had the title of President of the Company. He had subsequently put in other sums which brought him £25,000 worth of shares in the post-war company, making him the second biggest shareholder after Morris himself.

In 1912 Morris had welcomed his encouragement and frequent visits to his workshop. Now established and confident after the spectacular success of his gamble, he was increasingly irked by what he saw as Macclesfield's interference in things in which he, Morris, was expert.

Hylda Church who was Morris's secretary, and later married Miles Thomas, recalled that Macclesfield preferred wandering round the works to board meetings where he became fidgety and let his attention wander. The two men started to squabble, with Morris increasingly resenting Macclesfield's rather gruff questioning about decisions which Morris, never a committee man himself, had taken without consultation.[14]

One story has it that the final straw came when Macclesfield came upon Morris in the works adjusting carburettors, which were one of his continuing obsessions. The story has him asking Morris why he did not leave such matters to those whose job it was. If true, it was exactly the remark to send Morris into a temper.[15]

Whatever the final straw, in 1922 Morris consulted the bank and abruptly sent Macclesfield a cheque for his shares, which Macclesfield accepted with remarkable grace, particularly as it must have been obvious that the business was likely to make a great deal of money very soon.

On a happier note, the same year saw Morris make a key appointment to run the garage business in Oxford. This was one Cecil Kimber, a motor enthusiast who had worked for a number of engineering firms and whose early delight in motor cycles had been painfully terminated by an accident which left one leg shorter than the other.

The building of bespoke bodies and special features on standard chassis was a feature of the industry. The first time Miles Thomas met Morris was at a rally at Box Hill in 1920 when he arrived in a car with a polished body built 'like a boat hull of longitudinal narrow planks tapering to a pointed stern'.[16]

At Morris Garages, Kimber, with his keen interest in competitive rallying would develop modifications of the standard Morris for sporting use, giving them the initials of the garage name. So the first MG would be produced in 1923 founding a reputation which would lead Morris to complain after one overseas trip that his reputation as the maker of the MG was greater than that as the maker of Morris cars.

By 1925 Morris had won his patriotic victory over Ford, with production of his cars surpassing the Model T. Newspapers noted how roads which once had been dominated by Fords were now crowded with British made Morrises. It was a popular triumph; anti-Americanism was rife. When the huge General Motors company of the USA had attempted to buy the Austin works in the difficult days of 1920, the dealers had banded together to dissuade Herbert Austin even though the company had to go into receivership and be rescued by its creditors a few months later.

But in 1923 with security almost within his grasp, Morris saw another peril which might wrench it once more from his hands. This time it was politicians.

The McKenna duties, the 33 per cent tax on motor imports, had caused Morris problems with his American supplies when they had been imposed in 1915. But by now he saw them as essential protection against the hugely expanded and successful American industry whose long production runs enabled it to sell cars more cheaply.

He was keenly aware too of the extensive measures the French were taking to protect their industry with, for example, local authorities discouraged from buying anything except French made vehicles.

So when free trade and the end of protectionism became an issue in the 1923 General Election, Morris actually discussed standing for Oxford as the Conservative candidate, opposing the Liberals. Their candidate was none other than the Frank Grey for whom Morris had canvassed in the 1919 election, and who had accompanied him to America and advised him on the bus campaign. As it happened, Morris was advised by his doctor not to stand but that did not prevent him mounting a rumbustious campaign against Grey in which he heckled his meetings, paraded through Oxford and was even accused of importing strong-arm squads from his Coventry workforce.

It was a side of Morris much at odds with the image of the

dignified benefactor he later became and bears out the warning by Miles Thomas to beware of letting the view of Nuffield late in life obscure the vigorous passionate Morris of the first half century of his life.

The local Oxford papers record a series of fascinating exchanges between Grey and Morris, who was now well into middle age, past his forty-sixth birthday.

So on 5 December the *Oxford Chronicle* reported Grey at the Corn Exchange:

> I consider Mr Morris's attempt to subordinate the national interest to his own interests calls for exposure and it shall have it. There is no-one in Oxford who has bought so much American stuff as Mr Morris. The last car I had was American and I bought it from Mr Morris. He was the first agent of the Hupmobile and he has by importing and selling American cars made a fortune.

Grey reminded the audience that he had gone to the USA with Morris to buy engines and challenged him to open his books to show how many parts he imported from Germany.

He hit back at Morris's suggestions that repeal of the tariffs would lead to unemployment.

> He says he owes his prosperity to 33 percent protection. If he is prosperous may I ask him to tell the Oxford public how many unemployed men he has absorbed from the Oxford Labour Exchange. [Here a voice shouted 'None at all'.] I have my information from the angry men I addressed at the Labour Exchange today, the unemployed for whom he is venturing to speak.

It was a rough campaign. Morris attacked Grey for refusing a commission during the war, and when Cowley was leafleted he was accused of trying to start a class war. When Morris spoke at the Corn Exchange he was heckled just as he had shouted back at Grey when he spoke at the Town Hall. Morris offered £20,000 to Grey if he could prove his allegation that he had gone to Grey's Town Hall meeting with 'twenty picked men from Coventry paid to heckle'.[17]

The Liberals continually contrasted Morris business acumen with his political ineptitude, and attacked his public promise to take on another 1,000 men if the duties stayed as intimidation.

In the event Grey won the election quite comfortably and the Government was defeated. A Labour administration came in which was also committed to removing the duties. Ford, which was increasingly in difficulty with the sales of the aged Model T because Henry Ford would not allow modifications nor provide a more up to date replacement, made the most of it. In February they advertised that 'Ford passenger cars will be reduced in price when these duties are discontinued', promising to refund the difference. In the April Budget the Chancellor, Philip Snowden, announced that the duties would go but not until 1 August. Morris's campaign switched into higher gear.

A petition from 2,500 Cowley workers to the MP for Henley prayed that the duties 'be not abolished so rendering groundless their fears of unemployment.' Morris wrote to the *Daily Mail* that removal of the duties would mean loss of employment for a million men. 'I base this figure on the fact that although 300,000 workmen are directly engaged in the production of British motor cars ... four million men are engaged in the production of the materials from which motor cars are made.'[18]

Already he said he had cut his production schedule by 25 per cent and others would have to do the same or worse.

It was, of course, a gross exaggeration but the orchestrated campaign infuriated the Chancellor, Philip Snowden. He accused Morris of 'rampant raging propaganda'. Morris struck back in a letter in May that the manufacturers were already being forced to dismiss approximately one third of the 40,000 men directly employed in the production of cars. 'The British manufacturer of today is in the position of a man trying to climb a waterfall – so soon as he makes any progress he is swept back by forces out of his control.'[19]

It was a cry from the heart – and it could stand as a good description of Morris's experience and career so far. But it had no immediate effect. Labour abolished the duties on 1 August but they were reimposed the following year by Winston Churchill when the Conservative Government was re-elected. Imports actually fell in 1924 from 22,000 to 18,000 while home production went up by more than a half, from 71,000 to 116,000. In 1925, imports did indeed double with an extra 24,000 cars coming in, but home production improved by as much.

The implication is that Morris was wrong and exaggerated the dangers. His own view was that he had been justified, claiming at the Hollick and Pratt annual dinner in January 1926 that the removal of duties had meant sales of only 27,000 Morris cars in 1924 compared with the 35,000 they had planned. That was clearly affected by other factors.

There was no doubt however that the industry's fears were genuine enough. After the Budget, Austin approached Morris with a proposal to merge their two businesses with that of Wolseley to produce what would have been an early version of the British Motor Corporation. Morris, acknowledged as the best production man, would have run it, but the shares would have been allocated on the basis of assets. 'My only concern', Austin claimed, 'is to put the British car manufacturer in a position to meet foreign competition which we have not up to the present time had any experience of. In another year's time, the rivalry, particularly from Continental manufacturers will be fierce.'[20]

The proposal offended Morris on two counts; it entailed the sharing of control which he had determined always to avoid, and it put him in a junior position because although his sales were far greater than the others, their plants, though less efficient and more ancient, were much bigger. It would give them the lion's share of the new company. After the meeting his accountant wrote back to Austin that 'his business is entirely his own, to make or break, to mar or improve, and he does not feel that he can give up this position of freedom ... the organisation would be so great that it would be difficult to control and might tend to strangle itself.'

The rising market now seemed to have swept away most of Morris's worries about the duties. But his success in having them reimposed meant that the cycle maker from Oxford had become not only a manufacturing prodigy but a figure on the national stage. His opinions and activities would now be a matter of interest beyond the confines of Oxford.

He had had a taste of public acclaim and he had liked it. He had seen his beliefs in protectionism triumph, and it had given credence to his clearly stated, if limited, political creed. It would give him confidence to seek a series of industrial and political alliances to press it home, although his relatively easy victory misled him about the simplicity of political action.

Meanwhile, the foreigner defeated at home, he would attempt to fly the British flag abroad with a series of ventures aimed at opening up a world market for the cars with which he now appeared to have conquered the highways of Britain.

6   Flying the Flag

Morris was now at the height of his powers. What was most remarkable was the confidence with which he expanded at almost breakneck speed into all kinds of areas foreign to a man who had still spent nearly all his time in the provincial city of Oxford. He was now a nationally known figure, the kind of personality whom newspapers would invite to contribute a New Year's message; an instructive example of business success.

Against a background of national doubt and economic uncertainty which saw Britain's place on the world stage eroding abroad and social and financial woes piling up at home, the motor industry seemed an example of hope, a modern industry which provided new opportunities for the tens of thousands who bought its products. It was a phenomenon which seemed to grow and grow in spite of the slump, labour unrest, and financial crises which led to rapid changes of administration and eventually National Government.

The subsequent troubles of the British motor industry in the seventies and eighties tend to obscure the fact of its earlier success. When its post-war reconstruction was discussed by a Cabinet sub-committee during the Second World War, it was seen as one of the few industrial success stories between the wars.

So it was not surprising that Morris, for all his Edwardian ideas about Britain's place in the world, should be seen and indeed see himself as the archetype of the successful modern businessman with a formula which would bring success in all kinds of undertakings at home and abroad. His enthusiasm for modern production methods and his sharp appreciation of the need to keep costs under control were qualities whose application was long overdue in large parts of both the motor and other industries, and helped him to expand by a mixture of acquisition and organic growth in Britain.

But it was less obvious that the attraction of his vehicles to the British public, a function partly of the tax regulations which penalised the higher powered cars and partly of the liking for the small car with plenty of accessories, would transfer onto a world stage. This was particularly true, for all the publicity success of Imshi, in the rugged conditions obtaining in the colonies which Morris saw as one of his principal markets.

At the same time, as he expanded and started to spend more time away from Cowley, it was clear that Morris's insistence on tight control of his business was going to be increasingly difficult to maintain. What had been a crucial virtue in the tough early years was now in danger of turning into a liability. His idiosyncratic ways and unwillingness to let others take decisions was a recipe for managerial disaster as the business grew beyond the capacity of one man to control. Until now the company's success had been based on variants of the first two models he had produced, with Morris poring over every detail himself. Now decisions would have to be made on their replacements.

The pace of expansion was galloping. In 1923 Morris branched out into manufacture of trucks and vans establishing Morris Commercial Cars Ltd in the old Birmingham factory of his one-time supplier E.C. Wrigley. It had gone into liquidation because of the slump. In 1924 he set up an export office at Cowley and bought a French manufacturer, the Leon Bollee factory, at Le Mans. In 1925 he returned to the USA to inspect new developments which allowed steel bodies to be built by production line methods. The following year he established a joint company, Pressed Steel, with the American Budd company to build them at Cowley.

In 1926 he arranged the first public issue of Morris shares, and made the first of his big charitable donations. In 1927 he bought the now bankrupt Wolseley company, carrying through on his own terms, much of what Austin had suggested three years previously. At the same time he was widening his international horizons. In 1927 as Morris Commercial produced a special Empire car for export, Morris embarked for Argentina to inspect the South American market. Then early in January 1928, as the snow banked against the Oxfordshire hedgerows, the tracked Cowley fire engine was summoned to clear a way through; Morris was off again, on what were to be almost annual visits to Australia by way of the United States.

It was a brave and vigorous approach. But it was most successful on familiar home territory. The Morris achievement was to force the British motor industry to adopt the modern production methods pioneered by the Americans which it had disdained before the First World War. It was not universally accepted. Motor production techniques would have to be called in aid when the country started its rearmament programme a decade later because they were lacking in other industries. Some industries like shipbuilding seemed not to learn them at all. But at times Morris seemed to be leading the world. He was making a sharp break with attitudes prevalent before the First World War and enshrined in the techniques of production particularly of some of the armament companies who owned motor manufacturers – that it was not cost but final quality which mattered. British was best and so you might expect to pay more for it.

That was not a concept to which Morris subscribed. The greatest success of the foreign trips he loved was the new ideas he brought back; his hopes of great markets abroad for British cars would be disappointed.

In fact most of the initiatives he took as he eagerly branched out would come to grief. The Morris Commercial vehicles company never had the reputation his cars had won. The Empire car it built was an unmitigated disaster. The French project never caught fire and had to be wound up after consistent losses. As for the export drive, it was not sustained. The 1927 peak of 10,551 was not paralleled until the mid and late thirties. Morris fairly quickly sold his share of Pressed Steel although that was more a tactical move to encourage other manufacturers to make use of it than a token of its failure.

Where success was undeniable was in the way Morris kept Cowley in the forefront of efficient technical practice and continued to set an example of cost effectiveness. Miles Thomas, with some exaggeration, set out his opinion of the Morris skills like this:

> People have often asked me whether Mr Morris was an engineer. To that, I categorically reply that he was a far better mechanic. He could read a blueprint but only just. He certainly could not create a general arrangement on a drawing board, and while he could do rough indicative drawings by freehand, he showed no evidence of the freedom of style in design that first class engineers display today.[1]

Morris did however possess a firm grasp of the importance of factory organization and, from his experience with his suppliers, he knew where to find the experts who could carry out the work for him.

At the end of the war, Morris had reorganized Cowley. Pre-war assembly had been effected on the first floor of the old military academy with machining carried out on the ground floor. Individual cars were built up without being moved about; there was nothing like a production line. After the war, assembly was moved to the ground floor where the working area had been enlarged by the addition of the new steel building. Now cars were moved from work station to work station, a kind of rudimentary assembly line layout, but the cars were pushed from station to station by hand and only once they had been fitted with wheels.

This would become inadequate but mattered less while bodies were still built up by hand from a mixture of wood and steel. The chief benefits of modern production methods were to be found in the complex progression of precision engineering operations for production of engines. It was here that Morris made his greatest advances.

When dealing with his suppliers in the early days, he had been greatly impressed with the work of Frank Woollard, the chief designer at the body maker, E.C. Wrigley. Before he bought the Hotchkiss company in 1923, he had asked Woollard to look the factory over and judge how much production could be stepped up. It was on the basis of his three page report, handed over at the Motor Show, that Morris made the decision to pay £300,000 for the Hotchkiss factory, brushing aside the procedures suggested by the Hotchkiss lawyers and signing the detailed documents within an hour. Inevitably it was Woollard he installed as manager of what was now called Morris Engines.

Woollard's success in increasing production by two thirds within six months and reducing the manpower needed to produce each engine became a case study in the industry. He himself set out his views in a paper for the Institute of Production Engineers early in 1925.[2]

Quoting figures which showed that output had risen from 300 engines a week in 1923 to 1,200 in 1924, partly by the introduction of the twenty-four hour day which was then 'an unusual feature in British machine shops', he went on;

Regularity is the key note of continuous production. Regularity in sales as to quantity and type; regularity in material as to quantity, quality and time; regularity in processing, workmanship and inspection, and where continuous production also implies working the plant on a basis of 24 hours to the day regularity has a very special meaning, because a shortage means absolute loss of output, since there can be neither stock nor surplus time from which to make good.

Changes will take place in the most highly standardised product, but to make continuous production possible, such changes should only be made at regular intervals and after very considerable experimental work ... keeping the car up to date without upsetting the continuity of flow is one of the greater problems for the engineers of a large-scale production concern for unless the product of the factory maintains a certain, and in this country, a high quality, the flow of orders ceases and continuous production becomes impossible.

It stood as a text for motor industry managers for the rest of the century and it was this thorough production emphasis, the hallmark of the Morris enterprise, which set the standards for the British motor industry, and brought him huge success.

Morris was continually trying to extend the frontiers of production and salesmanship. His engine plant had introduced huge automatic transfer machines 180 feet long which were equipped to perform a range of different operations in sequence which turned out a particular component. They were in advance even of Detroit. But the arrangement also ran ahead of the available engineering techniques and was too complicated and expensive. American engineers judged them as twenty years ahead of their time, and it was not until after the Second World War that they were reintroduced into the British motor industry. It was a token of the breadth of the Morris ambition and vision at the high point of his career. He had a world view.

One of his most fundamental and far-reaching initiatives was the importing of the new technology of steel body manufacture from the United States. The practice had been for car bodies to be constructed with steel parts fitted to wooden frames. But Morris had closely followed the development of a process for assembling all-steel bodies on the other side of the Atlantic. In November 1925 he sailed for America announcing that his chief mission was to induce the Edward G. Budd company of Philadelphia, who had developed the technology, to send an organization to England to build a new steel sedan in a plant ready built by Morris Motors.[3]

Budd was unwilling to relinquish control of the process but agreed to set up a joint venture at Cowley called Pressed Steel. It proved a difficult translation. Although some of the 1927 Oxfords had the new bodies, the unpractised labour, the new techniques of welding and the raw dies spelt trouble.

When the first cars came through;

> The panels were ripped; the aperture for the windscreen was awry and would obviously leak in the first shower of rain; the doors only fitted where they touched, and although copious supplies of circular rubber tube filling had been sewn inside to give the door some semblance of fit, the whole thing was an impossible product. To heighten the gloom, someone wryly said we ought to advertise it as an all-weather body – it would let all the weather through. 'W.R.' was like a bear with a sore head – literally. He had a habit when he was worried – and that was very frequently in those days – of scratching the hair on the back of his neck.[4]

Morris was less ambitious with his car design. He went for reliability and proven design; it was curious that he was more adventurous in production techniques. Perhaps it was that the financial returns were much more quantifiable than improvements to cars which might or might not bring in more sales. Perhaps it was Morris's understanding of the British motorists' psychology, which was evidenced in many ways.

He set out his concerns for the customer in the *System* article.

> One continual source of anxiety to the owner is the cost of running repairs. A little garage in Cornwall may charge three times as much as a city garage for de-carbonising, grinding in valves and re-setting tappets, a process necessary to all cars, even the Rolls-Royce. We are therefore instituting a system of standardised repair charges. One of the things we have to impress on the dealer is the necessity for holding a sufficient stock of spare parts. Only under these conditions can we give service to the owners of Morris cars.
>
> It will be realised that most of the work attached to dealing with complaints falls under the same heading – the giving of services to the man who had once bought the car. The

satisfied owner is one of the best possible selling media in this trade for motorists are incorrigible talkers of shop. Only by service after purchase can you keep the owner satisfied – and get his selling force behind your product.[5]

That was Morris the old garage owner speaking. To assist his customers further he introduced a hire purchase arrangement in conjunction with a finance company, the United Dominions Trust, in 1923. Hire purchase was not unknown; there had been some use of it before the First World War. But now there was a vastly bigger market among the new would be car owners, of the middle classes scraping and saving to afford their first car. Once again Morris captured the tide of the times – by the mid 1920s half of all car sales were made on hire purchase.[6]

The company's own magazine, started specifically for Morris car buyers, declared, 'The system has an immense national and social significance. It has proved to many thousands of citizens ... that it is possible to save money and acquire property of which they might be justly proud.'[7]

To run the magazine, the *Morris Owner*, established in 1924, Morris made another shrewd appointment. He brought in a journalist from the *Motor Trader*, an enthusiast called Miles Thomas. He had won a DFC in the Royal Flying Corps during the war and Morris was impressed by his reporting of the new Oxford in 1922. Thomas had not taken any notes (explaining afterwards that it was all in the leaflet) but had noticed a last-minute change in the car's hood which other journalists had failed to spot. After a number of other encounters, Morris invited Thomas to join him at the end of 1923.

He would eventually become his deputy and a close friend, marrying Morris's secretary Hylda Church in 1924. His journalistic flair stayed with him and after years as a manager he produced the most colourful and incisive descriptions of Morris when he came to write his autobiography. At this point his presentational talents were exactly what Morris needed as he and his company moved onto the public stage. It was Thomas who a few months later would write the propaganda about the dangers of repealing the McKenna duties which would go out under the Morris name. Public relations was an important part of the company's success. Thomas gave it a sharp professional edge away from the traditional old school tie approach and became a key member of the team.

But for all the cossetting of the customers it was still price which remained the key weapon, just as it had been in the crisis of 1921. The *System* article which was written a few weeks after Thomas's arrival set out the Morris view.

> My aim is to keep ahead of the market. We have never waited for the public to ask for a reduction. We get in with the reduction first. Is it quite sufficiently realised in this country that every time you make a reduction, you drop down on what I may call the pyramid of consumption power to a wider base? Even a ten pound price reduction drops you into an entirely new market. If the man cannot pay the last £10 ... he cannot buy the car. The one object in life of many makers seems to be to make the thing the public cannot buy. The one object of my life is to make the thing they can buy.[8]

An example followed rapidly on the arrival of Thomas. The start of 1924 saw sales beginning to stagnate.

> Output seemed to be sticking at round about 600 cars a week when I joined. He wanted to get over this hump so we had an idea. He said, 'Let's say we can't guarantee that this low price will be maintained after March 31st or whatever day it was, unless more orders are forthcoming.' In other words anyone who wants the car at this low price has jolly well got to put the order in now. The orders came flooding in and that got him over the hump into the 1,000 and 1,500 a week mark, and from then he never looked back.[9]

It was still highly competitive. The Clyno company from Wolverhampton had grown as startlingly as Morris. Its first car came out in 1922 and by 1926 its production of 12,349, though still only about a quarter of Morris, was rising sharply and put the company's output ahead of Ford in third place in the British industry. To give Cowley more concern, the 1924 Clyno was regarded as better than the Morris equivalent and the company had a familiar-sounding slogan: 'A price level as low as any car of like rating in the world and a value vastly higher.'

The words were matched by deeds, as Clyno started a price war with Morris. Thomas recalled;

> Prices were often not fixed until the opening day of the Motor Show and there have been cases when manufacturers would go to the show with two or three sets of price cards for

the same model. Clyno always tried to match Morris prices. It got so bad I had to play a trick on them. They had found out who our cataloguers were and bribed somebody there to get them an early pull of our lists. So I had a false catalogue run off – with false prices, made them very much cheaper than we were actually going to come with. So when the Motor Show opened, Clynos came out with prices below ours and we knew were below a profitable figure. This was the beginning of industrial spying.[10]

Thomas's view was that Clyno went bankrupt not long after because they had tried a price war with Morris. The reasons were more complex. They borrowed heavily for a huge new factory, neglected to update models and finally produced a cheap car which was cheap and shoddy in other ways too. In short, they had made exactly the mistakes which Morris had taken care to avoid. Once more it pointed up his success.

In 1925 of 132,000 cars made in Britain, Morris made 55,582 and coined a pre-tax profit of £1.5 million; in 1926 he made 48,330 of 153,500 and his profits were £1.04 million; in 1927 he made 61,632 of 164,553 and his profits rose once more to £1.29 million, reaching the £1.5 million mark for the next three years.

It was not surprising that so patriotic a man as Morris should now turn his thoughts to the possibilities of world markets, particularly given his strong emotional belief in the British Empire. 'I find it difficult as a worker not to think in terms of my country and the Empire ... one of my dreams that I work for is to put England "on top" industrially again', he wrote in the *Daily Express* in 1927.[11]

It was still somewhat at odds with the realistic appreciation he had showed of American production techniques and the need for reliability that he should have embarked almost casually on the production of a car which turned out manifestly unsuitable for its purpose – the Empire car. Perhaps he was taken in by the apparent ease with which he had come to dominate the British market and the way in which he was managing to export about a fifth of his production. His conquest in Britain of the Model T Ford, so ubiquitous all over the world, may also have been an influence.

He could not have been unaware of the challenge. Back in 1911 the correspondent of the *Automobile Engineer* was writing that the

motor car trade of the Empire has gone to America in the

main through the greater commercial application of the Americans and through the greater suitability of the American car for rough country. It has so often been repeated that high clearance, standard track, great axle strength, exceptional strength of steering and great flexibility of springs are essential features for a successful colonial car. On the other hand, never yet have I seen a colonial motor car from a British factory which fulfilled these requirements.[12]

Morris commissioned what was to be called the Empire Oxford in 1926. It was to be built by Morris Commercial and it had some of the key features suggested by the *Automobile Engineer* to cope with rough road conditions – a high clearance and a wider track which would allow it to run along railway lines if flanged wheels were fitted. The prospects were enticing – some of the colonial markets were as big as those to be found in small European countries, and it provided a new market perhaps to balance the slump-prone home market.

In July 1925 *Autocar* reported Morris as telling a dinner party of overseas agents at the Holborn restaurant in London that 'he was heavily interested in the overseas market', and with admirable candour indicated what to his mind the main features of an ideal overseas car were, notably the 4 ft 8 in track. 'In five years', he said, he hoped 'the Morris car would be as well known abroad as at home.'

But when Morris commissioned the Empire car he had no first hand experience of the conditions into which he hoped to sell. It was not until the spring of 1927 that he was to visit Argentina where the first batch of Empire cars were shipped, and not until 1928 that he would travel to Australia which was intended as the prime market. He was to return from Argentina with the message that 'the motor car industry can never really hope to expand until roads in Argentina and Brazil are taken in hand.'

It is not entirely clear why the Empire car was such a spectacular failure. It had a 15.9 horsepower engine and was the first Morris with a four speed gearbox. It may have been thought underpowered for the colonial market and it rapidly acquired a bad name. Of the 1,740 produced in two and a half years, over 205 were shipped back unsold from Australia; some Oxfords were sold on the home market but as six cylinder cars were in fashion, not many of those either. The design was later adapted as the basis for a taxi but the Empire car was estimated to have cost Morris £100,000.

But it was only the beginning of his interest in conditions in the Empire. 1927 was to see the start of the custom of spending several months abroad every year, usually in travel to Australia. In spite of the failure of the Empire model the rhetoric about it seemed to grow stronger.

In the *Autocar* of 6 January 1928, under the bold heading of FORTHCOMING EMPIRE TRADE, Morris was quoted as he boarded the *Aquitania* to voyage to the United States and then Australasia;

> The success of the British light car industry in Australia is a striking example of how British industry and skill can by organisation and enterprise overtake the handicaps placed on them by the War. British light cars have triumphed in Australia because of their economy in operation, the ease of handling and high quality workmanship.

It was breathtaking stuff. Australia was the biggest market but British imports were far outnumbered by American. The same edition of the magazine carried a letter from an expatriate in Benares in India. British manufacturers, he wrote, had again missed the bus. He contrasted an Italian car which would romp up any hill with

> two well-known British cars in the neighbourhood (nearly everyone else runs Americans). The smaller will not go 10 miles under similar conditions without boiling like a kettle while the larger uses 4 gallons of water every 25 miles ... that is all there is to it. The first stands up to tropical conditions, the other two fail miserably. The first has an enormous world market while the other two are misplaced examples of misguided patriotism which their owners will never repeat.

While the effort to export to the British colonies is easy to understand, Morris's attempt to take on the French in their own back yard needs more explanation. Before the First World War, the French had for a while dominated the industry until overtaken by American mass production. Post-war, their motor industry was markedly less successful. Links between the two countries were quite strong with considerable import of French engines and components as well as built-up vehicles before the war, and Morris had travelled in France.

It would have seemed an obvious market yet in 1925 when the Morris office was established on the Avenue Malakoff in Paris, *Autocar* reported that Morris and its neighbour Rolls-Royce were the only British companies maintaining a selling organization in France, 'and curiously enough, one is the most exclusive and the other the most popular representative of the British motor industry.'

To establish himself in the French market, after a first unsuccessful attempt at an import business, Morris bought a French firm, the historic Leon Bollee company, which was based in Le Mans. Leon Bollee had been one of the pioneers of the French motor industry and patents to his tricycle cars had been bought in 1896 by the British Motor Syndicate as part of its efforts to turn itself into the first British motor manufacturer. Now Bollee was dead and Morris purchased the works from his widow.

It was a spectacular and confident move. The reasons given for it are various. One explanation was that it was a reaction to the news that Citroën were to set up in Britain. Another is that it came about through the Hotchkiss company, and Morris's contacts there. Whatever its origin, it was another striking failure, and again there are various reasons cited – French prejudice, a poorly judged model range, a decision to staff senior jobs with new recruits rather than seasoned Cowley men.

Morris himself was to blame French chauvinism and even to suggest that French suppliers had sent him the poorer quality of their production; certainly he could have nothing like the same hold on them as he had on his English suppliers who had grown with the company and depended upon it.

But the initial approach was full of optimism with Morris insisting he wanted a 'crack at the French' while public statements were designed to reassure an English audience. On 1 May 1925 *Autocar* reported that Morris did not intend to produce any Bollees for the British market and quoted him as saying, 'I feel that the primary consideration of all business at the present time should be to decrease unemployment in Great Britain.'

One of those who worked in the French operation was Carl Kingerlee. Later in life he would become Morris's influential private secretary. He worked for a firm which supplied Morris, another example of the well-trodden management route into the company.

Kingerlee's view of the failure was plain, effectively saying that

Morris had not done his homework.

He was rather pushed into buying Leon Bollee at the Motor Show, and the people who went out to look at it advised him it was a good buy. But in actual fact it was very wrong because Le Mans was a very long way from any coachbuilders. There were none in the town. So for the first seven or eight months we had to drive chassis to Paris to have bodies fitted on. It was paint and varnish in those days so that when they got back they weren't in a very good state to be tested and then sent out.

We built the wrong size car at the wrong price. He decided to fit the Hotchkiss four cylinder engine. We produced this car at the Paris Salon at the same time as people like Delarge and Hotchkiss went over to six cylinders at about the same price. All the American cars were becoming six cylinders and it became a six cylinder industry in France at that time.

By 1928 Morris was admitting defeat and started to run Bollee down. It was a bitter reverse and like the failure of the Empire car he did not like to talk about it.

Other British manufacturers were no more successful abroad than Morris was, although there was a steady trickle of exports. Where Morris was successful was in keeping the flag flying at home. He guaranteed a strong component supplier business and he introduced new technology to make the industry more efficient.

Kingerlee, though he knew Morris originally through connections with his well-known family in Oxford, was an example. He had had a small business making aluminium pistons, and after meeting Morris at a party on a Saturday night was summoned to see him at his golf club on the Sunday morning where Morris placed an order. A year later Kingerlee received two letters; one from Woollard cancelling the contract because the company was now to make its own pistons; the other from Morris asking him to join his staff in recompense.

It was characteristic treatment; supplying Morris was a matter of make or break. For those who were loyal the rewards could be enormous although margins were always tight. Morris took great delight in pointing out to would-be suppliers the advantages of economy of scale.

One of the companies whose fortunes especially rose with Morris was the Birmingham electrical firm of Joseph Lucas. The founder of the company, the original Joseph, had started by selling paraffin oil from a cart and then making a best-selling lamp for ships. Later Lucas had turned to bicycle lamps and then car lighting. Morris had not thought their equipment good enough for the Oxford but fitted it as standard on the Cowley. They were one of the companies which provided him with credit in the 1920 crisis, and he never forgot the debt to either Lucas or its representative, Charles Breeden.

By 1923 over half of Lucas's lighting and starting equipment was being supplied to Morris. So there was consternation when a boardroom row with his brother-in-law, Oliver Lucas, led to Breeden's departure, Lucas feared that Breeden's close connection with Morris might cost them the order. His replacement, Frank Thacker, who had worked for Rolls-Royce, was seen off by the two joint managing directors on his way to Cowley and interrogated on his return.

His account recalls his reception by Morris and makes clear how much a matter of personal contact the industry was. Everyone knew everybody.

> He was pleasant enough with me and I had no difficulty talking to him. He expressed his sympathy for me at joining Lucas and warned me I was working for a bigger humbug than Horatio Bottomley. I explained I should be the Lucas representative and he stated this was quite agreeable to him.
>
> The two joint M.Ds asked me particularly to report verbatim what W.R.M. had said to me. I am afraid I was very naive at the time and so I told them exactly, word for word. It was received in rather stony silence.

In the event, both Lucas and Breeden prospered. Lucas sales to Morris rose with the volume of production, from £94,725 worth in 1921 to £907,860 in 1925. The firm arranged for a design engineer and draughtsman to be seconded to Cowley to make any necessary modifications. Breeden formed his own firm, Wilmot Breeden, and Morris ordered temperature gauges from them. When they were sued for breach of patent by an American company and could not finance their defence, Morris took the case for them and won.

It was a difficult balance between supplier and assembler and Morris could play a difficult game. He was once asked if he had ever done anything dishonest. The closest he had come to it, he told the Professor who had asked him, was when a supplier, having verbally agreed a price, took Morris out for lunch and plied him with champagne – then produced the contract marked out for a higher price. Morris, still proud of his strong head for drink, stayed the more sober and ended up signing for a lower price than he had agreed. It was a story he relished as a warning to those who tried sharp practice with him.

Just how tough he could be was seen in the case of Triplex Glass, the company whose safety glass suddenly became in huge demand in what was called the 'splinterless boom' of the late twenties. When Morris's great rival Austin made a special agreement with Triplex in 1927 to make safety windscreens standard for all models, taking the output of the whole of the new Triplex factory at King's Norton, Morris moved.

Outwardly he played hard to get. He delayed placing any orders for his 1928-9 range and Triplex's founder booked a passage on the *Aquitania* to New York just so he could lobby Morris on the way. Finally Morris placed his order but for only a quarter of his output and then for the cheapest quality glass at a price on which Triplex made a loss.

Privately he played a longer game. Operating through nominees he bought a large block of a new issue of Triplex shares and continued to build his holding expensively as the share price was high, but without revealing his identity. He ended as far and away the largest shareholder and his nominee, a solicitor called Graham Cunningham, soon became managing director. Though he sold his shares gradually through the 1930s, Triplex knew where their interests lay.[19]

Morris won a greater victory over Austin in 1926, who by the mid-twenties was re-emerging to become Morris's greatest British rival, with his purchase of the Wolseley company. It was one of the great names of the industry. Originally the Wolseley Sheepshearing Machine Company, it had started to make cars as a sideline in the 1890s when business was slack, on the prompting, and to the designs, of one of its engineers, Herbert Austin. It had then been taken over by the big Vickers armaments company and a separate motor manufacturing subsidiary was set up. Although Austin later left after a technical disagreement, it went on to become the biggest British car manufacturer before the First World War, and grew even further with war work.

Post-war Vickers lost interest and sold out. The company had grandiose plans, built sumptuous offices and poor cars, and in 1926 went bankrupt to the tune of two million pounds.

It was a tempting prize for a growing motor manufacturer. When Austin and Morris had discussed merging in 1924, Morris's letter of refusal had talked of the 'admirable plant' offered by Wolseley and expensively re-equipped. He was growing rapidly and had had a successful experience of buying suppliers' plants and turning them to efficient use. Wolseley had a more up-market name than Morris and would complement his range particularly as Morris was planning a light six-cylinder car and admired the Wolseley version. For Austin there were similar considerations although his plant was already much more extensive, and there was also the poignant opportunity of acquiring the company he had helped found, returning as master.

There was also a final, and patriotic reason; to keep out the Americans. Austin had been persuaded to refuse the General Motors offer for his own company while Morris had also been sounded out about a sale for £11,000,000 but had rapidly refused. Now it was rumoured that General Motors, with its policy of buying companies all over Europe, was interested in Wolseley.

Morris was never sure whether he was bidding against General Motors though Miles Thomas subsequently held the belief that the third party was a speculator who would have resold, perhaps in parts. All Morris knew was that there were three bidders – himself, Austin and a foreign interest. His first sealed bid was for £600,000 but when the bids were opened it was found to have been topped by the foreign bidder. Although the time limit had expired Morris then received permission to increase his bid and an objection by the foreign interest was dismissed by a judge. Morris and Austin then matched bid for bid, watched by their staff, among them Miles Thomas.

So it went on, each leapfrogging the other until I noticed a whispered conversation between a rather tense-looking Mr Payton (the Austin financial director) and a very flushed bright eyed Mr Morris. From my privileged position I was able to hear the gist of the whispering which on Morris's part, with his chin well stuck out was to the effect that he was determined to outbid Austin. He repeated this assertion out aloud for all to hear. The Morris finances were very sound and so at £730,000 Wolseley Motors was knocked down to Morris.[20]

Thomas's participation did not end there. He and Morris had prepared a press release setting out what they would do with Wolseley. He hurried to the *Daily Express* to get it into the paper only to see through the glass panelled door that Austin and Payton were already with the editor, drawing up a statement. Thomas, his release ready, short-circuited the process by ringing the editor and dictating his copy from the outer office. Such was the enthusiasm and publicity sense of the Morris team.

In the event Morris sold off some of the Wolseley plant, moved Morris Commercial into one factory and concentrated car production in another. Beside the plant he once more inherited men who would become valuable members of his team including Oliver Boden, the executive manager, and an able design team.

One of the young Wolseley workers was James Woodcock. Later to become deputy chairman of the Nuffield Organisation, he was a month from finishing his apprenticeship when Morris bought the company.

> There was great relief. Thank God something had happened to us. The old owners had had their yachts and their engines in for repair and servicing, and allowed it to go bankrupt. My first sight [of Morris] was when he had just bought it, seeing him walk along what they called the old mill with Oliver Boden, in his bowler hat and a dirty old mac walking through, chin jutting out as I got to know so very well. That was it. The next thing we knew was that L.P. Lord came in as works manager. He was a brilliant engineer. At Engines branch in conjunction with Archdale he designed and brought into production big multi-spindle drillers, the first step towards multiple engineering. He was put in to reorganise the place.

The purchase of Wolseley came at the end of Morris's period of rapid expansion and it took longer than he expected to make the progress he wanted. One reason, he believed, was that he was moving upmarket away from his traditional market of those who wanted a reliable car at the most affordable price. The Wolseley buyer wanted something of more exclusive quality, and he had to be convinced that the mass production methods for which Morris was renowned would provide it. There was one major purchase that year, of SU Carburettors, but effectively the empire was complete.

Morris's progress had now put him on a new financial plane and the arrangements he had made after the war were no longer suitable. He was also to face a challenge from the tax authorities who pursued him for super tax on money he insisted was being ploughed back into the business. It was a difficult argument but it was to be conceded to Morris in strange circumstances which demonstrated what a national symbol he had by now become and how he was indeed seen as flying the flag for Britain.

The structure of the Morris companies was, like the man, idiosyncratic. Morris would retain parts of his empire, like Wolseley, the Morris Garages and MG as his own personal property as Morris Industries Ltd but in 1926 he turned the core of the business, Morris Motors Ltd, into a public company. Apart from the financial reasons and the money it would secure for him personally, there were the appealing grounds put to Morris by his accountant Thornton that if his persistent hypochondria was to be proved justified and he suddenly died, the business would have to be broken up subsequently for technical reasons.

The flotation took place in 1926 in a typically individual way. Morris insisted on doing it all his own way. The company's capital was fixed at £5 million with 2 million ordinary shares of £1 each and 3 million 7½ per cent cumulative preference shares. His advisors insisted that given the poor record of motor companies to date, issue of the preference shares with their fixed interest should be linked to the ordinary shares, and the whole issue underwritten by the bankers in case not all the shares were taken up.

Morris insisted that he would give up none of the ordinary shares, and was so sure of his reputation that he refused underwriting, declaring he would himself buy up any preference shares remaining. One of his principal stockbrokers then resigned but the issue was a triumphant success. Morris had proved he knew better. As the biographical memoir smugly remarked, 'This Preference issue provided his first contact with higher finance ... and there is no doubt that he thoroughly enjoyed an experience in the course of which he often found himself in total disagreement with expert opinion.'[21]

As Morris held all the ordinary stock, he retained complete control about how much dividend was paid each year and how much was retained in the business once the fixed interest preference shares had been paid out, something he saw as a key requirement for controlling his business.

Under the new arrangements it was laid down that once the

preference shares were paid out, a quarter of the remaining profit should be lodged in a reserve fund until that fund had reached a million pounds. It was the old Morris policy of ploughing his profits back into the business. In the first three years of the public company he did better than that, refusing to take any dividends and crediting two million pounds to the reserves. Now at last he was financially secure.

But his determination to put back money into the company rather than taking dividends was already bringing him into conflict with the tax authorities who saw it as a dodge to avoid paying super tax, the tax levied on people with particularly high incomes. Unlike income tax which was then levied at a fixed rate, super tax rose progressively. As companies paid only at the standard income tax rate, there were advantages in leaving money in the company.

The 1922 Finance Act had attempted to close the loophole by a stipulation that if the Inland Revenue judged that a company had not paid out a reasonable part of the retained income within a reasonable period, the whole income could be treated as if paid out to the shareholders and effectively become liable to the much higher rate of super tax.

Morris went through two long and costly cases in 1926 and 1929. The first hinged on provisions which allowed the tax authorities to allow not just for the running costs of the business but for its 'maintenance and development'. Morris brought a procession of witnesses to the box including Payton, the Austin finance director, to demonstrate just how perilous the motor industry was and how vulnerable to sudden shifts, so requiring large reserves. The Crown pointed to Morris's steady programme of acquisition but lost the case.

By 1929 and the second case, a familiar peril had reappeared. Two out of three political parties were proposing to remove the protective McKenna duties if elected at the forthcoming election. Meanwhile Ford, which in 1926 had declared itself 'licked in Britain' was making expensive plans for a come-back. New models were planned and a new purpose built factory with its own docks and foundries on the Essex marshes at Dagenham.

In the evidence he prepared, Morris, created a baronet just a few weeks earlier, made much of the threat.

It has been the aim and object all my life to develop these businesses and not to make money for myself but, so far as I have been able to do so, to assist in the development of British manufactures and industry. The main object of my life has been to manufacture a car which could be sold at a price which the ordinary man in the street could buy, and if I could, to compete with the Ford product, which at the time I started to manufacture and market the small light car was dominant in Britain.[22]

Sensationally the case was halted after a single day and the Attorney General, Sir William Jowitt, who was taking what was seen as a nationally important case, announced after a week's adjournment that the case would be dropped.

He declared:

It is not merely my function to win cases. I have to be quite satisfied in my own mind that the result ... is going to be conducive to the national good. I was impressed ... by the evidence showing that there was at least a possibility of serious competition between Sir William Morris and his companies and Mr Ford and his companies with regard to a market which must always be a more or less restricted market. Though it is certainly not for me to take sides in that controversy between those eminent gentlemen, at least equally it is for me to see that they are both of them fairly armed for the fight and I can well understand that for the purpose of that fight it is desirable that Sir William Morris should have at his disposal very large capital reserves.

Secondly something has been said by Sir William Morris with regard to the development of the export market. So far as that is concerned, he has no more sincere well-wisher than I am, and I sincerely hope that he will not allow his energies to flag or his determination to become less keen; because I am quite convinced that, with the ingenuity which he possesses, he may be able to develop for this country a very important market which we should all like to see, and which will do, if it is developed, a great deal to assist in the terrible problem of unemployment with which His Majesty's Ministers are faced today.[23]

After the case Jowitt and Morris strolled arm in arm down the street. The boy from the backstreet bicycle shop had received the ultimate accolade, if not the final one. He was a pillar of the establishment, the nation's industrial champion, for whom even legalities could now be set aside as he flew the flag for Britain. He was accepted and judged on his own terms.

7 Pillar of the Establishment

It had been a long road from the shed at the bottom of his parents' garden to the airy escarpment of the Chilterns in the village of Nuffield where Morris had now chosen to live; up above the plain of the Thames and Oxford itself. Just as his business was now well-established and a matter of national moment, so his own views and idiosyncracies had become a matter of national interest, his backing and advice sought out by an extending range of the prominent which included even the future king himself.

If the Morris character had been settled during the early struggle, the style was now established and would become increasingly well-known, but the marks of the long and perilous apprenticeship remained for all to see.

Enthusiastic, idiosyncratic, determined to the point of dogmatism, repetitive, frugal, and single-minded were all epithets which could be used of him. But the first impression most people had was one of restless energy.

Miles Thomas first met him in 1920 when Morris, in his early forties, arrived at a motoring club rally in a straw boater 'with just that touch of the unusual to make [it] stand out in the small crowd.'

> He was a dark, trim, dynamic figure, full of physical energy, rather shy in his casual conversations, and not really a very good mixer. While he was punctiliously polite, his public projection was that of a self centred withdrawn introvert ... I must confess that Bill Morris was nothing like so colourful a personality as some of those other aspirants to fame and fortune in the small car world and whose products have long since been forgotten.

Thomas was to be close to Morris until his death, 'in all his varying moods, at the heights of his exultations, and in the depths of depression. At all times he was mercurial, unpredictable, but inevitably sensitive and keenly feeling in human affairs.'[1]

If Thomas's view was considered coloured by later experience, the impression gained by Massac Buist of *Autocar* in 1925 was of a man in perpetual motion.

> In talking to you he may begin by putting one knee over the other until a perpetual restlessness makes him, within the next few minutes, fling his legs over the arm of the chair he is using, and rock his whole body to and fro. The next moment he jumps up, walks a few steps forth and back using nervous energy unnecessarily. Even when standing he will shake one leg at the knee continually while he is reading a chit from the works, discussing a carburettor, or telephoning. This is the only sign of nervous tension, happily now based on no serious cause, and only a subconscious condition.[2]

Another acquaintance, Richard Newitt, whose Wadhams firm became a South Coast distributor after the 1919 reorganization and frequently saw Morris passing through Southampton on the way to France or the USA, found him, 'temperamental, full of go, like a violin string'. But a man who had to have his own way and could be difficult to deal with.[3]

The underlying tension was always there. Thomas was startled by Morris's reaction to finding a piece of soap dissolving in an unemptied wash basin at the works.

> That bright-eyed tight little man fumed and swore and became tremendously hot under the collar. He cursed roundly the habits of people who did not leave wash basins in the state in which they would expect to find them. He cried to high heaven about the extravagance of leaving a piece of soap to waste.[4]

The suppressed feeling often showed as Morris went round the shop floor in the early days. George Walker started in the Cowley machine shops in 1920, in a section 'colloquially known as the rat's hole because it was down some steps'.

> We used to have an early morning visit from Lord Nuffield and we always knew if he was in a good or bad temper; the further his hat was on the back of his head the worse his temper. He used to stamp through the machine shop glaring at everybody and cursing the foremen. I always recall the

occasion when a man called Bob Lambert threw an apple core at me because I was working on a machine just by the door. He missed me and it hit (Mr) Morris in the tummy. Bob Lambert is the only man who can genuinely claim to have had his bottom physically kicked by Lord Nuffield. He chased him down the whole length of the shop kicking him up the behind.

In the early days you used to see a great deal of him just walking about. He would talk with any of his people; mix with any of his people, and he knew them. I admired him very much.[5]

Thomas was impressed too that until the age of about fifty Morris could remember the name of his shop floor workers, but then,

Inevitably as the business grew and the number of personnel increased, he could not memorise the names of all the workpeople. That seemed to give him peculiar discomfort. I do not pretend that he had any guilt consciousness but as soon as he found that he did not know all his workpeople by name, he ceased to walk through the shops. That was a pity because it would have done a great deal for morale. Indeed when he became Sir William Morris he divorced himself more and more from the running of the business.[6]

It was a benevolent paternalism, provided the employee knew his place. The quality Morris most valued from those who worked for him was loyalty. He remained particularly attached to those like Alfred Keen who had been with him in the early Longwall days but who would never aspire to a position of major influence.

'When taking over any man for an executive position,' Morris told an interviewer, 'the first thing I want is a loyal face. If a man isn't going to be loyal neither of us will get on together. I think perhaps I have an ability for reading faces, and for that reason I've made very few mistakes in my time.'[7]

The other side of the coin to that was put by Miles Thomas. 'Provided they were loyal, unquestioning servants who did not try to interrupt while the boss was talking and did not figure even in the fringe of the strong limelight that illuminated his personal image, all went well.'[8]

The problems came when those believed to be loyal challenged the boss; there was a steady drip of departures of those who were thought to have overstepped the mark or been disloyal, an anathematising of friends as well as colleagues – from the early ally Frank Grey who had dared to oppose protectionism right through to Reginald Hanks, a long-serving Vice-Chairman in the 1950s. Thomas himself was a victim when Morris came to resent his public prominence outside the Morris business.

For most of his life Morris lacked close friends, particularly in the business. The exception was Lancelot Pratt, the head of Hollick and Pratt which had produced the first bodies for the Oxford and had come to Morris's aid in 1919 with a loan of £10,000. He was more than a loyalist. When Morris bought his company in 1922 he came down to Cowley as deputy governing director. It was seen by all as an excellent move; Pratt came close to being the only man trusted implicitly by Morris. Morris's authorized biography describes it as 'a very happy arrangement, for he was an intimate friend'.[9] Thomas thought Morris suffered greatly when Pratt died of cancer eighteen months later.[10]

Morris kept until his death a poignant letter from Pratt which refers to an earlier bout of illness and clearly reflects the affection between the two men.

> Dear old man, please do not worry about me. Who has been talking? Somebody has, it is either Young or Grey. They both mean well but must not do it. I came over to try and help you, not to be an added worry. Although I thoroughly appreciate your anxiety on my behalf, I shall when I come to Oxford on Tuesday put a stop to the good people running to you with tales about my health.
>
> I have got shingles. They are very uncomfortable things to put up with, but as they are not catching, it does not matter so much. I shall come to Oxford as usual on Tuesday and bring the coupe price with me.[11]

It is the only letter amongst his papers with a trace of affection in it.

Without Pratt, management by Morris was autocratic, sometimes wilfully so. Thomas had an inside view.

> Essentially he was a lonely man, for the reason that he strongly preferred to think alone. Not for him a busy round of interviews and meetings and conferences. He became increasingly ill at ease at the head of the boardroom table. Yet equally he became more and more impatient when we

departmental directors got together for regular formalised exchange of views. It became more frequent for him, deliberately and mischievously, to call one of us out of our Wednesday afternoon management conferences to go to his office and answer some question which could quite easily have been left for another hour, or even another day.

He liked best talking to individuals – face to face rather than on the telephone. He liked to spur people on by telling them of the shortcomings of their colleagues.[12]

Morris had a dislike of paperwork. It was blamed for the restrictive distribution contract, which was the cause of the formal liquidation of the company in 1919. Thereafter he took care to have documents read or explained to him; he rarely read anything himself.

Robert Macintosh who met him as a young doctor in the twenties and became one of his few personal friends, said;

> He never did any reading. I have never known him read a book in the whole of his life; and when it came to the papers it was only the front page news. I honestly cannot remember him ever being interested or reading a book of any sort. Figures though. That was the extraordinary thing. He could read a balance sheet which completely baffled me. Whether it was two million or five hundred. Making up your mind from figures, but he had that curious flair.[13]

Miss Ena Berry, his secretary from 1939, said he never read a letter nor dictated a reply. He wanted to hear the meat of it and then just indicated a reply.[14] It put a heavy responsibility on Nuffield's private secretaries, Wilfred Hobbs and later Carl Kingerlee. Hobbs was private secretary or personal assistant to Morris from 1924 to 1945. Discreet, self-effacing, but clear-minded and decisive, he was a key go-between between Morris and his executives, and a filter for approaches from outside. He effectively decided what and who Morris saw. He also acted as discreet eyes and ears for him, alerting him to sensitive issues. When the business of charity bequests swelled to huge proportions, Hobbs became the man who sieved the proposals.

Leslie Farrer-Brown, first director of the Nuffield Foundation says, 'In many ways one felt the only man who could guide him was Wilfred. He shunned the limelight. He was another of those shy men, who lived in a village with his sisters. He was completely devoted to Morris; his personal confidant, almost his offsider.'[15] One senior executive taking over his position made sure he had Hobbs' support, describing him bluntly as 'the power behind the throne'.[16]

Morris retained the same office throughout his time at Cowley in what had been the old Manor House. As one visitor described:

> You went through number one gate past the tin shed where he had made his early cars into the Nuffield Press, up a rickety staircase to the second floor to this little room, through his secretary's office and you were ushered into the presence. My first impression was of this man with a jutting jaw standing up and telling me 'Sit down'. There was a plain desk, a couple of tin ashtrays on the desk, a valuable clock which I gather he had given to him, a side-desk with a roller-top and a threadbare carpet.[17]

Others noted the cycling medals displayed in a case over the fireplace, a dial which indicated wind direction and later they would sometimes be taken through a door to see the Revd Francis Pilcher's original bicycle, rescued from a jumble sale.

There was also a drinks cabinet, containing the ingredients for his favourite drink, gin and vermouth for making 'gin and it'. Morris was never a puritan although sometimes his hypochondria held him back, and Thomas recalls days when 'the bottles were in very easy reach in his office at anything after eleven o'clock in the morning. Sometimes he would smoke heavily, enwreathing himself in clouds from his pipe for the whole day. At other times he would go completely anti-nicotine and make curious cigarette holders with all kinds of filters in them. One, I remember, was about nine inches long and had three separate filtration systems which were so efficient that practically all that came through was pure tasteless air.'[18]

Once more his love of gadgets was evident. But he would not give up smoking until the very end of his life. He took to a patent cigarette made by a Birmingham firm with special ingredients which ensured that if dropped on the floor or put down it would go out. It became a mannered party piece which Morris endlessly performed, to the increasing irritation of those who had seen it hundreds of times before.

His attitudes to his workforce were paternalistic, slightly sentimental, but uncompromising. He believed in paying good wages but that done, saw no need for extra welfare provision and he opposed trade union organization.

'I have no particular reverence for tradition,' he wrote in the *Daily Express* in 1927,' especially for industrial tradition. I never allow trade unions to interfere with me. The sins and shortcomings of the employer a generation ago are nothing to do with me. I disown the past in this respect emphatically. The laying down of standards is anathema to me.'

Morris could afford to take this line for two reasons. First, he paid over the going union rate, and higher than parts of the industrial Midlands by means of a bonus scheme devised in the early twenties by Landstad and proudly exhibited by Morris in his *System* article. Secondly Oxford had not previously been an industrial centre.

Before Morris, the largest industrial employer had been the university press and a study of his workforce showed that a third had come from low-paid agricultural backgrounds. The unions found great difficulty in organizing – indicated by the way the Morris plants worked on during the 1926 General Strike. It was not until unemployed miners with a tradition of active unionism began to arrive in Oxford in the later twenties that the unions began to find some steam, but the Morris policy of high wages still had its effect.[19]

'A low wage is the most expensive method of producing. A moderately high wage gives a man an interest in life. Men are only going to work if they are going to earn more comforts, hobbies and amusements.'[20]

The result was wages double those on farms around Oxford, which even surprised Woodcock when he came down from the Wolseley plant in Birmingham. 'When I first went to Cowley, he had taken people in from the surrounding farms to do a simple job, tightening up two or three nuts and he was paying them five guineas a week. Now at that time the skilled engineer's rate was forty-six shillings plus ten shillings national award – £2.16. So, of course they didn't strike.'

Morris regularly praised the British worker.

The men I employ hold, I hope, a good opinion of me. I hold a high opinion of them. I expect as much from them as they expect from me. There are no workers in the world to touch our British workers as men and as workers. They are simply in a class by themselves.[21]

But his belief that it was enough simply to pay good wages was disputed by some of his management. 'Much has been said and written about welfare schemes for workers,' wrote the man whose later benevolence would endow hundreds of different schemes. 'I do not believe in overdoing it. You cannot intermingle work and pleasure. Pay a man a good day's wage for an honest day's work and he will soon find out how to enjoy himself properly.'[22]

That was not always the case in Cowley where there was an influx of people from depressed parts of Britain eager to find work in the burgeoning new industry. 'Large numbers of young single men are continually being absorbed into the motor industry,' said a letter to the *Oxford Mail* in 1937. 'They have to find lodging near the works and often they get accommodation in homes that are already overcrowded. After working hours there is no comfort in such places and in most cases they are expected to be out of doors in the evenings.'[23]

Thomas and others working away both in Cowley and other plants ruefully reflected that whatever the governor wrote, it was they who had the day to day responsibility for labour relations.

> We had considerable difficulty in persuading [him] to allow money to be spent on putting up canteens, sports pavilions, playing fields and all that kind of amenity which, in the emergent years of industry between the wars, became not only a status symbol of a company, but a very real necessity if labour was to be attracted and held.[24]

Morris had himself now moved his own private accommodation out of Cowley where he and his wife had lived for a time in the manor house adjoining the works. They had transferred to the village of Nuffield, fifteen miles out of Oxford on the Henley road.

The village stands on the great Chiltern escarpment which curves round from Buckinghamshire and through Oxfordshire until it is cut back by the course of the Thames. The common which runs up to the village from the main Oxford to Henley road is occupied by a fashionable private golf course called Huntercombe which was founded at the beginning of the century.

Morris had been advised to join the club after his post-First World War illness. It was to provide exercise and some fresher air on the heights above the damp Oxfordshire plain in accordance with the club's own early advertisement for 'health-giving breezes, a perfect seaside course inland'.

It proved congenial, and he took to the place. When in 1925 the Norwich Union who owned the Huntercombe estate announced a development of the site with building plots for sale, Morris told his private secretary, Wilfred Hobbs, to buy the estate. Hobbs is supposed to have asked how much he might spend, Nuffield to have replied, 'the best price you can'.[25] In the event Morris paid £32,500 for 967 acres and soon he and his wife moved to live there in a flat built onto the already extensive clubhouse.

Originally the property was registered in Mrs Morris's name and those close to the family heard it described as a present to her. It certainly provided an interest and a focus for both partners in what was now a difficult marriage.

Discussing the Morris marriage is difficult. Both partners were very protective of each other. No interviews were permitted of Mrs Morris and she is allowed less than a page in the authorized biography. Morris wanted nothing at all. Being married to a man who is married to his business is never an easy situation, and Lilian Morris, shyer than her husband and an even worse mixer was destined to be lonely. The move to Huntercombe provided them both with a new interest, with Lilian taking on responsibility for the management of the clubhouse. She did not cook and so the opportunity to have meals provided for them in the clubhouse plus ready-made company for them both made a great deal of sense.

A tall, rather gaunt woman, sometimes giving the impression of brusqueness because of her shyness, Lilian Morris was preoccupied with the worry that her husband's business, already close to ruin at regular intervals, would one day come to final grief. Her nephew's wife, Margaret Hawes says, 'She was tight with money. She was very worried that it would all disappear one day. You can understand it. Growing up in a family where you have had to be very careful because there is no father. It rather sticks.'

She had a reputation for parsimony. There were Cowley stories of her gathering in the canteen scraps for the chickens, and then selling the eggs to the men; of having a room papered but the wall left bare behind the wardrobe. When out to lunch with a friend she would enquire the price and choose the cheapest and there were soon complaints about the catering standards at Huntercombe when she took over.

Macintosh, whose first wife was a close friend, thought highly of her, like Mrs Hawes. 'She was quite forthright. As honest as the day. She wasn't mean but if there was a question of price she would go for the cheap thing. I could not tell her that to her face.'

There were no children of the marriage. Thomas was the only one to speculate in public about the reason. Saying that their home life was not very happy he told one interviewer that Mrs Morris 'had made up her mind not to have children because she had a horror and fear of childbirth'[26], while he suggested in another interview that there were no children because she had decided not to have any because she resented the time he spent at his business.

Soon after the move to Huntercombe Morris started the practice of going to Australia by ship almost every winter. He would leave in January, returning in March when his cash book would show a flurry of activity as he dealt with subscriptions and other bills. Lilian did not usually go with him. He was accompanied often by Wilfred Hobbs, and sometimes by other members of the organization, or a relative. While he was away Lilian Morris would often be driven to the south of France by Maule the chauffeur with her sister and brother-in-law.

There was a little talk of other women but it was very discreet. There was a relation who claimed to have travelled to London to buy a mink coat for one lady friend; a younger woman who talked of being offered an MG if she returned Morris's affections; there were shipboard flirtations. There is however one hard piece of evidence; the fact that Morris had a woman friend in Australia was common knowledge among the Cowley circle, and was confirmed by one of those who travelled to Australia with him. In addition, Miles Thomas's daughter, Dr Sheila von Bergen says, 'Everyone knew there was a woman he used to go out to every year. Certainly my parents knew but not much about it. Whether Lady Nuffield knew I simply don't know. I thought she did but she never ranted or raved or got at him about it.'

That was not in any case the Lilian Morris style. She was happiest, her friends said, in her garden, with her dogs and doing the needlework which had once helped her earn her living. She did not relish the public arena into which her husband was increasingly being thrown and would rarely accompany him to dinners and functions. But when Miles Thomas organized a visit to a film studios she was enthusiastic and enjoyed herself demonstrably.

His daughter remembered her as a 'nice woman'.

She was a very upright woman. She had a schoolmistressy air to her. A fine woman but she didn't do anything with herself.

She was neat and tidy but she didn't refurbish herself at all. She was a bit of a stickler.

She used to take over the skating rink in Oxford at Christmas and give children's parties down there which were nothing to do with the works, and gave us all very nice presents.

He was always kind but not good with children. He just never met them. He didn't know how to behave. He was very inept at handing over the half-crown. He knew he should do it, but even as a child one realised it wasn't going well. You got it but everyone felt embarrassed by it.

The village of Nuffield had divided views about the Morrises. Tom Streak, the greenkeeper, remembered Morris as having no time for anyone who wouldn't work but bothering about his employees in a human way. When the golf course staff had difficulties with their housing, he had four cottages erected for them. Lilian Morris would spend hours in the garden, dressed 'like a gypsy', frequently having differences of opinion with her gardeners about where plants were to be put.

Ivy Vernon became a 'between maid' for the Morrises when she was fourteen, doing cleaning and washing-up. By then they had moved to a nearby house, though they continued frequently to take their meals at the club.

She found Lilian Morris penny-pinching over housework. She complained that the servants had to clean the windows with plain water and the baths with hard soap, and furniture was allowed only a smear of polish from a tube.

Once when the Morrises were away she and another maid were left instructions to turn and vacuum the mattresses. They found an evening bag tucked between the mattresses, 'to check we had done it'. She also remembered Lilian Morris checking that she hadn't used too much water in her bath. She was often hungry, the Morrises ate little and the larder stayed locked. After a year she left mainly because of Lilian Morris. 'I couldn't stand her. She was behind you all the time.'

But she also remembered the Morrises' help when her brother Reg was knocked off his bicycle and stayed unconscious for a month. A car was provided every day to take her mother to the hospital and Morris arranged for a specialist from Guy's, and paid all the bills.[27]

Kathleen Francis was cook and personal maid to Lilian. She

stayed with the Morrises for thirty years, becoming the housekeeper. Her sister, Miss W. Francis, who was frequently in the house and sometimes slept there, recalled Morris frequently saying to them, 'And what are you ladies doing today?' and driving them to Oxford on his way to Cowley or to Reading on his way to London. Her view of Lilian Morris was that her husband would not have got where he had without her behind him, and that she was not so difficult to get on with as others made out.[28]

Mrs Hawes, a frequent visitor to Nuffield who lunched with her every week in later life says:

> She was shy that maybe she had rather a brusque manner to overcome it. She didn't really like public life. I went to visit her regularly to accompany her to these occasions. Once I had to dig her out of the garden. She loved gardening and spent as much time there as she could, doing all the jobs, even the heavy digging. She was very shy so I went with her on many occasions and saw many people receive their degrees and went to Henley Regatta and Wimbledon, which they liked.

The village of Nuffield was to be the Morris home. They moved a few hundred yards from the clubhouse to Merrow Mount, a large house which they renamed Nuffield Place in 1933. Amongst their few close friends there was Kennerley Rumford, a popular baritone singer married to the much more celebrated Dame Clara Butt, a singer who was a national institution between the wars and for whom the words of 'Land of Hope and Glory' were written. Rumford had joined the club at the same time as Morris and was later put in by him as secretary.

At Huntercombe golf course, Morris was his old idiosyncratic self. The club records say he managed a handicap of twelve, but he played without a back swing and seemed impatient to get on with the game. Macintosh who met him first at the club said, 'He was apt to forget his backstroke. He paid little attention and rather prided himself on just putting the club down. There was none of the addressing of the ball. He was a practical man; it was unnecessary.'

'I have never known him play a full round. He would play a few holes then say, "Come in and have a cup of tea". And I have known him then go over and repair my car. He rather took pride in that.'

Tom Streak who worked for him at the club said Morris was such an impatient player, barely waiting for the tee to be put in, that the caddies would joke that one day he would hit their hand rather than the ball. He never addressed the ball but hit out at once. Nor did he keep score, simply asking the caddy from time to time, 'How do we stand?'[29] No church-goer, he played most Saturdays and Sundays and had a regular female caddy, Edie Davis.

Although Mrs Morris also played and became President of the Ladies Section, enjoying weekend foursomes, the move to Huntercombe was to have a wider significance. It brought the Morrises into the company of a different group of people, a ready-made set of acquaintances. Many of them were doctors, and the contacts made at Huntercombe were to lead to many of the most important benefactions Morris was to make.

The principal group was a collection of doctors from Guy's Hospital in London. One of them was Robert Macintosh, an anaesthetist from New Zealand who had served in the Royal Flying Corps during the war and been a prisoner of war.

> One or two of the senior people had been going down for a very long time. We all dined together in the clubhouse and Mr and Mrs Morris used to join us. It was a communal dining-room and they lived there and joined our table. Rather unusually they had no staff, no cook. They lived very simply. We used to discuss different things and paid no more attention to him than anyone else there, then he did begin to get interested in some of the things we were talking about.

Morris was to develop a voracious interest in all things medical. There was a clue already in his hypochondria but his conversations at Huntercombe were to make it all-consuming. It was an area forever to be closed off to him as far as practice was concerned but one where his bequests would give him a vicarious involvement. There was perhaps another attraction; there is traditionally little deference to be had from a group of confident doctors, secure in their own profession, not inclined to bow down to a man who never read a book.

There is a story which has been often repeated, not least by Morris himself, that as a child he had always wanted to be a surgeon but family circumstances and his father's illness had prevented it. Morris even caused it to be written in by hand to the biographical memoir but early interviews do not mention it. Macintosh said bluntly it was 'Complete baloney, an afterthought'. He insists that it was only gradually that Morris was drawn in.

The doctors were of course aware of the Morris wealth and also of the embarrassment it caused him. He was fond of telling them, and many others, how cheaply he bought his suits. 'He used to say "I have never paid more than £5 for my suits – what's wrong with this one?" Now there we shut up. We could have told him what was wrong but no-one liked to contradict him. When you are talking to a peer of the realm, silence was converted to approval,' said Macintosh.

Morris was to make his first tentative bequests in 1926. In 1927 he set out in public in a *Daily Express* article, headed 'Life is a practical job' his uneasiness about charitable giving, which revealed he had already had contact with the Rockefeller circle, on which his own Foundation would later be based.

> Being, I suppose, what is called a rich man, there is one thing in life that troubles me a good deal. That thing is charity. I remember a secretary of Rockefeller's voicing no doubt his chief's view saying to me recently in New York 'You know Mr Morris, it's the easiest thing in the world to make money. But it's damned difficult to know how to get rid of it.'
>
> This is my experience. The man who would give money is compelled to do a great deal of hard thinking. Is his gift going to do good or harm? Money has tremendous power and can do either. The responsibility of the would-be giver is great. If he is a decent man, he cannot escape it ... I am approached each day for monetary assistance. I disregard all of them. When I give, I give collectively and not individually.

The first Morris excursion into large-scale charitable giving came in the summer of 1926. By this time he had become used to the appeals for assistance which all businesses receive. His first cautious toe in the water was not one of the medical charities with which his name soon came to be particularly associated but was a matter of almost straightforward business encouragement. He provided £10,000 to establish a Chair of Spanish Studies at Oxford University. It followed a visit to Spain which had included a meeting with King Alfonso after whom the Professorship was to be named.

It fitted with his current enthusiasm for expanding his activities into the export markets of Europe. The Crown Prince indeed had purchased an MG. But he also saw it as a hint to the university, with whom his relations were always ambiguous, that it should be more involved with studies he saw as appropriate to the modern world. This battle would be rejoined later.

The first of his hospital benefactions came the following year. It was reported in January 1927 that he was contributing £104,000 to St Thomas's Hospital in London for general finances. The annual running costs of the hospital were £175,000 and only £73,000 had come in. Sir Arthur Stanley, the hospital treasurer, described it as 'the largest individual gift received by the hospital for years'[30] and it was an astonishingly large sum from a man whose company was only just establishing itself.

Later in the year he was being hailed in Birmingham after contributing £25,000 to the city's General Hospital and further sums to the Coventry and Warwickshire Hospital. These were both cities where he had major manufacturing sites, and the Birmingham donation was announced as he was opening a large new depot there. There was more apparent connection and cynics could say, more obvious self-interest.

This could not however be said about another of the first benefactions. In 1926 Morris gave £10,000 to provide fares for parents of boys sent to Borstal establishments to visit them. It was a direct response to a conversation with Sir Alexander Patterson, the Commissioner of Prisons. He was one of a new group of people with whom public recognition was now increasingly bringing Morris into contact – the society of the good and the great. It was company which he increasingly enjoyed.

Morris gave in much the same way as he had raced his bicycles, floated the shares in his company or directed his managers; in his own way and on his own terms. He very rarely gave if pressed and delighted in making surprise, or surprisingly large, donations. The classic case, perhaps, is his reaction to being told a story by the doctor Sir John Conybeare about nurses whose savings had been embezzled by a con man. Out of the blue Morris wrote them a cheque. He clearly enjoyed the sensation the unexpected brought.

At the same time he relished the social approval which he now began to receive from some of the highest in the land. He was something of a social snob. Late in his life the Nuffield Foundation organized a function to which Morris declined to come. When it was known that the Queen Mother would attend he made a surprise appearance. It was a paradox. Alongside the cheaply bought suits, the advertised liking for bread and dripping, the cult of ordinariness, lay a great concern to be seen as a grander figure to which the expensive search for a worthy genealogy attested. As Macintosh noticed, beside the £5 suits sat the court cases of robes and honorary uniforms which recognition brought.

Carefully kept amongst his few papers are the royal acknowledgements of his benefactions. They include a copy of the telegram sent by King Alfonso to express 'heartfelt thanks' for the first donation. It was heady stuff for the motor maker who five years before had been uncertain whether his business would even survive.[32]

And there was better to come. A brief typewritten note addressed to The Cottage, Nuffield Common and dated 26 June 1929 came from St James's Palace.

> The Prince of Wales is to be in Oxford on the evening of Friday July 5 for the Rhodes Scholars Reunion Dinner. HRH desires me to ask you whether you would care for a game of golf that afternoon. If I hear from you that you are free I will write again and say what time HRH would like to play.[33]

It was a marker for a new relationship; one of a series of meetings between Morris and the future King Edward VIII. The first was probably on 24 May 1927 when the Prince had been shown round the Cowley factory and watched while the giant tyre fitter 'Tiny' fitted a tyre in forty seconds. From 1929 onwards the *Court Circular* recorded regular audiences of Morris with the Prince, and there seem to have been other informal meetings. In 1930 Morris Commercial fitted out a six-wheel shooting car for the Prince with 'sleeping quarters, two enormous tanks for a shower, lavatory fittings and a specially skilled Morris driver-mechanic'. Water was propelled by a mechanical tyre pump.[34]

But the economic and political clouds darkening over Europe could not but press themselves upon the consciousness of both Prince and motor manufacturer alike. Morris's successful factories were besieged by the casualties of older industries seeking the employment others could not provide.

There was a contrast between his successful formula and the continuing economic failures of successive Governments. It would have been surprising if anyone in his position, emboldened by the establishment accolades he was now receiving, should not now be tempted to try his hand at influencing the political process. Morris was not a man to duck the challenge particularly when his protectionist creed was threatened. Nor was he one for a half-hearted attempt.

Just as in 1924 his approach would be enthusiastic and single-minded but it would have unlooked for consequences. The qualities which brought Morris business success were not suited to the careful manipulation of the political process.

8   The Political Dimension

The approach Morris took to politics was crude, direct and simple. It had much in common with his raucous electioneering of 1924, what Philip Snowden had described as a 'ramping, raging campaign'. His very success at that time helped him to believe that single-mindedness was perhaps the quality most needed for political achievement. What his political beliefs were was rather more difficult to establish. They were essentially a mix of imperialism, paternalism and above all protectionism – the touchstone of it all was the effect he believed it would have on his business. Essentially he was a right-wing Conservative of an imperialist stamp. But mistrustful of the performance of Conservative Governments, he was tempted by alternatives.

He told Miles Thomas that he believed in 'benevolent dictatorship'[1], an easy enough phrase, which might have been applied to his own conduct of business, but one lacking much political content. It was the kind of remark which dozens of his peers might have passed. It was however an extremely loose political philosophy for a man who was actually thinking of using his position and his wealth as a political weapon.

His first attempt at political bribery, as it were, had come in 1924 when he had promised to employ an extra thousand men or make a contribution of £10,000 to the Radcliffe Infirmary in Oxford if the moves towards protectionism were defeated. By the time he re-entered the political arena at the end of the decade, he had available much greater sums of money and was potentially much more of a loose cannon.

Morris set out some of his thoughts on politics in his 1927 article in the *Daily Express*, appropriately headlined 'Life is a practical matter'. Handling politics, it seemed to appear to Morris, was much like handling a car.

I look upon life essentially as a practical man. Frankly I have not much use for philosophies. Theories of any sort leave me cold. What knowledge, beliefs and feelings I have are the result of experience. I mistrust any other sort. Life is a practical job. Thinking about it may help some people but the longer I live the more certain I become that a man can only find himself in the work to be done.

Needless to say, I am an individualist. I find it hard to avoid politics. Politics are bound up so intimately in the lives of all of us. Every man, I hold, should have definite political views but like his sport, they should be kept outside his job. For myself, I am an out and out Protectionist. I believe we could have every man in England employed tomorrow if we had protection here. It has been my lot to see other countries with a tariff prosperous, their working people earning high wages and happy while my country, with Free Trade, staggers along under her immense burden of unemployment. There must be reasons other than free trade to explain this away but the coincidence strikes me as queer.[2]

Like many of his declarations, it was economical with the truth. Although he might point to the surging American motor business, it was about to turn down, and while protectionism had not prevented the French industry fading away, Morris's own business enjoyed the huge protection of the McKenna tariffs.

In retrospect, he would play down his political activity, insisting to his official biographers that it was only reluctantly that he was shifted from a belief that 'a manufacturer who tried to sell to all his citizens, whatever their beliefs, should himself keep out of political life',[3] and claiming to have refused the Conservative nomination for Oxford in 1924. In fact, as contemporary reports make clear, he was chosen as the Conservative candidate at the end of 1923, only withdrawing later on doctors' advice.[4]

The two factors which drew him back into an active role at the beginning of the 1930s were protectionism and the concern shared by a number of leading industrialists about the growing divisions between what came to be known as the two sides of industry. To Morris and his acquaintances, it seemed that the whole industrial system as they had known it was collapsing, and that socialist doctrines were rapidly finding acceptance (as the rise of the Labour Party showed) with industry's case going by default.

For Morris running his business in a paternalistic way, and successfully resisting the introduction of unions, the idea that, as his biographers put it, 'any idea of complementarity between management was increasingly shouted down'[5] was a threatening one.

The confrontation had been seen at its starkest in the 1926 General Strike. The trauma of those happenings had produced a drawing back from confrontation within industry although not from the Government. While the King's appeal for a 'peace that will be lasting' did not discourage the Conservative administration from ramming through a law restricting trade union rights and strikes 'designed or calculated to coerce the Government', some industrialists had formed a joint committee with the very TUC which had led the strike.

Led by Sir Alfred Mond, one of the founders of Imperial Chemical Industries, they formed a joint committee to discuss ways of improving the efficiency of British industry. Mond, who had been a Liberal MP, was renowned for the enlightened practices of his own firm, which had introduced a formal committee system for workers to discuss the business with management as well as wide-ranging welfare provisions. In left-wing circles, Mondism was to become a term of abuse.

Morris was neither important nor interested enough to become involved in the Mond-Turner talks, as they became known. In due course the impetus behind them had slackened as the economic situation improved and British industry enjoyed a period of growing success until the economic crisis of 1929 brought all the old concerns and arguments flooding back.

This time Morris was deeply involved. 1928 had marked something of a peak in inter-war prosperity with British industrial production increasing for the third year running and unemployment at its lowest since 1920, at little more than a million. Comparative prosperity continued until the Wall Street Crash of 24 October 1929. The drying-up of American money had a rapid effect on world trade and British exports quickly felt the pinch. By July 1930, unemployment had doubled to over 2 million and there was talk of 3 million out of work by the following year.

The Labour Government which had been elected in 1929 struggled to set an effective course amid the storm. A junior Minister, Sir Oswald Mosley, produced proposals which bore many similarities to the kind of New Deal package later successfully introduced by President Franklin Roosevelt in the United States. They included the planned use of credit and public works to promote expansion, some public direction of industry and planned foreign trade. It was too radical for the Cabinet, and Labour was still in favour of Free Trade. After the Cabinet rejected it in May, Mosley resigned to fight for his policies, set out later in a manifesto, in party meetings and its autumn conference.

It was against this backcloth that on 19 September there appeared in *The Times* a letter signed by twenty-two prominent businessmen whose chairman was Sir William Morris. It announced a meeting a week later to set up a National Council of Industry and Commerce 'to further by all possible means the economic and financial prosperity of Great Britain'.

> The proposed meeting calls for no excuse. The depth and persistence of our industrial depression demands immediate action. The British people today are tired of the waste and extravagance of successive Governments and the slavish adherence of political parties to economic theories which have lost all relation to the facts of modern business life. The National Council will be a body of British businessmen determined, if it is humanly possible, to restore prosperity to the country and ensure employment for its people. To this end, its object will be to secure the adoption of proper measures for protecting the home market and to advance the cause of inter-Empire trade by every possible means. It will endeavour in our own time to achieve some of the blessings which flow from the concentrated will of the nations of the united British Commonwealth.
>
> The Council will be entirely free from party politics and will welcome assistance from members of all parties ... It will seek to bring into political life the measure of practical commonsense without which the business of Great Britain and of the Empire cannot be concluded.

It was an almost classic statement for the case which was heard in a succession of British economic crises in the course of the century for 'businessman's Government', sometimes phrased as a 'Government of Great Britain Ltd'.

Those who signed it represented something of an alliance between protectionists like Morris and supporters, like Mond, of the crusade by the newspaper proprietor Lord Beaverbrook for a system of Empire Free Trade to balance the United States and what some could see as an emerging European grouping of trading nations.

Amongst the signatories were Mond (now raised to the peerage as Lord Melchett), a close Morris associate in Gibson Jarvie of United Dominions Trust, Sir Harry McGowan, the chairman of ICI, and half a dozen other knights of industry including the chairmen of GEC, AEI, and BAT, a representative of the Mining Association and the chairmen of Harrods and Debenhams. The last two did not obviously stand to benefit from increasing tariffs on imports except in so far as it might contribute to general economic spending power.

The initiative led on to the formation of The League of Industry the following year. Morris was its president and provided most of the funds until it was wound up just before the 1935 General Election. It was very much his own vehicle. Melchett had died a few months after the letter to *The Times* and Gibson Jarvie appears to have been one of the few other signatories to have played a very active role.

Plans for business involvement with the administration of the country were very much the flavour of the times. Winston Churchill, not long before the Chancellor of the Exchequer, declared in his Romanes lecture at Oxford on 19 June 1930 that although Parliament had been supreme in handling the political questions of the nineteenth century, it had been less successful in dealing with the economic issues of the twentieth and he went on to propose an economic sub-Parliament, 'free altogether from party exigencies and composed of persons possessing special qualifications in economic matters'.[6]

It was now that Morris began a series of meetings with Mosley, not long after his resignation from the Government, encounters which would soon immerse him in much deeper water than a mere industrial pressure group. He would provide the funds for Mosley to establish a new party.

At this point, before he became a fascist, Mosley was one of the brightest and most original of the younger politicians. Radical Conservatives like Harold Macmillan and Robert Boothby were among his political friends while the seventeen Labour MPs who would sign the Mosley Manifesto later in the year included Aneurin Bevan.[7]

Morris was introduced through Colonel Wyndham Portal, later Lord Portal and a wartime minister, a guards officer who had become a successful businessman and acted as a fundraiser for Mosley. By September and the formation of the National Council

Morris was talking of the need for strong Government and 'a real leader'.[8] When Mosley, having failed to carry the Labour Party, published his manifesto in December, which included proposals for a five-man Cabinet ruling by order with only a veto from the House of Commons, Morris described it as a 'ray of hope' and saw it as the basis of an 'industrial party'.[9]

Mosley, he said, was 'a courageous young man'. His own mind, he claimed, was 'harassed day and night by the plight into which this England of ours is rapidly falling'. The 'one bright spot' was the 'forceful gesture of a young and virile section of the Labour Party, providing concrete evidence of the possibility of the formation of the foundation of a vigorous Industrial Party.'

'Show me a successful business anywhere in the world, that is operating on the principles utilised a century ago. You cannot. Then what hope is there of a Parliamentary system which has remained unchanged for so long?'[10] The following month he provided Mosley with £50,000 which allowed him to form the simply named New Party towards which he had been inexorably moving.

It was a characteristic Morris gesture, being prepared to commit himself while others with a more subtle political instinct, waited, and not hesitating to give his gratuitous advice to the recipient.

In his autobiography Mosley goes so far as to describe Morris as 'our chief backer'[11] at the start of the party, and a man prepared to let it be known unlike more cautious financial supporters, whom Mosley declined to mention even thirty years later. For all Portal's efforts, the only major contribution at the very start came from Morris.

Mosley's description of his dealings with Morris is revealing. After protracted negotiations, he says he had practically given up hope of assistance 'as nothing ever seemed to come out of our talks' when he suddenly received a telegram inviting him to lunch at the Huntercombe clubhouse.

> We lunched alone and as usual the conversation roamed widely over general political questions. Like Lord Rothermere he was a genuine and ardent patriot, but he was even less well versed in the technique of politics, a business genius who seemed rather lost outside his own sphere. His success rested on an extraordinary and inventive flair for mechanical processes ... and a remarkable capacity for picking men, particularly business executives. Political conversation

tended consequently to be tedious, as the only real contribution he could make was through the power of his money, and that point seemed never likely to be reached.

However ennui flew out of the window when at the end of lunch he pulled a cheque from his pocket and handed it to me across the table. It was for £50,000. He said he had been studying me for a long time – the object of the seemingly pointless conversations were now clear – had developed full confidence in me and had decided to back me. Then came one of those white-light observations which reveal a whole career, in this case the long and dusty road from the little bicycle shop to the motor empire. 'Don't think my boy that money like this grows on gooseberry bushes. The first ten thousand took me a lot of getting.' I bet it did, I thought and was deeply touched. He was a good and honest man, as well as a business genius; a combination which can occur.[12]

It is not clear how much Morris gave Mosley in all, or for how long the contributions continued as Mosley progressed towards violence on the streets and outright fascism. In the middle of 1931, Morris agreed to back the weekly newspaper *Action* which the party was starting to try to get round what it saw as a press boycott and the refusal of the BBC to give the party airtime. He provided £5,000 for launch costs and guaranteed £15,000 a year for two years.[13]

He had also guaranteed several years' salary for one of Mosley's working class Labour MP supporters, W.J. Brown, the MP for Wolverhampton West.[14] Brown, the founder of the Civil Service Clerical Association had been warned by his union executive that he would be sacked from his union post if he joined the New Party. In the event Morris's pledge was not redeemed. Although Brown resigned, he decided at the last moment not to join the New Party.

Morris also provided money to support the controversial youth clubs which Mosley planned as part of a New Party youth movement. The mix of political and physical training they were to provide seemed to some early supporters such as John Strachey to be a potentially explosive combination with fascist overtones. Though few clubs were set up, a few of the members and instructors joined the 'biff boys', the heavies who were to keep order at the Mosley meetings which increasingly were disrupted by Labour supporters. In a letter to the author Colin Cross two years before his death Morris claimed that the total extent of his support for Mosley had been a substantial sum to the clubs. It was clearly not true.[15]

By the end of 1931, the New Party was effectively finished. An economic crisis in August had brought a National Government, and in the ensuing election in October Mosley and his supporters had been heavily defeated, losing all their Parliamentary representation. The circulation of *Action* collapsed and Morris now refused to provide any more money.[16] He was distancing himself from his political gamble but there was more to it than that. The National Government was embarking on a programme which incorporated some of the policies for which the National Council had been formed.

It is not clear whether this marked the end of the Morris involvement with financing Mosley. In July 1934 Morris wrote a letter to the *Jewish Chronicle* denying that he was anti-Semitic and had ever supported fascism, and enclosing a £250 cheque – a small amount by his standards – for the Central Fund for German Jewry.

The political scene was darkening. On the day *The Times* reprinted the letter, the paper had been confiscated in Berlin by the Nazi authorities and it recorded the sacking of a German opera house director because a new opera by Richard Strauss was rumoured to have a Jewish librettist. Morris wrote of 'rumours in circulation to the effect that I have given financial support to the Fascist movement in this country and that my tendencies are therefore anti-Jewish'. The rumours had been reinforced by a recent cartoon in the London *Evening Standard*.

Boldly he continued that there was not 'an item of truth in these allegations. I never subscribed to the Fascist movement nor supported it in any way neither do I have the least antipathy to the Jewish race. It occurs to me that the best way of evidencing the foregoing statements may be for me to make a subscription to a Jewish charity'. It was a crude and disingenuous rebuttal, almost contemptuous in the way it suggested that what was for Morris a very small tip would put everything right.[16]

Later that year Mosley would complain at a public meeting that big businessmen had said that they could not support him publicly because 'if I did the Jews would ruin me and my business' but it seems to have been Rothermere he had more in mind.[17]

A thread of anti-Semitism did however run through the establishment of British industry – and it persisted in some quarters after the war. There is evidence that Morris shared it.

Amongst his papers are to be found copies from the early 1930s of a magazine called *Patriot*. This was published by the Duke of Northumberland from 1922 onwards to foster the views of what were called 'Diehard Conservatives', who looked nostalgically back to the so-called 'diehards' of Edwardian politics. They had stood for tariff reform, stronger armed services, and for opposition to alien immigration. Their policies of protection for British industry and Imperial preference were obviously grist to Morris's mill, and he cannot have been displeased with their aristocratic flavour and the whiff of landed gentry.

The 'diehard' groupings were anti-socialist, pro-Empire, and also markedly anti-Semitic; in the First World War they had attacked British citizens with Jewish and German backgrounds.[18]

The *Patriot* melded the various obsessions together. Its edition of 17 May 1934 attacked what it called 'the dominant influence of a body of revolutionary minded Jews from all parts of the world'.

Morris appears to have shared the concerns. Along the margin of his copy is written in the pencil he favoured; *It is a well-known fact that every government of my England is Jew controlled regardless of the Party in power.*' Again, in his copy of 5 August 1937, the reference to Russian involvement in the Spanish Civil War are marked up and a section on a speech at a miners' rally by Professor Harold Laski has Laski's name underlined and 'Jew' written in the margin.[19]

These were views which Morris denied in public and they were to some extent balanced by the evidence of the Morris personal cash book of further donations to Jewish causes as the Nazi persecution of them became evident. They include small sums in 1938 for a Jewish art exhibition and the London Jewish Hospital and a larger donation of £5,000 to the Jewish Refugee Fund at the end of the following year. Early in 1939 Morris had first-hand experience of what was happening when he found a group of refugees travelling to Australia aboard the same ship, the Blue Star liner, *Ulysses*. The cash book records a donation to them of 1,050 Australian pounds.[20]

Morris's cash book plus that for Morris Industries which were his own private companies is the main source for his private and political donations, recording sums as little as £5 for his cousin Marjorie Pether or as much as £20,000 in later contributions to political parties. Of the Mosley monies there is no record. However, there are large payments at about the same time to the

A young William Morris on his first bicycle, an out-of-date penny-farthing

A photograph of the Morris family, probably taken in 1896. From left to right:
Emily, Alice, Frederick, William and Emily (later Mrs Yockney)

The staff at the bicycle shop, Morris's first business.
Morris (far right) characteristically keeps a cigarette in his mouth

A letter from Morris offering to build a bicycle at cut price for a young woman

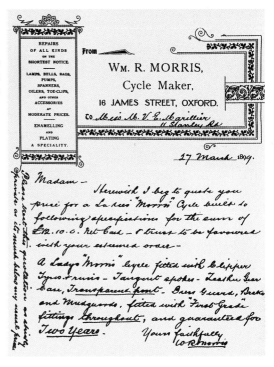

Morris in the 1913 Oxford, his first car

The first factory, with a week's production lined up outside

The Prince of Wales visits Cowley on 24 May 1927. Rowse stands behind him and Hans Landstad and E.H. Blake are to his left

Morris playing deck quoits on a voyage to the Argentine in 1927

The Morris image. Under Miles Thomas the company was a pacesetter in the use of advertising and public relations to attract customers

MORRIS for Happiness

PRICES MORRIS MINOR £125 MORRIS OXFORD £200
MORRIS COWLEY £160 MORRIS SIX £365
TRIPLEX AVAILABLE ON ALL MODELS   DEFERRED TERMS ARRANGED

Cartoon by David Low in the *Evening Standard* on 29 June 1934, depicting Mosley as conductor of a choir of apparent fascist supporters with Nuffield in the front row. The back row is made up of Labour and Communist leaders. The cartoon caused Nuffield to write to the *Jewish Chronicle* protesting that he was not anti-Semitic or a Mosley supporter

Cartoon in *Punch* of Lord Nuffield as he liked to be seen, distributing a modern cornucopia to embarrassingly eager Oxford dons

Sir William Morris with the Duchess of York, later Queen Elizabeth, and William Goodenough, at the opening of the Oxford Infirmary, 22 October 1931

Nuffield hands over the 100,000th Morris 8 in 1936, the bestselling small car in Britain before the Second World War. Leonard Lord (standing behind Nuffield) who designed it, proved to be the nemesis of the Nuffield Organization after the two men fell out

Nuffield at the opening of the college he founded and which bears his name

The final years. One of the few pictures of Lord and Lady Nuffield together

National Council of Industry and Commerce. On 20 January £5,000; on 5 February another £50,000; on 6 February a further £15,000. They show Morris pressing ahead with his own lobbying and propaganda at a time when he was also giving strong support to Mosley. They are such large sums however, far greater than those provided for the League of Industry in subsequent years that there must be a suspicion that this was a way of channelling the money to Mosley.

Mosley himself remained sphinx-like about the sources of his money. Home Office papers reveal that a Special Branch investigation in 1934 under the Head of MI5, General Sir Vernon Kell, reported to the Permanent Secretary at the Home Office that 'it has not been possible to obtain reliable information on this matter since the facts are known only to Sir Oswald Mosley and his most trusted assistants.' But referring to Morris himself, it said, 'it is generally believed in blackshirt circles that he has contributed considerable sums.'

Under cross-examination by Lord Birkett during his appeal against wartime detention in 1940, Mosley was protective of Morris, saying, 'Lord Nuffield, as was common knowledge in the early days of our party, gave us large sums of money but he went as far as to publish in the *Jewish Chronicle* that he was not supporting us because his cars would have been subject to a boycott. I do not say that Nuffield supported us afterwards but those men were at colossal pains to hide their connection with the movement'.

The next day Birkett asked Mosley specifically whether Nuffield had contributed to the British Union of Fascists. Mosley replied, 'Not to my knowledge.'[21]

The aims of Morris's League of Industry, as formally set out, included a special emergency tariff, a fiscal policy which would open and preserve empire markets for empire produce, an independent economic tribunal to decide the form of protection for each industry, cooperation between employer and employed, and an organization to watch over the interests of those engaged in industry.

Morris particularly enjoyed the conferences the League ran when its supporters came together for discussions and he found himself in a ready-made community. He was particularly active in sing-songs round the piano late in the evening. As well as industrialists and attempts at factory branch membership, there was also a token scattering of Labour representatives. The most prominent was the former general secretary of the Miners' Federation of Great Britain, Frank Hodges, a moderate who had resigned his post back in 1924 and become a junior Labour Minister.

But politically the wind was taken out of the League's sails by the election of the National Government in 1931. It adopted a protectionist line; there was an Import Duties Bill, with a special Import Duties Advisory Committee rather as the League had suggested, while government encouraged the reduction and deconstruction of some traditional industries. The League occupied itself more with encouraging discussion of industrial problems in conferences and study schools. In 1935 it was wound up in anticipation of the General Election, though Morris's last donation came almost a month later, presumably to settle final accounts.

The reason given by the official biography is that the 'party allegiances of its members would have caused an impossible strain so that the independence of the League from party politics might have been endangered'.[22] That had never previously seemed a concern of Morris. The real reason was that the League had outlived its usefulness and there was no obvious rallying point for it once the narrow Morris rallying call of protection had been achieved.

After the disastrous adventure with Mosley, Morris would confine his attempts to influence the future of industry through politics to two channels; donations to existing political parties and a major and successful programme of financial support for re-establishing industry in areas like Cumberland and South Wales which had been particularly badly hit by the depression.

The cash book makes clear that after the Mosley debacle Morris hedged his political bets though broadly he backed those who believed in national or coalition Government. So three weeks before the election he paid £20,000 to Sir John Simon of the National Liberals, a further £4,000 went to Lord Portal for transmission to Ramsey Macdonald's National Labour Party while another £1,000 was paid to the Conservative Neville Chamberlain for the Birmingham Conservative Party.

In 1938, just before Munich, he was providing much larger sums. As much as £75,000 went to the National Party on 5 August, another £25,000 to Conservative and Unionist Central Office and a further £75,000 to Lord Plender for the National Publicity Bureau. On 11 November the British Democratic Party received £5,000. This was the occasion of the celebrated Oxford by-election in which Morris predictably backed the Conservative supporter of National Government, Quintin Hogg, against the former vice-chancellor of the university, A.D. Lindsay, who stood as an Independent Progressive. By now Morris had worked closely with Lindsay on his major benefactions and a rumour was put round that he would support him. Another Morris letter disabused the electorate.

Reasserting his whole-hearted admiration of the Prime Minister, Neville Chamberlain, he announced, 'My political opinions favour no individual party as I am convinced that the continuance of a National Government is our best assurance of the furtherance of the successful legislation and statesmanship which we have enjoyed since its inception'.[23]

His political donations were now comparatively small beer compared with the resources Morris had by then provided for relief in depressed areas.

His first excursion into supporting a depressed industry had been a disaster. In February 1927 after the end of the miners' strike which had precipitated the General Strike, he had been induced, perhaps by Hodges, to buy a coal mine in Gloucestershire – the Hornbeach Colliery, near Lydney in the Forest of Dean.

It was a quixotic gesture. Although it was suggested it made business sense, providing some kind of vertical integration, in reality there was a glut of coal, the colliery was flooded and it made no economic sense. Less than two years later the Morris Industries minute book was recording the sale at a loss of the grandly named Morris Collieries. 'The best price that he was able to obtain ... was £1,800.'

Morris learnt the lesson. His next moves were straightforward assistance not cloaked by business interest. His work with the League of Industry had brought him into contact with people grappling with the problems of the depressed areas and he was made aware of the emigration from them only too graphically by the queues for work at Cowley.

He donated £30,000 to a scheme for self-help for the unemployed in South Wales which helped with craft training and marketing. But in December 1936, he announced a £2 million Trust for the Special Areas.

The special areas had been defined by the Special Areas Act of

1934 which established commissioners to promote public works schemes and other help for Tyneside, West Cumberland, Central Scotland and South Wales. The act had followed a report by three special investigators who included Morris's old political go-between, Lord Portal. In 1936 the Government went further and set up a Reconstruction Association to encourage small business development with loans of up to £10,000. This was pump-priming; Morris's Trust was intended to top up this assistance with private capital and supply loans which could be much larger.

It was generally reckoned an outstanding success. Morris brought in a powerful set of trustees including Portal and the social reformer Seebohm Rowntree and it was seen as a pioneer of new methods of financing. It eventually disbursed over £2.3 million. Amongst the ninety-three businesses it supported were new factories in South Wales and the reopening of the collieries in the Cumberland port of Whitehaven which had been closed for two years. One of the satisfactions for Morris was to see the revitalization of the town and the achievement was formally recognized after the war when he was given the Freedom of the town in 1953.

Thereafter, though he continued to be a spokesman for the motor industry and crossed swords with the Government over policies which directly affected the Morris business, he did not take part in such broadly based political activity again. In any case the thirties saw him facing a major task in retaining and reconstructing his own business which was coming under greater challenge from within and without. The policies and practices which had led to his success in the 1920s were now the general standards and markers for the industry. It was time to adjust to a new situation.

9   Reluctant Delegation

There is a compelling group portrait of the Morris management taken on the occasion of a visit by the Prince of Wales in 1927. In the centre stands Morris in a rather ill-fitting suit and a trilby hat. Beside him is the Prince with his bowler hat and walking stick, like a slightly apprehensive Charlie Chaplin. Around them stand the confident managers: Daniel Young, the square Witney engineer, who had backed the original W.R.M. Motors and did most of the factory construction work; E.H. Blake, formerly the sales manager of Dunlop, who had come in as Morris's deputy; Landstad who had worked with Morris on the design of the first car; Arthur Rowse who had learnt from his wartime Government work to plan production. Miles Thomas ducks into the picture from one side like a slightly nervous curate.

There is undoubtedly a feeling of establishment and pride about the picture but it marks a high water-mark of the Morris business – the moment when the original inspiration had reached its apogee. Within a very few years most of the key members of the team would be gone and the apparently inexorable rise of the company bogged down in stagnation.

The bald statistics tell part of the story. In 1927 Morris production of cars amounted to 61,632 out of over 164,000 cars produced in Britain. Between then and 1935, by which time British car production had doubled, it only exceeded that figure once. At the same time the pre-tax profit level of £1.59 million achieved in 1928 would not be surpassed until 1936.

The worldwide slump of the early thirties was only a little to do with it. While British car production did fall back in 1930 and 1931, the industry was far less affected than its American and Continental rivals. There was an underlying growth in the market and when it came through strongly in the middle thirties Morris took a much smaller share of it.

The basic problem was that the original formula for the Morris success had grown stale. His empire had been carried on the backs of two successful cars – the original Oxford and the Cowley which, with adaptations, had been the backbone of the business. Although they had had a remarkable run, they were now dated and the market represented by the would-be car owner was looking for a different size and shape of car. Morris Motors was floundering as it looked for alternatives – as Ford was in the early twenties when it was slow to replace the Model T to which Henry Ford was emotionally committed. It was a mixture of a genuine shift in the market and a proprietor's autocratic stubbornness.

And while parts of the Morris armour – notably its concern for customer service and tight supervision of costs and dealers – remained potent competitive weapons, others, like its manufacturing techniques, were now being copied by others. It was a penalty of success; Morris had achieved his intention of building a British motor industry reliant on modern techniques which were as up-to-date as the rest of the world.

The consequence was that other British manufacturers could now take advantage of not only his techniques but the concrete benefits of the network of vigorous component suppliers Morris had encouraged and facilities such as the Pressed Steel works. Henry Ford even made an inspection of Cowley when he visited England in 1928 though Morris significantly was not there to greet him, meeting him in London the following day.

Competitive advantage in business is rarely still, particularly in a young and technically evolving business with an immature market as the motor industry then was. It could scarcely be expected that the domination which Morris and his great rival, Herbert Austin, exercised in 1928 when they held 60 per cent of the British market, could be maintained. A decade later the big two had become the big six as a series of shake-outs of smaller manufacturers consolidated the British industry and the large American companies, Ford and General Motors, turned their attention, along with their technical and financial resources, to Britain.

Henry Ford's 1928 visit to Britain was about more than collecting antiques and having an audience with the King. It was an inspection of the strategy for re-establishing Ford as a major force in Britain. From its pre-war domination, its reliance on the obsolescent Model T and a succession of insensitive American managers had led to disaster. In 1926, Ford's son Edsel had crossed the Atlantic to report to him that, 'We have been defeated and licked in Britain'. Old Henry Ford's stubbornness and the determination of William Morris were the principal causes.

Ford could not compete as it had pre-war by bringing in cars from the United States to assemble in Britain. The McKenna duties and the particular liking of British owners for smaller cars had seen to that. The strategy was for a purpose built new assembly plant on the Dagenham marshes east of London, with its own docks, foundry, engine shops and the full range of integrated production which could be found in Ford's Michigan plant. It was formidable competition, acknowledged as such by the Government in the dropping of the super tax case against Morris.

It was part of a general overseas expansion of the big American firms. General Motors had tried unsuccessfully to buy both Austin and Morris, and its management had been divided about whether to buy a British company at all. But at the end of 1925 it made the plunge and bought the much smaller Vauxhall in Luton, paying two and a half million dollars and making it the company's first manufacturing plant outside the USA. Its challenge would take some time to build up, with a switch from the traditional large Vauxhalls which had sped the wartime army generals about their business to smaller models.

But the Vauxhall switch of strategy showed an appreciation of the principal problem which the Morris empire now faced – a change in what the car-buying public wanted.

Back in 1913 the new Morris Oxford had been hailed as 'a new miniature light car. Without attempting to enter the field of the cycle car proper, it aims at being essentially a miniature motor car, possessing all the attributes of a full size car but – and here is where it differs from many of the small cars on the road – it is also made with all the care that is bestowed upon the highest priced cars', was the verdict of *Autocar*.[1]

Its reliability and price had enabled it to tap a new market of middle-class car owners. During the 1920s Morris had consolidated round the rather larger Cowley range with immense success. But the new generation of young first time car owners, growing at a rate which surprised commentators in the 1920s, were after something much more like Morris's original conception. With improved road surfaces and advances in car and component manufacture, it could be smaller and as reliable.

The trend gathered force at the end of the 1920s under the

double impact of the economic slump and the system of taxation of motor cars modified in 1920 which penalised the larger cars by assessing tax by horsepower. Petrol duties pushed in the same direction. In 1928 a quarter of all cars sold were 10 horsepower or under; five years later the proportion was as high as 60 per cent where it remained. As one study put it, 'it was necessary for any large-scale manufacturer, actual or potential, to produce a small car.'[2]

Morris Motors at first did not have one at all, and then not a satisfactory one. It took its place at the starting line with its competitors with all the advantages of its experience and well-oiled manufacturing machine but handicapped by squabbles amongst its team.

The official biography records that the company developed five new models between 1926 and 1929 which it describes as 'a very rapid pace for a business whose mainstay had continued to be the 11.9 horsepower Cowley'.[3] But these were almost all larger cars, variations on earlier themes and not all successful. They included the disastrous Empire Oxford.

The manufacturer who had taken over the reputation of producing the reliable small car was Morris's old rival, Herbert Austin. In the early twenties he had persisted with large over-priced cars but had been saved from bankruptcy by the invention of the Austin Seven, which he designed in his own home. The small car was at first derided even by its own distributors as 'a bath on wheels' but its performance and accessibility to what *The Economist* called 'the new strata of demand ... surprisingly responsive to the advent of the cheap and reliable family car'[4] turned it into a cult, a symbol of the increasing social freedom of middle-class young people in the twenties and thirties.

Austin had described the Austin Seven, launched in 1922, as a model which 'would knock the motor-cycle and side-car into a cocked hat and far surpass it in comfort and passenger-carrying capacity'[5] but it could equally well have been summed up in the words applied to the first Oxford; 'a miniature motor car possessing all the attributes of a full-size car.'

The huge Morris success of those years discouraged any need to respond. It was enough to cope with the problems of turning out enough vehicles from Cowley to meet demand. But when business slowed down, the motor business was agog to know whether Morris would have an answer.

The man himself was reluctant. He was pressed by his managers but with a sharp eye to the business practicalities he continued to insist into the 1930s that it was in the larger cars used for business that the lucrative market lay, and that once motoring ceased to be a novelty among the lower-middle income groups the trend would be to bigger engines as it had already been in more developed markets. He was also still pursuing the British car which would have real export potential – and that would be a larger engined vehicle.

But in 1928 he had accepted that his engineers should produce a small car. The 8 horsepower Morris Minor was duly launched for the 1929 season. 'Some people,' said Morris, 'think my idea is to crush the Austin Seven off the market – which is absurd. But I say this – the price will not be higher.'[6]

It was typical combative stuff and *Autocar* trumpeted on 31 August 1928, 'At last a day long awaited has arrived when it is possible to give a full description of a car that may well make history, not only in the land of its birth, but throughout the world'. It was a tribute to the reputation Morris had earned. If there was a touch of disappointment that 'there is nothing unusual in its appearance ... just a little car, complete in every detail' then 'an all-too-brief trial of the little car's road capabilities left an excellent impression'.

In fact, the car came close to being a disaster. The engine, developed at Wolseley, was over-complicated, with design ideas from a large wartime aero-engine. The dynamo was too small, the battery frequently ran down in winter, and the company paid the penalty of saving on the expense of a new steel body. Instead the car had a light fabric covered body with felt and wool padding rounding off the corners. Unfortunately in springtime, birds found it an ideal lining for their nests and pecked holes in the fabric to get at it.

Miles Thomas, sales director at the time, described it as 'a troublesome baby' and by the early thirties forced through a redesign to provide what he called 'a more rugged and less costly' car which included a new simple engine which was shamelessly copied from the new Ford Eight.[7]

It was a blow to the Morris reputation which had been built on meticulous attention to detail. But Morris himself was less and less involved, while his managers found themselves trapped in a double bind. While they were increasingly left to their own devices, particularly in the plants distant from Cowley, their decisions were still subject to belated scrutiny by the autocratic proprietor when he returned from his now regular absences. They had the worst of both worlds; deprived of his acknowledged judgement in the first place, they were subject to his capricious interference at a late stage in the process.

'We had learnt over the years,' said Thomas, 'to get things done without waiting to be told what to do by "the boss"; but, believe you me, we had to keep our minds attuned to the idea of what we thought "the Governor" would like. We all suffered from the knowledge that there would be impending hindsight and post hoc comment.'[8]

Apart from the disappointment of the Minor, a larger sister was also a failure. A six cylinder car launched in a 15 horsepower model, again with a fabric body, it had been developed by Cowley in part because of increasing rivalry with Wolseley to show what Cowley could do. In the event the engine was not built with sufficient room for cooling and hot oil disintegrated the clutch and poured onto the road.

In the early days these were the sorts of things which the alert and ever-present Morris would have picked up on. But the business had grown beyond that, and in any case the governor was increasingly absent. The car had been developed while he was abroad and was only shown to him on his return when the tarpaulin curtains which had masked it from general view were dramatically pulled back.

Thomas remembered, 'He took one look at it and developed an abiding hate, but he allowed himself to be talked round'.[9]

Morris had now developed a regular pattern of wintering abroad. It was quite a common practice among successful British industrialists to go on long overseas journeys during the winter; as late as the seventies one merchant bank had the greatest difficulty in reaching the board of a major components company over a take-over bid because they had all gone on a winter cruise.

Morris, most often accompanied by his secretary Wilfred Hobbs, was particularly fond of Australia. His first visit was via the USA in 1928. The *Sydney Morning Herald* of 15 February recorded his arrival.

At the age of 50 years, Mr W.R. Morris, a smiling mercurial little Englishman, who arrived in Sydney before dawn yesterday morning is the greatest manufacturer of purely

British motor cars. He has a vigorous forceful personality but in meeting him one is more attracted and impressed by his blue eyes than any other feature. Their darting, fresh, glistening glances are a sufficient introduction to the brain that has built up his wonderful British business.

Morris warmed to the attention and pursued his dream of major empire trade. Australia was far and away the biggest overseas market for British cars in the twenties, consistently accounting for a quarter or a third of all British exports. In 1926 the 15,498 vehicles the UK exported there accounted for over 46 per cent of its motor exports, though they still took far more American cars.

Morris had left England in January 1928 declaring that, 'British light cars have triumphed in Australia because of their economy in operation, the ease of handling, and high quality workmanship.' Now that British manufacturers had successfully fought for and consolidated their home market, they had breathing space to look overseas. 'It is only by personal contact and experience of actual conditions that our manufacturers can continue to compete successfully in the Dominions.'[10]

He returned in April singing a different tune; the need to buy more Australian goods. 'If we are to sell more from our kinsmen, we must buy from them.'[11] He had picked up more than the caution induced by the failure of the Empire Oxford in Australia and the frequent complaints of dealers about British delivery; he had also encountered the protectionist arguments of which he was the great exponent in Britain.

Privately he told his accountant Thornton that import duties were imminent and that they would have to spend a quarter of a million on a body shop if they wanted to continue to import significantly into the market. He also admitted that 'we had not got quite the right class of goods and some of our dealers were not of sufficiently good standing.'[12]

The worldwide slump later in the year and import duties in Australia precipitated a decline in exports. Although Morris took steps to consolidate his business, spending £100,000 on reorganizing distribution, concentrating sales on a slightly larger engined model, and establishing arrangements for assembly of parts shipped from England, the dream of a huge new market was gone.

Morris however had discovered the delights of the long sea

voyage, and he would visit Australia another half dozen times that way in the thirties as well as taking passage to South Africa on various occasions.

His wife rarely went with him, and he discovered in leisurely shipboard life on the smaller liners the kind of ready-made social life which he seemed unable to construct for himself. It was a kind of seaboard mixture of the Huntercombe Golf Club with the late night jollity of conferences of the League of Industry.

Morris did not find socialising easy. On an earlier voyage to Argentina on a motor industry mission to investigate the (poor) prospects for British sales, another passenger was the motor dealer, Reginald Rootes, who would later compete with Morris as a manufacturer. He remembered;

> Morris was a more popular man in the trade than Austin, but a man of not much personality, he couldn't talk much, but he was very honest, very straightforward. He was admired by his dealers. He never left the boat. He just sat on it, and didn't mix with other people at all. I had dinner with him; he had nothing to talk about except the motor business.[13]

Now however the annual voyages became a focus of Morris's life. He usually chose a slow ship with good facilities for deck quoits in which he competed fiercely, and which would remain an active passion with him beyond his seventieth birthday. It was a welcome diversion from a business rapidly approaching crisis.

Back home the crunch came at the start of the thirties. Under the impact of slump and differential taxation, the sales of the larger horsepower cars on which Morris had based his strategy started to collapse. The 11 and 12 horsepower cars which had taken a quarter of the market in 1928 took only 15 per cent by 1933, while 13 and 14 horsepower models collapsed from 23 per cent to 8 per cent. Meanwhile the small 8 horsepower cars rose from an 18 per cent share of the market to 26 per cent and their slightly larger 10 horsepower sisters from 8 per cent to 34 per cent – an almost wholly new market.[14]

At the same time, the old Morris marketing ploy of undercutting the competition was no longer so effective. Others, particularly Ford, had access to as up-to-date facilities, while the public made clear they did not simply want the cheapest version; they were looking for the extras and the pieces of distinctive styling which made a car slightly different – a tendency which would become familiar to post-war salesmen, and which they found a British characteristic, more pronounced than in other European markets.

Morris Motors discovered it when Thomas marketed a stripped down basic version of the Minor for £100 with a limited gearbox, rudimentary windscreen wiper, and no clock. There were few orders; buyers preferred the better quality model. Thomas concluded that, 'No one wants to keep down with the Joneses'.[15] More staidly, the economists called it 'long term price model competition'.[16] The consequence would be a plethora of new, or at least slightly differentiated, models produced by the industry throughout the thirties, which reduced individual production runs and the scope for economies of scale.

Although Morris had become adept at modest alterations on his basic Cowley design and had indeed made a feature of making sure there was something slightly new for every Motor Show, unlike Austin, this was something much more demanding. And it came at a time when the man who had for so long been single-minded, as Rootes had noticed, was increasingly letting other interests take him away from the business.

It was not simply the shipboard absences; he was elusive in Britain too. 'He divorced himself more and more from the running of the business. He was much more ready to accept an invitation to visit a nurses' hostel or look at the wards of some new hospital or something of that kind than continue intimacy with his own organisation,' was the Thomas complaint.[17]

Within the business too his interests were shifting. Before the First World War two industries, motors and aircraft, had seemed the taste of the future. In between the wars it was apparent that the greater excitement and technical challenge lay with aircraft.

Morris had purchased an entry into aircraft knowhow with Wolseley which had constructed aero-engines under licence during the war. Now he revived construction establishing a new Wolseley aero-engine factory. It was a pricey and not very successful start. The Wolseley engines were named after signs of the Zodiac with titles like Scorpio or Leo but their prospects cooled when the Government made it clear that it was unlikely to order from Wolseley and would stick to its four preferred military suppliers.

James Woodcock found himself being put in charge of aero-engine production, and protested he had never been near an aero-engine before. He got a blunt reply from the Wolseley works manager, Len Lord. 'It's about bloody time you were.'

Woodcock's view was that the company had gone into aero-engine production because it believed it could utilize its existing resources, skills and economies of scale to make them economically and effectively.

If so, it was disappointed. *The Economist* judged, 'His aeroplane factory, originally designed mainly for civil purposes, was not producing an engine suitable for the air force ... there was no reason why the Ministry should have bought the Scorpio engines.'[18] It was another example of the slipping capabilities of the firm.

Matters came to a head in 1933, and now at last Morris moved decisively. The catalyst was probably the launch of the new Ford small car, the 8 horsepower Y. Designed and brought into production within six months, with the prototypes built across the Atlantic in Ford's River Rouge works at Detroit, it excited the public. Exhibited at the Albert Hall in London, it drew 50,000 visitors, who paid to see it. The promised threat from Dagenham, delayed while Ford management had squabbled about what car to produce, was now a reality.

Morris now had a major purge of his management. Out went Woollard, the great expert of factory production methods after five years on the board; out went Edgar Blake who had been Morris's deputy; out went Arthur Rowse after seven years on the board; Thomas moved from sales director to run the commercial vehicle plant.

The man Morris chose instead was Leonard Lord, a ferret-faced, ginger haired Yorkshireman who had been a key member of Woollard's team on planning new factory production methods. They included the state of the art experiments with grouping machine tools which led to the first automatic transfer machines. Lord was a brilliant design engineer who would be responsible for the two most successful inter-war small cars – for rival companies. But he was a proud, spiky, and brutally direct man.

Morris's decision to pick Lord was exactly right; another example of his ability (knack is too strong a word) of appointing the right men once he had seen them in action either as a supplier or working for a subsidiary. His choice would save Morris Motors, yet ironically would seal its fate. Another Morris characteristic, his inability to allow anyone to stand within his shadow, or to delegate in full, would lead to a fierce alienation of Lord. In turn Lord would wreak his revenge, destroying the power of the Morris empire when its founder weakened in his old age.

The two men had marked similarities. Single-mindedness, social awkwardness, an instinctive grasp of engineering and works organization, an arrogance, unforgiving memory and a compulsion for tobacco. Thomas, working closely with both, saw other psychological similarities – Lord like Morris had had a strong mother fixation. He had taught evening classes when he first started as an engineer at Courtaulds to provide her with extra money.[19] In some ways Lord could have been the son Morris never had.

Lord had refused to take over at Cowley unless he had full control. Thomas recorded his arrival;

> He awoke people to the hard facts of life. Most of them had never worked anywhere else except at Cowley and were stiff in their attitudes. He swiftly made them flexible. Everyone admired his methods, if not his manners ... He walked roughly over the toes of anyone who got in his way. He wore a lighted cigarette constantly in the corner of his mouth, blowing off the ash without taking it from between his lips.
>
> He loved sketching ideas for fascia boards, instrument mountings and other details on pieces of scrap paper, then getting the drawing office to work out the practical designs. New Morris models swiftly began to take shape.[20]

The results were quick to show. Lord had been brought in after profits had slumped. Trading profits halved in 1931 from £1.16 million to £662,000 and though they rose slightly in 1932, in 1933 they were down to £343,000.

His answer was a wholesale reorganization of Cowley to the most modern standards, surpassing Dagenham in many ways, coupled with the design of a new small car to make the most of the facilities. This was the Morris Eight, which became the bestselling inter-war car.

The Cowley reorganization was long overdue. Cars had continued to be pushed from work station to work station by hand. Now, for the first time, a mechanised assembly line was installed and overhead conveyors delivered parts. It cost £300,000.

Morris, who was created a peer in 1934 (choosing Nuffield because the titles of both Morris and Cowley were already being used by other peers), conceded more control to Lord than anyone before. He even agreed that two of the companies which he still privately owned, Wolseley Motors (but not Aero Engines) and MG should be transferred to the public company, Morris Motors.

Lord had argued that the relationship between the various Morris companies was anomalous. They were closely linked in day-to-day business relationships, both as major suppliers and customers for each other, but were also competitors. Morris had been pondering the move for some time, and the purchase price from his private company, Morris Industries, provided him with more shares for a major flotation which he was considering.

It was the transfer of MG which caused the biggest heartaches. It had been the creation of the enthusiastic Cecil Kimber, who had continued to develop it as it moved from the central Oxford site to Cowley, and then to a new factory in Abingdon. It was always a double-edged relationship. Morris had been keen as a young man on distinctive coachwork and rally performance but he was also a fundamentalist about production. He was as delighted as anyone about the cars' remarkable successes on the race track but insisted that they must share standard parts with the rest of the company to provide economies of scale. Further he believed that unless the MGs seen at rallies and race tracks were recognizably the same as those in the showrooms, the sales benefit of the racing expenses would be lost.

At the same time, he had an affection and respect for Kimber. A letter from Kimber in the Nuffield Archive which accompanied a present for Morris in 1925, talks of the difficulty of buying 'an appropriate gift for a man of your simple tastes and vast resources … for me at any rate it is easier to sell a Morris car.'[21] Kimber settled safely, but unsuitably, on a book.

An entry in the personal cash book also records a loan from Morris to Kimber, a unique event. There is no other record of a loan to an employee. It took place on 2 Aug 1935 and was for £800, at exactly the point when the business was transferred to the public company.[22]

Morris was a regular, if not frequent, visitor at the factory. Albert Smith, a former Chief Accountant at MG recalled:

> I think he rather liked the factory because it was such a nice friendly place, so he'd ring me up and say 'I'm coming to lunch.' So we'd have a lunch and a little natter and a chat, and he was terribly easy to entertain. Afterwards I would

escort him back to his car and I knew I should be asked the same question, 'Are you putting up any new buildings, Smith?' To which I would always reply, 'No, sir', and he would then say, 'That's it me boy, keep the walls bulging.'[23]

In 1935 however Lord's entry was much less cosy. He marched round the shops, looked at the racing bay, and announced, 'That lot can go for a start.' The official biographers record a more considered judgement based on the way the racing models were increasingly moving away from standard production models, a tendency encouraged by continental rivals whose vehicles were increasingly pure racing machines. It was a symptom of the new more puritan Lord regime, what Kimber saw as 'the soul-deadening hand of big business'.[24]

Lord's reorganization brought swift results and an economic upturn helped. When *The Economist* produced a supplement celebrating the industry at the end of 1935 Morris Motors advertised, 'The triumph of specialisation. Over 108,000 Morris cars sold in 12 months. Britain's motor industry has never before known such sensational sales figures as these – because British motoring has never before known such a sensational policy as Morris – specialisation.'

'From the Morris Eight which has the largest sale of any one car in this country, to the Morris Big Sixes, the finest cars ever produced at their price – every Morris has a measure of value which bids fair to establish new conceptions and conventions in motoring.'[25] The old flash and sparkle and confidence were back, and so were rising profits. In May 1936, *The Economist* recorded the largest ever figure of profit earned for dividend of £942,700.

It was now that the explosion came between Morris and Lord. The flashpoint was the improvement in the company's finances. Lord argued in a way which nowadays would seem commonplace that his success should be rewarded by a share in the profits. He suggested a relatively modest basic salary with scope for a large performance-related bonus when profits started to reach levels he correctly anticipated.

It was a disastrous misjudgement of one awkward man by another. Lord had tried to intrude on Morris's most treasured sanctum – his total financial control of the business. He may have been encouraged by Morris's agreement to put some of his private companies into the public company, but it was a monumental miscalculation. Morris was the only one who benefited from increased profits once the preference shares with their fixed rate of interest were paid. He was already planning how to spend the money he intended to realize from that. He might regret he had no son to whom to hand the business; he certainly was not going to allow anyone else to have a guaranteed share in it, and Thomas estimated Lord's scheme could have made him a million.

The result was that they parted company. Lord went sulking to the Isle of Wight. There were efforts to repair the breach; both men realized how much they stood to lose, but their similarities made matters more difficult and their hang-ups made proper reconciliation impossible. Wilfred Hobbs, personal secretary to Morris and a key man in the difficult chemistry between him and his senior executives, first had to break the news to Lord; Morris characteristically had declined to do it himself. Hobbs then drove wretchedly backwards and forwards trying to patch things up. He failed, and Lord departed to America to visit motor companies and compare the latest methods.

On his return, a deal of sorts was made. Lord became head of the new Nuffield Trust for the Special Areas with a salary of over £5,000 a year. He said later:

> Lord Nuffield sent for me and told me he wanted to do something for the special areas, and he offered me a cheque for two million pounds and got me to go and do the best I could for him. Typically Lord Nuffield of course but I didn't know what to do with two million pounds.
>
> He told me to put it in the bank; I don't quite know what he expected to happen after that. So I told him the logical thing was to get some trustees together and set the thing up properly and that is what eventually happened.[26]

Thomas saw the move as more Machiavellian. Morris had realized how valuable Lord could be to a rival, particularly with his new American knowledge. 'Nuffield had backward glances and thought it was a bad thing having this extremely capable man roaming around without any ties and possibly going to a rival. He was furious at not having tied it up legally that he could not go to a rival.'[27]

In the event it was short-lived. In 1937 Lord joined Austin and was designing the Austin Eight to compete head-on with the Morris Eight. Thomas found him one day in his office, blowing the ash off his cigarette and announcing, 'Tommy I am going to take that business at Cowley apart, brick by bloody brick.'[28] That in effect would happen. Morris had made a fatal enemy.

Lord was succeeded at Cowley by Oliver Boden, who had been an executive manager with Wolseley and had continued to run the company under the Morris regime. Widely respected, he would work himself to death within a few years. He provided a sure touch for a business which was now increasingly being run without Morris, who was concentrating on the aero-engines side.

Morris was now very much a public man. When he announced the Trust for the Special Areas he said grandly that it was an 'expression of goodwill towards the new King', George VI.[29] His utterances on a range of subjects, as well as his bequests, were now reported more widely but also more critically. The first thoughts of the emergent motor manufacturer had been greeted with interest; the pontifications of the established magnate were subject to more searching examination once the novelty had worn off and since he had been seen to have feet of clay in both business and politics.

So when he returned to a well-worn theme in 1934, *The Economist* picked him up sharply. 'Lord Nuffield now reiterates weekly that it is the patriotic·and apparently moral duty of every Englishman to refrain from buying foreign goods. We are not clear Lord Nuffield's convictions extend in this direction. Does he consider all international trade immoral?' Questioning whether he might not purchase raw materials abroad if he could not find them so cheaply at home, it concluded, 'Is it his belief that all countries should be allowed to import but only Great Britain to export? ... Lord Nuffield should expound his code of ethics more fully. For we cannot suppose that the whole duty of an Englishman consists in buying British cars.'[30] It was uncomfortable for Nuffield; his simplistic views did not enjoy cross-examination.

And there was an increasingly tetchy edge about his public pronouncements. He attacked the prices charged by the big steel companies as a 'steel ramp' run by 'gentlemen with big cigars and nothing to do'.[31] He also waged a running war against the Government for its refusal to order aero-engines from Wolseley.

The Wolseley aero-engine factory had been started in 1929, long before the big rearmament programme of the mid 1930s. Morris had been disappointed not to win Air Ministry orders and had blamed it on resentment of remarks he had made suggesting that the Ministry was paying too much to its selected supplying firms.

He was enraged by a letter in November 1933 in which the Ministry told him that it was improbable that it would be able to order either of the Wolseley engines on offer. As Morris continued to nag, a further letter in March 1935 pointed out the difficulties the Ministry was finding in keeping its five designated suppliers in work.[32]

This was not the kind of argument that appealed to Morris, who believed that his production techniques were more efficient, though his engines in fact lagged behind the rapid technical improvements being made. He sought an interview, complaining that if no orders were forthcoming, he might as well close the factory down. At the interview with the Air Minister, Lord Swinton, he offered to manufacture under licence either an American or a Bristol engine. Again he was refused.[33]

Resentment spilled over to outrage the following year when the Government decided to enlist the help of the motor industry in aircraft production as part of the rearmament programme. Under the 'shadow factory' scheme the Government financed the building and equipping of new factories on or close to the sites of existing car plants. The factories would be run by the motor companies and make aircraft components but when the Ministry's requirements had been met they would be mothballed and kept in case of war. As far as engines were concerned, they would produce parts to a Bristol company design, but not whole engines, so economising on machine tools.

It was in one sense a tribute to Morris, a recognition that the industry whose mass-production techniques he had led was the best fitted for the production of the key element in Britain's defence. But it was on the Government's terms.

When the scheme was announced in March 1936, Wolseley Motors was among the firms which put in tenders. At the same time Morris repeated his demand that the separate aero-engine concern, still part of his own private company, should be given work on a separate basis. When this was again refused, he took his bat home.

He announced that he was closing down the plant and insisted at the same time that the motor company withdrew from its detailed discussions about a shadow factory. It had not helped that the row had coincided with the quarrel with Lord.

Thomas, who had been involved with the talks, was now brought in to draw up a long statement attacking the shadow scheme, which he gave in Morris's name at a press conference, cleverly pre-empting the Government version. It criticised the scheme as technically and strategically unsound and was particularly scathing about the idea of assembling engines from parts made in several different factories.

There was a bitter meeting with Lord Swinton, reported by the press in the Morris-Thomas version.

> 'There was no excitement and there were no high words,' said Lord Nuffield, 'I took up my hat and gloves and left but before I went I said, 'Well, God help you in case of war.'
> 'I said to the Air Minister, "Do you want our engines?" He said "No". I then said, "Do you want us to make Pratt and Whitney (American) engines?" He said "No, that is your business." I said, "Is there anything you would like me to do?" Lord Swinton replied that he did not think so.'[34]

The Times suggested that 'a certain unfamiliarity with joint effort on the part of one who has been the sole controller of vast productive processes might have been countered by more persuasive methods on the part of the Ministry'. *The Economist* was more blunt about Nuffield's dictatorial temper and pointed to the differences of opinion within the Morris organization. The Morris criticism of the shadow scheme struck home however. Lord Swinton conceded that in time of war factories might turn out complete engines while *The Economist* called for an independent enquiry.[35]

Two years later, Swinton's successor, Sir Kingsley Wood, succeeded in repairing the breach. The popular press reported that reconciliation was sealed with a cough drop proffered by the Minister and accepted by Morris. 'This picture is NEWS because it shows you Britain's Number One giver, Lord Nuffield, BEING GIVEN SOMETHING.'[36]

More significantly the two men agreed that Morris Motors should take part in the scheme although it would build aircraft rather than engines. A shadow factory was to be built at Castle Bromwich to turn out a new fighter called the Spitfire in cooperation with its makers, Supermarine, which was a subsidiary of Vickers. But Morris was careful to save face. There was an agreement, which he insisted Boden committed to paper, that the factory would be run rather differently from others in the shadow scheme.[37]

The row over the aircraft programme did not prevent cooperation over other rearmament measures. Swinton, in an effort to calm the dispute, had been careful to say in his Parliamentary statement on his shadow factory refusal that he had the authority of Morris to say that he held himself ready for other important work. Morris briefly intervened to say that his aero-engine plant would be used for manufacturing tank engines.[38]

In the following months it was also agreed that a new factory on the Wolseley site would make prototypes of a new breed of tank, the so-called 'cruiser' tank. These were fast moving lighter vehicles whose abilities in Russian exercises had impressed British observers. An example was shipped to Birmingham from the USA, travelling minus its turret and classified as a 'tractor' to avoid restrictions on US exports of arms. Morris took a keen interest in its design and modification, personally recommending some important changes in the positioning of the wheels on which its tracks ran.

And he was soon involved too in another example of importing effective foreign designs, as he had been before the First World War. He arranged the manufacture of the Swedish Bofors gun to remedy the lack of a suitable anti-aircraft weapon for British defences.

In a speech in 1937 to the Institution of Production Engineers, Morris reflected on his relations with the Government.

> My experience of Governments in the past, and I am going back quite a long time before the war, is that they would not listen to such people as ourselves. We were really non-existent until we were wanted to produce something. Then we were really wonderful. They stroked our backs and we purred like kittens – but we purred because we had to.[39]

The motor business was now more and more in the shade of Morris the public man and his high profile as a benefactor. Even the *New York Times* compared him with Rockefeller and Carnegie.[40]

The Wolseley advertisement for *The Economist* motor industry supplement in 1935 showed a picture of the factory under the headline, '72 acres of practical idealism'. It declared:

> We have sought always to remember that our responsibilities towards the Public are bound up with those we owe to our employees, the industry as a whole and above all to our

country. Whilst raising the efficiency of our plant to the highest level possible, we have endeavoured to improve the conditions under which our employees work, to take our share in lessening unemployment and to frame our policy towards the common aim – world leadership for British cars.

Such is the Wolseley policy – instigated by Lord Nuffield. 'An institution,' said Emerson, 'is the lengthened shadow of a man.'[41]

There had never been much doubt about that as far as the Morris Empire was concerned. But managers were becoming increasingly concerned about the effect of benevolence outside the business on industrial relations within. It was particularly acute at Cowley. There workers openly compared the lack of funds for their recreational and welfare activities with the bequests to university chairs, nurses' homes and London hospitals.

When the spire of the new St Luke's church in Cowley, financed in memory of Emily Morris, started to rise above the streets which led to the factory, the complaints became vociferous. The result was that Morris was persuaded to set aside a special fund of a million Morris Motors shares which would provide workers with an annual holiday bonus. It was portrayed as another Morris first for British industry – holidays with pay, and the workers were described as 'shareholders'.[42]

It was not only workers who now had designs on the Nuffield millions. On 25 May 1938, many of the popular papers carried banner headlines which announced, 'Attempt to kidnap Lord Nuffield'.

The *Daily Herald* reported:

An attempt to kidnap Lord Nuffield is alleged to have been made last night. He was sitting in his office at the Cowley works near Oxford between six and seven o'clock when a large saloon car driven by a chauffeur drew up. Two men alighted and entered the building. It is alleged they ordered Lord Nuffield to leave and enter the car. A friend of Lord Nuffield, Mr Kennerly Rumford, husband of the late Dame Clara Butt, was in an adjoining room. Because of what he heard, he ran to a phone and called the police. Within a few minutes, four cars with about a dozen police arrived. The office buildings were surrounded and two men were taken away by police.

The report was true in substance, if not in detail. There had been an elaborate plot laid by an experienced blackmailer, Patrick Boyle Tuellman. His plan had been to abduct Morris to a yacht moored off the Suffolk coast. However his accomplice got cold feet and went to the police, who much to the delight of Morris allowed the attempt to continue.

An appointment was agreed at Cowley but then a quarter of an hour beforehand the accomplice rang the police to complain of a hangover and to say he would arrange a later interview.

After a rapid review of the evidence, the Chief Constable of Oxford, Charles Fox, then decided to act. To the chagrin of Morris he arrested Tuellman in his parked car before he reached the factory. Fox said later, 'Lord Nuffield was excited by it. He rather wanted me to allow him to be kidnapped because he said he could deal with the person concerned with a "mechanic's punch". I took the view that if he was unsuccessful, I should be walking about, looking for a job.'[43]

The extent of the Morris wealth had been highlighted by his decision to turn some of his controlling interest in the company into cash by selling ordinary shares which he had for years refused to put on the market. In October 1936 there were scenes of pandemonium on the floor of the Stock Exchange when he sold a quarter of his £2,650,000 holding of ordinary stock. He was careful to retain control of the other three-quarters, but he made a huge profit. Five shilling units had been priced at nearly eight times their face value – at 37s 6d; the price closed at 41s 10½d.

After the reorganization business had continued to improve. In 1938 Morris added to his personal company the firm of Riley with its distinctive range. It had run into financial difficulty and its owner, Victor Riley, a friend, had appealed to Morris for help. After the take-over, he continued to run it.

So at the Annual General Meeting in May 1939, the newly-created Viscount Nuffield could report gross profits for the year of £1,751,181. He announced, 'The delivery figures for the first three months of the current year created a new record in the history of the company and I am hopeful, provided the international tension eases, that the company will enjoy a greatly improved year in 1939.'[44]

As he must have sensed, it was not to be. The Second World War would throw up challenges which he was no longer capable of meeting. Although the Nuffield Organisation became a huge contributor to the war effort, it was mainly through the work of others. The war saw the beginning of the decline of William Morris, and it would be the old battle over the shadow factories which precipitated it.

Before war broke out however, the Government sought the services of Morris for further help. The military planners had changed their views on the practicality of repairing damaged aircraft in a war. Once thought a waste of time, it now began to assume strategic importance. In March 1939, the RAF decided to establish five major repair depots of its own and to have a sixth run on its behalf by private enterprise. Morris agreed to take this on, with Cowley as the designated depot, with extra facilities and an airstrip.

After the outbreak of war, there were greater responsibilities still. The Morris team successfully argued that the work should be more widely spread and should be given to a network of carefully organized specialist suppliers, which included some of the company's own distributors; in other words the original Morris formula.

Morris received the title of Director-General of Maintenance, RAF, and a uniform to go with it. But he declined the offices at Bush House in London and remained at Cowley. There was a strongly symbolic flavour about the appointment and the work was mainly done by others; in any case he did not keep the post for long. By the end of 1940 the personal participation of Morris in the aircraft programme was largely at an end and he had resigned as Director-General.

The parting came over the Castle Bromwich shadow factory. During the spring of 1940 it was apparent that there were major differences of approach between the motor manufacturers and the aircraft designers. The motor men's approach, as set out in the earlier arguments, was that to get a rapid flow of production, proper jigs must be made to provide for as many standard parts as possible. This meant rapid production once established but a considerable time-lag while the arrangements were put in place, and little flexibility.

The plane makers had other priorities. As they strove to improve the performance of both the aircraft and its engine and assimilated the lessons from combat, they produced a string of modifications, so negating the advantages of the standardization required for long, rapid production runs. Overlaying the argument was the demand from the RAF's hard-pressed squadrons for fighter aircraft immediately.

The situation went from bad to worse. There was uncertainty about what other aircraft the factory should make and it had to switch production from Spitfire parts to whole aircraft. The Morris men complained that the Vickers representatives were attempting to ride roughshod over them and that the drawings they provided were insufficiently detailed.

Breaking point was reached on 17 May 1940. Miles Thomas, who had been appointed Vice-Chairman after the death of Boden in March, found Morris on the telephone to Lord Beaverbrook, another industrial autocrat, who had become Minister of Aircraft Production a week before.

> Lord Nuffield was vociferously defending his Castle Bromwich organisation and making it abundantly clear that in his opinion the Minister could have either Spitfires or modifications, but he could not have both. The moment of truth had arrived. Sarcastically, certain that he was putting the ace of trumps on the table Nuffield shouted, 'Maybe you would like me to give up control of the Spitfire factory?' In a flash, came the reply: 'Nuffield that's very generous of you. I accept.' There was a click in the earpiece – the line went dead ... Nuffield's face was ashen.[45]

Morris did not take it lying down. In an echo of his encounters with Swinton, he went up to London and marched into the Ministry's headquarters at Stornoway House, where he told Beaverbrook he would have him sacked. Beaverbrook's cool rejoinder was that he would like nothing better.

Next Morris went to the Prime Minister, Winston Churchill, and with a typical crudeness which demonstrated his continuing lack of political judgement, chose to remind him of the sums he had contributed to the Conservative Party. He got predictably short shrift. Churchill told him, 'I cannot interfere with the manufacture of aircraft.'[46]

Thomas had no doubt about the significance of the episode. 'From that moment on, he seemed to lose the vital force that drove him inexorably to greater and greater things.'[47]

10 Town and Gown

Relations between Morris and the university which dominated the city in which he lived were always contradictory. There was respect and condescension on both sides, but much of the time distrust and downright dislike, fanned by political suspicion. Morris could wish one of his academic adversaries to be tossing in his grave; academics would talk of Morris paying damages for the changes industrialization had caused to the city of dreaming spires.

Yet both sides sought out the other. University dons looked for patronage and assistance and a link with the modernizing world. Morris himself was attracted by reputation, influence, and the possibility, exceedingly rare at the time, of having a college named after him.

There was a constant tussle between a university pleased to receive assistance but insistent that it must use it in the way only it could judge best, and the characteristic Morris 'bull at a gate' approach. Just as in politics, he believed he knew best and distrusted tradition and subtlety. It was his way or not at all. It was a recipe for prolonged disagreement between men who prided themselves on their good judgement and were not accustomed to backing down.

Two pictures sum it up. One, a *Punch* cartoon by E.H. Shephard, illustrator of Winnie the Pooh, on 2 December 1936 entitled 'The Horn of Plenty' shows Morris pouring a stream of coins into begging bowls thrust out by beaming academics. Others hasten up. The second is a description in the *Oxford Magazine* after Morris's death by Sir Douglas Veale, a former registrar of the university, who was one of his principal antagonists. It describes Morris in a college setting.

He never was at his ease. His mere presence imposed constraint. The other members of the common room would be conscious, some perhaps guiltily conscious of the current criticism of his benefactions, most of them would be anxious to make a good impression in the hope of more favours to come. He himself would be on his guard against being inveigled into hasty promises. In the result, free and forthright conversation was impossible.

He never became more than an honoured guest even in the common rooms to which he belonged. Not even there could he be heard expounding his plans with the clarity and confidence he could display in private conversation. If he could have done so, there would have been fewer critics, and far fewer vocal critics, of his benefactions.[1]

Morris had been brought up on the outskirts of a city which was the creature of the university. Before 1914 its population of around 50,000 would be swelled by 10 per cent during university terms due to the influx of undergraduates. The University Press was the largest single industrial employer, printers were the largest group of skilled workers but far and away the largest source of employment – 26.9 per cent was domestic service, much of it associated with the university. Out of term college servants would often travel to find work in seaside hotels.

For the boy from Cowley the university's domination was impressive and so was its economic clout. It was no accident that when he opened his first bicycle shop it was right in the centre of academic Oxford, and it was there too that he started to garage cars.

There have always been tensions in the ancient university towns between town and gown. Morris and his family remained, and remain, decidedly and proudly 'town'. How much he felt the division when he first came into business contact with members of the university it is impossible to say. Probably there was a mixture of the pleasure Morris noticeably took in contact with the establishment, with resentment of being patronised and what seemed a free and easy way of life.

Life was to Morris, above all else, 'a practical job'. In sport, as in business, he played to win. It is hard not to see a reflection of his view of the university and its crowds of blazered undergraduates in his *Daily Express* article in 1927. 'I think there is too much sport in England. It seems to me that the ideal of so many young men today is to stroll through life in a blazer.'[3]

Any distrust of undergraduate attitudes he may have felt at the start was reinforced in spades by his disastrous experience with the Oxford Automobile and Cycle Agency. As he stood in the rain to buy back his tools, he could reflect that his business was in ruins due, as he saw it, to his undergraduate partner's 'endeavours to stimulate business by efforts mainly staged in the hostelries of Oxford'.[4]

The iron bit deep into his soul. Amongst his papers was a newspaper cutting about another spendthrift undergraduate some years later. It reported the adjournment of the bankruptcy hearing of Derrick J Wernher, described as a millionaire's son. 'Upon the debtor leaving Oxford in June 1910, his father paid debts of £25,000 and since then the debtor has amassed further liabilities amounting to £80,000 for money lent, extravagant living, racing and gambling.'

A covering letter to Morris from a London solicitor enclosing the cutting says, 'I hope you have been successful in getting your account settled', but suggests that otherwise he should prove in the court for the amount involved.[5]

One of the Morris anecdotes has him telling a meeting that he would never employ a graduate as a manager and then sacking one of his team when, following the speech, he explained that he had a degree.[6] The story may be fanciful but graduates were as scarce as hen's teeth in the British motor industry of the time and there is little doubt that the story broadly reflected Morris's own view.

His reservations about university students were also coloured by the way that left-wing politics in Oxford drew on support and encouragement from both junior and senior members of the university.

Morris had a horror of communism, and he could find activists from the university at the gates of Cowley. Confronting one group in 1934, he offered to pay for them to go to Russia to see conditions there provided they remained there.

The Times recorded:

At a meeting of the Friends of the Soviet Union at Oxford last night, two of the three Oxford men who accepted Lord Nuffield's offer to send them to Russia provided they were willing to stay there declined to be deported by the wish of an employer.

Mr D. Brown of Ruskin College said that he would go to Russia any day as a delegate of the working class but he was not going to be got rid of in the way Lord Nuffield had suggested. Mr Jones, an Oxford unemployed man, said that reflection had shown him that it would be an unwise thing to do because if he stayed in Russia, he would be unable to help the British working man.[7]

So there were a mix of emotions in the Morris approach to the university – respect, perhaps even awe, an impatience with what he saw as the irresponsibility of many of its members and a determined desire to push it into the modern world of which he saw himself and his business as exemplars.

It was the last of those reasons which lay behind his first bequest to Oxford University which was also the very first of his thousands of major charitable donations.

This was the £10,000 to establish the Chair of Spanish Studies named after King Alfonso, which the official biography says was to encourage the university to pay more attention to modern studies. Even as early as this, in 1926, Morris was already under attack for the industrialization of Oxford. When the approach had been made to him about the chair, it had been suggested that he might like to make some recompense for 'what he had done for Oxford'. In a sharp reply in a letter now lost he criticised instead the city and university authorities for not taking greater care over the development of the city for which they shared responsibility.[8]

It was to be a theme to which the university constantly returned, with perhaps the most vituperative attack coming from the future Poet Laureate, John (later Sir John) Betjeman. His book, *An Oxford University Chest*, sneered at 'pale-faced mechanics in Oxford bags walking down the Cornmarket' and 'the muddled pretentiousness which passes for a town'.

But Betjeman put his finger on the difficult relationship.

It has always occurred to me that the great black wall of the University has shadowed his life. He has stormed it and won. Oxford is no longer primarily a university town but primarily an industrial town. The shade of the wall may now seem grateful to Lord Nuffield. He is able to bolster its crumbling bastions, to mortice it with gold.[9]

Certainly there were those who saw it that way. Perhaps the least dignified approach to Morris for assistance came from the group of Evangelical clergymen who were attempting to found St Peter's Hall, later to become St Peter's College.

It broke all the rules which he had laid down for bequests. 'I will never be persuaded into giving anything for any purpose – I like to make up my own mind, and for that reason I do object to so many people writing to me asking me to subscribe to this, that and the other, when in the first place they could write to other than myself who have never given anything.'[10] It is difficult to see quite what changed his mind in this case unless it was a connection with his mother, which was shamelessly played on.

The approach came from the Rev. C.M. Chavasse, the son of a bishop who would later become Bishop of Rochester himself. He was rector of St Aldate's, the Evangelical church in the centre of Oxford where Morris's mother Emily regularly worshipped, and Lilian Morris sometimes accompanied her sister there. Morris had provided a new organ for the church in 1925.

Christopher Chavasse was now part of a group which was setting out to establish a foundation in Oxford which would promote the low church version of anglicanism in a similar way that Pusey Hall stood for the high church vision of the Oxford Movement. But there was also a clear intention that the institution, initially a hostel, should later become a college.[11]

Morris was no church-goer. When Chavasse first wrote, he received a reply from Hobbs which said that Morris 'considers that the hospitals situated in the neighbourhood of his many works have the next call on him and it is probable that he will consider these to the exclusion of other matters'. However, he left the door politely ajar saying he would be happy to talk with his father.

Another man may have taken it as rejection but six months later Chavasse was once more in correspondence, talking of urgency and asking for the 'promised interview'. It was the wrong tactic. A cold reply from Hobbs apologized if he had given the impression that Morris was more interested than he actually was, and pointedly returned the outline of the scheme. 'He has interested himself in so many schemes of a similar character during the past year, it is impossible to add to them at the present time and he regrets therefore that at the moment he is unable to render the assistance which is suggested by purchasing the land shown on the plan.'[12]

A year later Chavasse tried again and was again brushed off. But he continued his futile bombardment of Morris with St Aldate's annual reports and even copies of his sermons. In November 1930 he asked again for 'a short and quite private' interview. Again it was refused and a weary letter from Hobbs referred to many requests 'of exactly similar nature' which, it said, 'convinces him that the way of the would-be philanthropist is even harder than he previously supposed.' Still Chavasse continued his campaign, sending Morris an even more unsuitable present – a book of his father's sermons, while continuing to visit Emily Morris.

Finally in April 1934, the seven year campaign brought a cheque for £10,000. There were special circumstances. It came three months after the death of old Mrs Morris, and Chavasse had officiated at her funeral. It was relatively little but helped to pay off part of a mortgage. Shrewdly, as well as thanking Morris, the council of the hall requested permission to name one of the hall's buildings after his mother, and later a bust of her was unveiled there. It was the right move at last. In November the following year Chavasse, who by now had performed a marriage service for Morris's niece and saw himself as a family chaplain, invited Morris to become a member of the council. Morris accepted. He only attended a single council meeting. But it was enough.

Chavasse was advised to consult with Hobbs and a further £12,161 was found to pay off debts, and this was followed by a gift of £50,000, significantly unsolicited. Morris, with his usual delight in surprise, had taken Chavasse aside at a university garden party. 'If I lived 100 years,' wrote the excited cleric, 'I could never find words to express my thanks to you for founding St Peter's Hall in Oxford – for that is what you have done.'[13]

Pedantically one might say that Morris was responsible for the foundation of two Oxford colleges – a unique record in modern times. But the real significance of the St Peter's episode is to demonstrate both the pressures on both Morris and Hobbs to make major donations and the way that the university community could be as importunate as any. St Peter's really was 'morticed with gold'.

The correspondence with Chavasse makes plain that the thrust of the first wave of benefactions was, and was intended to be, medical. It was not until the mid-thirties and particularly until after the sale of some of his holding of ordinary shares in 1936 that Morris was able or willing to widen the scope of his giving and provide huge sums for Oxford University. When he did so however, it was on a much more prescriptive basis with money given on his terms with conditions attached.

His greatest donation to the university was for medical purposes, springing out of two sources – his conversations with the doctors at Huntercombe and his desire to improve the medical services provided in his own city.

Back in 1930 the Radcliffe Observatory in Oxford had moved its operations to the clearer skies of the southern hemisphere and Morris had provided £100,000 for the purchase of the site to enlarge the neighbouring Radcliffe Hospital, the city's principal medical centre. But it was still a limited facility. Sir Robert Macintosh described it as

> the poor little country hospital which Oxford was. When I used to come to Oxford I knew people who had to have operations and they went up to London for them. Until then medical students in Oxford did what were known as pre-clinical subjects. They did anatomy and physiology – nothing to do with patients and then they went to London or Liverpool or Birmingham.

The suggestion that the Radcliffe might be turned into a full-scale teaching hospital was made to Morris by the Regius Professor of Medicine, Sir Farquhar Buzzard in July 1936 but both men had been involved in plans for upgrading the hospital facilities for years before. Morris's purchase of the observatory site had been accompanied by the proposal that a Trust should be formed with the purpose of holding the site but also encouraging medical teaching and research work, including the possibility of an Institute for Medical Research.

The ideas owed much to a major political figure with whom Morris had become associated and who would be responsible for the professional guidance and structuring of the bequests. This was Will, later Sir William, Goodenough. The son of the chairman of Barclays Bank, he became the manager of its Oxford branch and Morris's banker when Barclays took over the family-owned Gillett bank which had given Morris such consistent support. Goodenough, who was chairman of the County Council and also much in demand for leading civil service committees provided the weight and good sense needed to coordinate Morris's impetuous giving, and crucially, retained his trust.

Goodenough was closely in touch with Buzzard who had been involved in an earlier attempt to find support for a post-graduate medical centre.[14] This had involved the American Rockefeller

Foundation which had had discussions with the then Minister of Health, Neville Chamberlain in 1928, but had turned down an application. Ironically the Foundation's own preference had been for Oxford but it had been unable to find anyone with whom to open confidential discussions in the university. Now Buzzard, who had subsequently moved to his Oxford post, was determined not to let matters slip again.

The ground had been well prepared. Detailed plans for a complete School of Clinical Medicine were thrashed out by Hugh (later Sir Hugh) Cairns at meetings with Buzzard, the university vice-chancellor, A.D. (later Lord) Lindsay and the registrar, (Sir) Douglas Veale.

In 1936 it was Buzzard's turn to become president of the British Medical Association. The annual banquet was held in Oxford and he invited Morris to be guest of honour. In his speech Buzzard talked of 'an ambitious dream' for a school of clinical medicine at Oxford and after the dinner he slipped a copy of the Cairns' proposals into Morris's pocket saying, 'Read this when you get home.'

The energetic Cairns had already buttonholed Morris at the pre-dinner reception and arranged to talk about the scheme with him at Huntercombe the following weekend. Cairns was an Australian and an enthusiast. After an hour of explanation Morris told him he was a man with 'fire in his belly' and he would back the scheme. He had wanted to do more for Oxford medicine.

But then came a typical Morris twist. With the university's hats still in the air, he decided to make a radical change to the scheme they had spent two years working out at a series of meetings. Instead of three professors, there would be four, and the fourth should be a Professor of Anaesthesia. It was unheard of. There were no Professors of Anaesthesia in the British Empire, and Oxford medical opinion did not regard it as a subject of sufficient standing to merit a professorial appointment.

But like so many of Morris's actions, it was founded on the imperative of his personal experience, and once decided he clung to his scheme with a tenacity that rocked the university back on its heels and came close to wrecking the whole enterprise.

As a young man Morris had had an appalling experience of rudimentary anaesthesia, when he had had all his teeth removed. He had told Robert Macintosh, the anaesthetist amongst the group of Guy's Hospital doctors at the Huntercombe Club about the ordeal – one by no means uncommon at the time.

> He had neglected his teeth and he had them all taken out.
> Incidentally one of his statements was that we would all be
> better off if we had all our teeth out. I think they were taken
> out in two separate lots. The gas – that was the only thing
> going – was given by the local dentist – local gas doesn't last
> very long – and he had horrible nightmares. He developed a
> terror. He just remembered being suffocated on these two
> occasions by a dentist who naturally wanted to take out as
> many teeth as he could. It is a very short-acting gas. The
> dentist had to drop the apparatus and get cracking. There
> was a horrible feeling of suffocation.

This seems to have happened when Morris was twenty. It was in
1897 that he explained to a rival cycle racer that the extractions
had affected his ability to race.

The experience stayed with him and it sharply contrasted with
the experience of another operation in the thirties. This time
Macintosh was the anaesthetist and things went so smoothly that
Morris regained consciousness afterwards demanding to know
when he would be taken to the theatre. He was immensely
impressed and by now Macintosh was an increasingly close
personal friend. Morris seems to have found it easier to get on with
New Zealanders and Australians who made up a number of his
medical acquaintants, perhaps because they were more direct
and he felt less class-consciousness. In the case of Macintosh, there
was another factor; Mrs Macintosh became one of the very few
close friends of Lilian Morris.

The proposal for the Professor of Anaesthetics was a product of
the dinner table conversations at Huntercombe. Morris, bursting
with the still unannounced scheme for the clinical school, spilled it
out to his doctor friends.

Macintosh remembered;

> He said they had asked for these three chairs, and without
> the slightest ulterior motive, I said, just to keep the
> conversation going, 'They have forgotten anaesthetics
> again'. I am absolutely sure that was the thing which put the
> idea into his head. I took no notice and the conversation just
> went on. But there is no doubt that it struck a chord. He
> thought about it and was determined to have that chair.

It was an extraordinary idea at the time. There was one

other chair at the time, in America, but nothing in Europe. One had to say to him 'I don't know whether this place has advanced sufficiently to have a university standard for a chair of anaesthetics; you have got to have the background for it'. And his reply was 'You won't be; your successor won't be, but the third in line will hold his ground'. And by Jove he was right.

So little did Morris understand university politics that Macintosh remembers that he expected his suggestion would be automatically approved.

He was much surprised when Buzzard called on him at Huntercombe on a Sunday afternoon to tell him that deeply grateful as the University was ... the creation of a chair in a subject such as anaesthetics would expose both the University and Nuffield to ridicule. Nuffield's reaction was entirely typical. In a friendly way, he thanked Buzzard for taking the trouble to point this out, otherwise he might have pressed for something obviously undesirable and Buzzard left, well satisfied with his mission.

Some two weeks went by, after which a slightly worried Regius Professor telephoned to enquire when the University could announce its Medical Benefaction to be told by Nuffield that at their last interview he had understood that the University had declined his offer. And then it became crystal clear that his offer was for four chairs or none.[15]

The university caved in, but Morris had still not done. He brushed aside the formalities of the election of professors on which much university tradition was based, and made clear that as the proposer of the new Chair of Anaesthesia he wanted also to nominate the professor – naturally his choice was Macintosh.

Once more the university was upset – while Macintosh was taken by surprise. He had a thriving private practice in London and saw little attraction in a transfer to academic life in Oxford where he feared he might be a fish out of water. But he was wary of causing a breach between his medical friends and Morris, and he knew that if he refused Morris would consider himself betrayed. After arranging to keep an option on his partnership, he moved to Oxford.

It proved a major success. The onset of modern warfare called for new techniques of anaesthesia to be developed to assist surgeons, and Macintosh was in the forefront. He travelled to Spain to assist in plastic surgery for Franco's wounded, and the techniques he pioneered were developed in the Second World War.

Veale himself conceded that, 'Lord Nuffield's insistence turned out to be fully justified.'[16]

The seal was placed on the enterprise on 1 December 1936 at a packed meeting of the university's congregation under the presidency of the university chancellor, the Cabinet Minister Lord Halifax. In the middle of the meeting there was an unscheduled interruption when Morris, unqualified to speak although he held an honorary doctorate, asked for permission to address the meeting and announced that he was increasing his benefaction from £1.25 million to £2 million. It was pure theatre of the unexpected. The crowded chamber cheered but there were those who resented the way Morris seemed to be playing with them.

There was one more battle to fight – a revolt by the medical staff and governors of the Radcliffe hospital against having the new university medical school imposed on them. The ubiquitous Goodenough, who was becoming almost indispensable in pouring oil on waters agitated by Morris, called a meeting and quelled the protests. There was now no question that Morris had stormed what Betjeman called 'the great black wall' of the university which had shadowed him. And once inside he was determined to plant his standard for all to see. The next step was to found a college to bear his name, which would follow his interests. He wanted an engineering college.

It is not clear when he first formed the idea but there was little doubt among those who negotiated the foundation of Nuffield College that the actual college was the thing: simply to support a major university department, in some ways more appropriate, would not have satisfied him. He wanted a traditional college bearing his own name as founder.[17]

Leslie Farrer-Brown who was to be the first director of the Nuffield Foundation says 'he wanted to found a college and he wanted it in Oxford.'

The approach was made at a meeting with Lord Halifax who then referred the matter to Veale, the registrar, with instructions to bring in the Vice-Chancellor A.D. Lindsay, later Lord Lindsay. Sandie Lindsay was a forceful and controversial don who stood for many of the things Morris hated. Later Morris would accuse him of cheating him over his desire for a college of engineering. Farrer-Brown remembers, 'More than once Nuffield said to me incidentally in the course of conversation, "If that fellow Lindsay can turn in his grave, I hope he is turning all the time".'

Lindsay, the Master of Balliol, was a Labour Party supporter, a Workers' Education Association lecturer, who stood as the Independent candidate backed by Labour against the National Government (which Morris supported) in the 1938 by-election. As his biographer put it, 'it would be hard to think of two people more likely to disagree about everything than Lindsay and Nuffield.'[18]

In one respect however they shared a common conviction. Both wanted to make Oxford studies more relevant to the modern world. Lindsay had been involved with the establishment of what were called 'modern greats', the study of the modern disciplines of politics, philosophy and economics to parallel the study of classical civilization and philosophy known as greats. He was anxious to promote social studies and to tie together research and practice, evidenced by the way he used a Rockefeller grant to undertake a survey of current Oxford social services. Here there were congruities with Morris's approach.

Indeed the two men had worked relatively harmoniously together over the plans for the medical school where they were both agreed about the need to marry activity in the labs with that in the wards. Lindsay himself wrote, 'the Nuffield benefaction in medicine is intended to put an end to a separation which is doing great harm in medical research – the separation between the scientific researcher ... and the clinical practitioner in the wards.'[19]

Halifax set out Morris's proposal in a letter to Veale. A former civil servant who had been Chamberlain's private secretary at the Ministry of Health, he was a politician to his fingertips, central in smoothing the way for the benefactions. His function was emollient, oiling the wheels to make things happen. Morris came to distrust him too but not with the abiding hatred he held for Lindsay.

The letter of 8 July 1937 laid out Morris's proposal at a meeting that morning. 'He had it in mind to offer to build on the waste ground he has recently bought below St Peter's Hall a College of Engineering. He had been much impressed with what seemed to him the gap in the equipment of Oxford on these lines, and felt that Oxford compared in this respect very unfavourably with Cambridge with the result that she lost many good men.'

He had offered a quarter of a million pounds to build the college
and a further three quarters to endow it. Halifax reported, 'I told
him that I was not equipped to speak about the way in which such
a school could be fitted into the Oxford scheme of things'. He had,
of course, expressed his gratitude at the 'repeated shocks' of
Morris's offers.[20]

It was a determined approach. Morris had even bought the site.
Ironically it seems first to have been drawn to his notice by the
plan for St Peter's Hall sent to him to encourage him to buy the
site for them. It was a glum and messy part of Oxford, opposite the
old castle keep and the prison. It contrasted sharply with the
approach to the city centre from the Cowley direction over the
handsome sweep of Magdalen bridge. Morris's idea was that his
college would similarly improve the approach to the city from the
station.

The problem was that the proposal did not at all fit into 'the
Oxford scheme of things'. Neither the university's own Survey of
Needs drawn up in 1932 to plan its development nor its current
appeal had any plans to invest in engineering.

Indeed, as Veale wrote to Halifax about the engineering
proposal: 'For us to set up a rival school would not only be
contrary to the arrangement to which we have come with
Cambridge that we should not unnecessarily duplicate services but
would, by sterilising capital sunk in the Cambridge School, be
thoroughly bad policy from the public point of view.'[21] In other
words the money should be used for another purpose.

The university authorities now moved with lightning speed to
divert the Morris proposals to something which would fit into their
plans. Halifax had telephoned Veale about the offer before writing
the letter, and he had mentioned that Morris had proposed that
accountancy should be part of the new institution's study. This did
not appear in the letter but was rapidly seized on by Veale.

He telephoned Hobbs that afternoon, arranging to see Morris
the following day, and spoke to Lindsay the following morning. By
the time he saw Morris he had a scheme to put to him which
'carries out the essential parts of his idea in a way which is far more
acceptable to us than a residential engineering college.'[21]

It was fast footwork by any standard. Morris was snookered,
blocked off from what he really wanted yet willing to proceed with
the game because of his dream of his own college.

Veale's proposal was twofold. If Morris really wanted to help

Oxford compete with Cambridge he should contribute to a new £100,000 laboratory for physical chemistry. Oxford believed itself pre-eminent in this, and it had engineering applications. Significantly its inclusion in the Higher Studies appeal had brought no response.

Secondly the college form should be changed from residential undergraduate to post-graduate. Veale envisaged it as a centre for Modern Studies to which 'the practical man is brought to give the benefit of his practical experience to the dons'. That, it was calculated, would appeal to Morris and fit in with the university's own concern to tie the study of local government to its practical working and to approach political economy through the way that its problems struck the businessman. 'This, you will see, gives effect to what Lord Nuffield meant by "Accountancy".'[22]

It was a far cry from a College of Engineering but Morris appeared to have been persuaded. Veale arranged for him to meet Lindsay and wrote to Halifax with breathtaking condescension towards Morris. 'I think I can safely say that he accepted this scheme as fulfilling what he really had in mind, when talking to you in all essentials, much as it differs in details.' At the end he scribbled by hand. 'Excuse a rather incoherent letter. I am in rather a flutter of excitement.'

Morris too appeared to share the excitement. When the scheme was formally announced on 12 October, the *Oxford Mail* reported 'three times his enthusiasm overcame his diffidence and he broke out with "this is the thing which may well go down through the ages ... it was too early yet to predict its outcome".'[23]

Lindsay's formal announcement in congregation on 16 November drew an explicit parallel with the medical benefaction's link between laboratory and ward. 'This College is concerned to bridge what I think is an even more disastrous gap in our modern life, the gap between the theoretical student of society and those responsible for carrying it on.'

The university's gratitude to Morris was expressed in a curious way which said much about Morris's wish to be accepted. Already the holder of an honorary doctorate – the obvious resort – he was granted the status of MA as if he had been a member of the university. He formally paid the matriculation fee and was now allowed to take part in the official administrative gatherings of the university. As Lindsay put it, he was now an 'ordinary member of the university'.

It was the formal acknowledgement that he was now inside the wall and the tone of Lindsay's announcement of the college's function was very much in keeping with Morris's vision of himself as the practical man who would bring modern common sense to ancient practices. But his pleasure in the foundation was soon curdling into distrust, dislike and effective divorce.

There were a number of reasons – the details of the scheme, the personalities involved, but probably most of all the simple fact of delay.

The medical school bequest had been rapidly implemented because the scheme had already been worked out by the university – the college proposals by contrast had sprung far from fully-formed from Morris's and Veale's heads. They were the subject of detailed discussion by the committee of ten set up by the university in October 1937.

Two of the committee's first tasks were to appoint an architect and a warden to head the college. Both were to run into trouble. The chosen architect was Austen Harrison who had been architect to the Palestine Public Works Department. Morris approved the choice and the design was accepted by the university in January 1939. Morris was in the southern hemisphere and it was not until June that he got to see the plans. Then he exploded. He declared that it might be suitable for Cairo but not for Oxford, it was un-English, out of keeping with tradition and he would not allow his name to be associated with it. Veale remembered it innacurately as the only stormy interview he ever had with Morris.

It was an appalling start. A new design, more mock-medieval, was eventually approved but not until March 1940 – well after the outbreak of war when any building work was out of the question.

By then the college was leaderless. The man chosen to be the first warden was Harold Butler, a distinguished civil servant who was director of the International Labour Office. Appointed in January 1939, he was called away to war work at the outbreak of war, returned briefly for a few weeks in 1942 and resigned in the middle of 1943 after another year away. The consequence was that the college trod water. Six part-time Fellows, who were already Fellows of existing colleges, were elected in June 1939 and six visiting Fellows chosen including the TUC General Secretary, Sir Walter Citrine and a couple of industrialists.

Half the tiny part-time team disappeared into the civil service at the outbreak of war and the running of the college was left largely to Lindsay and the most active of the Fellows, G.D.H. Cole. Veale was by now writing of 'Lord Nuffield's obvious dissatisfaction with the complete stagnation of the college for so long a period'. Dissatisfaction however was soon to turn to fury.[24]

If Lindsay had been guaranteed to raise Morris's suspicions about left-leaning academics, Cole was a caricature of everything Morris disliked. A nationally known Labour Party activist and polemicist, along with his wife Margaret, he had written a pamphlet backing an Oxford tram strike as long ago as 1913, and was exactly the kind of enthusiast Morris found lobbying his workers at the gates of Cowley. Indeed in October 1940 he gave a speech to the university's Democratic Socialist Club which the *Oxford Mail* headlined, 'Mr G.D.H. Cole urges socialist methods. Tells Oxford capitalism is unable to conduct war well'. It was difficult to envisage anything more guaranteed to infuriate Morris – except perhaps the jibes of his conservative friends, which were not slow in coming.

The former Governor of the Bank of England, Montagu Norman, was said to have chaffed him about the 'little Kremlin' he had created in Oxford while in private conversation Morris referred to 'that lot of bloody reds'.[25]

Goodenough and Hobbs began to be seriously alarmed about his attitude and Morris started to talk of changing the nature of the college back to engineering. Goodenough pressed the college to arrange research work for the Government. There was limited enthusiasm from the Civil Service and Goodenough lobbied Halifax and Whitehall as well as stressing to the college that if it did not initiate research work it would be 'failing to meet our obligations to Lord Nuffield'.[26]

The absence of a warden increasingly infuriated Morris, and by early 1941, Goodenough, his confidant, was warning that unless Butler threw himself with vigour into the college's work or made way for someone else, he would resign and Morris would be expected to be outspoken in public about the use of his benefaction.[27]

The tension was temporarily eased in February with the setting up of the Social Reconstruction Survey to be run by Cole to examine the consequences of the social and industrial disruption caused by the war, in conjunction with the Cabinet's own reconstruction committee. Cole threw himself enthusiastically into the work, recruiting large numbers of staff and spreading his enquiries out widely. While the university authorities soon became concerned about the cost and found Cole difficult and overbearing, the survey gained public recognition and when it was proposed in May 1942 to appoint Cole as sub-warden, Morris was persuaded by Goodenough to agree.

> I must confess that when I first heard of the suggestion that Cole should deputise ... I was caused a little uneasiness by a thought that his past ideas and activities might to some extent reassert themselves, but on this point I have gained assurance from the knowledge that the Vice-Chancellor [now David Ross of Oriel] will be associating himself personally with the development of the College.[28]

It was wishful thinking on someone's part and Goodenough's patching up did not last. In November 1942 Morris called on Veale and spent an hour and a quarter in furious conversation with him. Veale's account was that he was 'boiling with rage about the college, saying that he was thinking of publicly dissociating his name from it, and making it plain that the university must never expect to get another penny of his money'.[29]

He was particularly angry that Cole was so much in charge of the survey, although this in fact had always transparently been the case. Veale attempted to reassure him, and pointed out that if he was known to be critical of the college others would always run it down to him.

There were coincidentally increasing university doubts about the survey, and an enquiry was put in hand about the attitudes of Government departments to it. When the Treasury withdrew its grant, and other departments were cool, its days were numbered. A bitter Cole remained to wind up the survey, resigning from the college in March 1944. A new warden, Henry Clay, was appointed but Morris was now so out of sympathy with the college that its Fellows never saw him.

The controversy came close to derailing the whole idea of Nuffield College as a centre for social studies. It is clear that it took strong persuasion to discourage Morris from attempting to revert to his original idea of an engineering college. A question in the university's Hebdomadal Council in June 1943 reflected rumours in Oxford when it asked whether the Vice-Chancellor had reason to believe that 'Lord Nuffield is dissatisfied with the decision of the University to associate Nuffield College with the subject of social studies.'

In his reply the Vice-Chancellor pointed out that the original offer specified social studies and this was enshrined in the trust deed, but he acknowledged that 'rumours had come to his ears to the effect that Lord Nuffield now regretted this decision and it was known that Lord Nuffield had serious misgivings about the Social Reconstruction Survey.'[30]

It is difficult to see how the legal foundation of the college could have been unscrambled to change it into an engineering college, without an extraordinary change of tack by the university. But Morris, as he had already demonstrated to the authorities, was nothing if not determined. It was not until early in February 1944 that a letter from Hobbs to Goodenough, which lies close to a press cutting of a Labour Party speech by Margaret Cole in the Nuffield papers, informed him that, 'When I saw my Lord this morning he appeared to understand the position entirely and there is apparently no longer any thought in his mind of transforming the college into an engineering institution.'[31]

Veale's view was expressed in a letter to Butler in 1942.

We failed to keep alive, perhaps even to realise the burning ardour with which he founded [the college]. All his enthusiasm cooled during the months when nothing overt was happening and he heard nothing from us. If that had been done I believe Cole could have preached the class war from the steps of the college and Nuffield could have borne it.[32]

But the damage had been done. The exhilaration about his conquest of the university had passed. He turned his face away from the college and would not be reconciled to it until the very last years of his life after a skilful and sustained wooing by a later warden, Sir Norman Chester.

Leslie Farrer-Brown, establishing the Nuffield Foundation as its first director in the early forties, recalls, 'He couldn't reconcile himself; he kept away. We in the Foundation had to get involved at one stage because it was clear that the endowment which they had thought was adequate was not'. Morris did not stop the assistance, but his attention had shifted away from the university. It was other benefactions which occupied him now, particularly in the medical field and the founding of an institution which would commemorate him and his name to a far wider audience than Oxford and the university.

11 Towards the Foundation

The reasons why Morris became such an extraordinarily prolific benefactor were never clearly and cogently explained by him. It would have been surprising if they had. They were so obviously a confused mix of emotions and intentions accompanying a generosity rare among the British motor manufacturers and most industrialists of his time.

There was for example what he himself recognized as 'the pleasure obtained from giving assistance to a needy and praiseworthy cause.'[1] There was the recognition it brought both from the public in general and the establishment in particular. There were the doors it opened into the unknown and secret worlds of the university and medicine, and their enclosing societies and rituals. There were the elements both of surprise and of power; the domination from the dispensing of patronage. There was also the strong sense that Morris was trying to chisel out for himself some lasting memorial in the absence of children to follow him.

Requests for donations seem automatically to have followed his achievement of secure wealth in the mid 1920s and to have doubled after his first bequests. In his *Daily Express* article in June 1927, he was already talking of being overwhelmed by requests, insisting he only gave collectively and not individually and complaining of the responsibility of giving. 'The man who would give money is compelled to do a great deal of hard thinking. Is his gift going to do good or harm? ... the responsibility of a would-be giver is great.'[2]

Three years later Hobbs, on instructions from Morris, was writing that 'the way of the would-be philanthropist is even harder than he supposed', and that 'money so given can best be expended in directions in which it offers prospects of benefiting the greatest numbers of the community, with preference always for his own work people. It is this conviction which has allowed him to regard the needs of the hospitals as unequalled.'[3]

If one grants that the principal gain to Morris work-people was the provision of better hospital services, it is a reasonable summary of the pattern of his early giving. It was concentrated on the local Oxford area, plus cities like Birmingham and Coventry where he had substantial works. It then developed in the direction of the particular special interests of his own – the Special Areas Trust flowing from the League of Industry activity – and perhaps his thwarted political intentions, his later benefactions supporting the welfare of the armed services during the war, and above all medicine, a fascination becoming almost all-embracing after his unhappy experiences with the university.

The roots of the obsession which Morris had about matters medical lie in his own hypochondria, his juxtaposition to the doctors at Huntercombe, and a recognition of the need for support for the very rapid medical advances which were being made in the period. He was made well aware of these both from the treatment he received himself and his conversation with the doctors.

Add to that the concern of the practical man to improve both the limited local hospital facilities available in Oxford and to encourage the rationalization and coordination of provincial hospital services, and a recipe emerges which broadly encompasses the benefactions.

The most vivid picture of Morris's hypochondria is given by Miles Thomas. By the beginning of the war Morris had got into the habit of testing his own urine, sometimes three times a day, for diabetes. Thomas went to see him one Tuesday to discuss a Ministry of Supply contract for several million pounds worth of anti-tank guns.

> He said, 'Don't stop talking, I'm listening', went into a corner of the office, produced a specimen, mixed the solution and started jiggling the test tube over the flame of the spirit lamp in a very chemist-like fashion. Something momentarily distracted his attention. Before we knew where we were, the test tube had hit the glass of the spirit lamp and broken and the 'specimen' was flooding the Ministry of Supply contract, rapidly obliterating some of the very sizeable figures.[4]

Thomas described Morris as ever ready to discuss his medical problems with medical or even quasi-medical men; and his executives commented on the huge amounts of bicarbonate of soda he would ingest for apparent stomach ache. The prescriptions and medical cards from years before and the X-rays among his papers confirm the same impression of a man who was obsessed by his own health – and other people's. He would encourage his own workers to have their urine tested as well and try to dictate to a surgeon what operation his sister could stand.

In fact his own medical history was not particularly remarkable. Apart from his loss of teeth and the problems with his eyes, perhaps from overwork, his most striking early experience of doctoring seems to have been with the celebrated Regius Professor, Sir William Osler. Morris, who serviced Osler's car and had frequent dealings with him, consulted him after a long period of strain. After listening to lengthy details, Osler struck Morris a sharp blow in the solar plexus and told him he had a peptic ulcer which he fully deserved from his life style and that he was 'bloody lucky' it had not perforated. When Morris told the story he joked that Osler himself had been lucky he had not burst it there and then. But he would also insist that no doctor was worth consulting who did not have Osler's books on his shelves, and wanted to name a building at the Radcliffe Infirmary after him.[5]

Sir John Conybeare dated the incident to 1905 but it may be that it relates to 1918 when Morris was advised to go to Germany for his health. Subsequently he was dissuaded from standing for the Parliamentary election in 1923 for health reasons, and he had his appendix removed in the thirties. It did not seem enough to justify the continual concern about his health which Thomas and others noted. However, their criticism of him was muted when it was found close to the end of his life that he had an apparently long-term constriction of his bowels, perhaps caused by his early cycling exertion. It could have been responsible for what Thomas described as 'the gnawing pain which on and off had beset him for more than sixty years', and could affect his judgement.[6]

Macintosh, with a doctor's perspective, said,

> I don't think he really suffered the effect of any particular disease but he would express an opinion about medicine which had just come into his head. He had funny ideas and of course it became increasingly difficult to contradict the man who had given hundreds of thousands to your hospital.

Some of the medical benefactions showed the typical quirky Morris surprise approach. An early example, which would have major ramifications and lead to a large fund to assist cripples, was one of the two first Oxford donations, to the Wingfield Hospital where Dr G.R. Girdlestone was carrying out pioneering orthopaedic work on crippled children. Hospital was a grand word for what was a collection of ramshackle wooden huts and Morris decided to step in.

Late one night in 1930 Girdlestone was called to the door by his maid to find Morris on the doorstep with a cheque for a thousand pounds. The two men developed a friendship and after the huts had been patched with the first donation, substantial buildings were erected three years later with a further donation of £70,000. As a result, in what became something of a pattern, the name of the hospital was changed to the Wingfield-Morris hospital. It caused some resentment amongst local people who, while grateful for the assistance, did not see why the name of the familiar establishment should be altered to accommodate the donor.

Morris liked to boast that he employed good men and then let them get on with the job. While this was palpably untrue as far as his business was concerned, with managers being repeatedly second-guessed and a failure to bring on young men, it was much more the case with the benefactions. Girdlestone and Macintosh were two obvious examples of individuals whose abilities were recognized and backed by Morris. The difference was that Morris could not presume to second-guess them.

The relative success and lack of major controversy over his medical benefactions as compared with the bitter battles with the university was partly due to this, but it was also considerably influenced by the confidence Morris had in two powerful men. Sir John Conybeare of Guy's Hospital and Sir William Goodenough the banker. Goodenough was deeply involved in the administration of most major Nuffield charities as well as in the hospital administrative committees, locally and nationally, which paved the way for the National Health Service.

Both were in a sense chance encounters. Conybeare had had his car garaged by Morris as an undergraduate and renewed acquaintance at Huntercombe as part of the Guy's party while Goodenough had become Morris's banker and financial advisor while still in his twenties.

Of Conybeare, his colleague Macintosh said, 'He had very good relations with Cony. They could not have been better. He could say anything to him, and he to Cony.' There were few of Morris's acquaintances to whom that right was allowed.

Goodenough was an even more substantial figure, the son of the chairman of Barclays, with the establishment connections which Morris prized and wide political skills. Leslie Farrer-Brown who worked closely with him before and after the creation of the Nuffield Foundation described him as 'energetic, always wanting things to happen'.

> He was a big man physically, very genial but he liked a sense of power. He was one of those chairmen who somehow or other was able to get a committee to come to a decision which he thought was right, even on matters on which he was not expert. I have known powerful men, members of high powered committees, say before a meeting 'Will won't get away with this', but somehow without breaking bones or creating hurt, he brought them round. That was true both of his wartime work on the Interdepartmental Committee on Medical Schools, which was part of the early preparation for the Health Service, and on the Board of Trustees of the Foundation.

> He had exactly the mixture of determination and political skill which Morris needed, and could not provide himself. Thomas once said of Morris that it was 'his inability to speak other than emotionally which prevented him from being an orthodox chairman at the top of a boardroom table or the conventional member of a council or committee. He was not a good functional Chairman.[7]

Goodenough more than plugged the gap, intervening with the university authorities or the Radcliffe staff to smooth things over and make sure Morris's wishes were followed within reason, while at the same time adroitly playing Morris himself, nudging him into reasonableness, and not averse to using him for his own causes.

Goodenough was very much younger than Morris. His family connections had made him manager of the Oxford Branch of Barclays in 1923 when he was only twenty-four – and it was extraordinary that he should have been so trusted by Morris. But then his 'remarkable talent with people' was picked out in his entry in the Dictionary of Business Biography. 'He was regularly in demand when there was disputation in one or other of the bodies in which he was associated, or on occasion, in a troubled Government Department; seldom was he unable to reconcile the disputants.' His subsequent influence on Morris's philanthropic activity was enormous.

Goodenough was a man in a hurry, who became chairman of the County Council and swiftly focused on the need to improve medical services. He was encouraged by a local politician, an Alderman William Hyde, and together in 1927 they established the Oxford and District Provident Association, a local forerunner of the BUPA medical scheme designed to provide insurance against sudden medical bills. Morris provided £1,000 for a reserve fund which allowed the scheme to be launched.

Morris, with his strong belief in self-help, went on to guarantee schemes of the same sort throughout the country in 1941 with £150,000 for a Provident Guarantee Fund, which in turn provided a further £50,000 guarantee to BUPA when it was formed in 1947. It became so associated with his name that it was known in its early days as the 'Nuffield scheme' or 'the Nuffield'.

The association with Goodenough and Hyde likewise prospered. Hyde was actually provided with an office at Cowley for his work, while Goodenough was soon a trustee of the newly acquired Radcliffe Observatory site and chairman of the Oxford Medical Trustees. Their concern about medical administration reached its culmination in December 1939 with the formation of the Nuffield Provincial Hospitals Trust, which once again had arisen from a local initiative.

Morris had shown his desire to improve Oxford hospital services by the acquisition of the observatory site and the establishment of the Oxford Medical School. Hyde had been involved in the work of the Oxford and District Joint Hospitals Board which in the days before the National Health Service attempted to coordinate work and facilities at nearby hospitals. It was a further step in providing better services in the region. Hyde and Goodenough then persuaded the health authorities that a network of similar schemes throughout the country would be of value, particularly under the strain of war, and Morris agreed to put up a million pounds in Morris Motors stock to finance it. Naturally Goodenough became chairman and Hyde secretary.

The Trust became of major importance. It acted as a stepping stone to some of the major organizational changes of the NHS with its 'demarcation of the country into a series of hospital regions, each having as the focus of the hospital and health services a university medical school and a "key" hospital'. It also backed a series of groundbreaking initiatives – university chairs in social, child and mental health, surveys of general and group practice, bureaux of health and sickness records and experimental health centres.

It was an important test-bed and focus of research for ideas which would find fruition in the NHS. It all accorded with Morris's liking for backing schemes which appeared to bring modern thinking and modern organization to bear on old problems. It was a theme which ran through his medical benefactions, whether to the Wingfield or to the Radcliffe, but it reached a controversial climax just before the war.

Morris, visiting Macintosh's unit at the Radcliffe in 1938, had been shown a film about artificial respiration. It featured a device called a Both respirator, after its Australian inventor, but which was more colloquially known as the 'iron lung'. This, confusingly, was a largely wooden piece of equipment into which patients were placed with their heads projecting to assist their breathing. By coincidence, when Morris returned home that night he saw an evening paper headline about an iron lung arriving too late at a hospital to save a life.

He promptly telephoned Macintosh the next morning to ask whether if all hospitals had the 'lungs' two lives might be saved a year. When Macintosh said yes, Morris announced that he would have 5,000 made and distribute them to any hospital which applied. It was a typical Morris decision – spur of the moment, idiosyncratic and blockbusting. It did not, however, please the doctors. The device was still only experimental and Morris was bitterly attacked by the medical press for jumping the gun and forcing the iron lung on the profession. In the event about 1,700 were made, some at Cowley, and distributed to hospitals in Britain and the Commonwealth. With characteristic thoroughness Morris also arranged a cheap flat-rate scheme for servicing the respirators.

Alongside the grander coordinated schemes, often associated with Goodenough and Hyde, a stream of other benefactions poured out. There were donations to the Navy League, to the Scouts, to village schemes for settlements and centres, to the Kipling Memorial Fund, to the University of London Students' Union, to nurses' homes, to the Institution of Production Engineers to set up a research department staffed by an emigre German engineer who was reputedly the world expert on production machine tools.

But the overwhelming interest remained medical, and, outside

Oxford, with Guy's Hospital. It was an association which Morris relished, and which brought him inside a recognizable – and apparently adoring – community. On the eve of the coronation of King George VI in 1937 he had left it too late to book a hotel room. Instead he and his wife stayed with the superintendent of Guy's, Sir Herbert Eason.

His daughter, Mrs Cook, who was then fifteen, later recalled, 'He was drinking champagne. The whole dinner was hilarious with Lord Nuffield putting the prefix 'eggs' instead of 'ex' for every word he could think of and we ended up parading round in his coronation robes, sword and all'.[9] It was a side of the man not often seen, but at Guy's he seems to have felt at home, and the hospital took care to court him in a way that Oxford University seemed not yet to have learnt.

In spite of his regular dinner table contact with the Guy's doctors at Huntercombe, the first benefaction to the hospital did not come until 1934. The doctors were well aware of Morris's antipathy to being approached directly for money and kept a social relationship while discussing general medical developments and needs. The first project was much in line with the Oxford work of Hyde and Goodenough in helping those who were neither in occupational health schemes nor sufficiently well off to meet sudden medical bills with equanimity. It was to provide accommodation at the hospital for those who in Morris's words were, 'neither entitled to come into this hospital as ordinary patients, nor well enough off to pay the charges in nursing homes.'

Morris had agreed to provide £45,000 for a seventy-three bed block. At the laying of the foundation stone he said, 'I would like to pay the highest tribute to the staff of Guy's Hospital. I have known some of them for many years and they have always appealed to me as being hard workers in the cause of humanity. That is the reason why I am here today and why I am making this gift to the hospital.'[10]

At the same time, in a move which foreshadowed his famous intervention at Oxford University two years later and which makes that appear less spontaneous than it seemed, he announced that he was increasing his donation by a further £20,000 so that the number of beds might be doubled.

The ceremony finished with three cheers for Lord Nuffield and the singing of 'For he's a jolly good fellow'. The hospital took care to remain on good terms with their benefactor. A policy had to be taken out on his life in case he died before the block was completed – an awkward matter but it was deputed to Conybeare to explain – and Morris was invited to become first a governor and then the hospital's treasurer in December of the following year.

Eight years later at a special meeting of the hospital's court of governors, the chairman, J.E. Humphery, described his donations as 'less important than the new energy and outlook which have been infused into the affairs of the hospital since the Treasurer's tenure of office began'. He continued, 'He comes to the hospital. He takes an interest in everybody and everything in it; you do not find his name on subscription lists but when anything special is needed for any department he is always ready to help; and the many things he has given to the Hospital and the number of small things he does (particularly for the Nurses) are a very real assistance and encouragement to us all. This is what makes him such a great friend of all of us.'[11]

Later in the year the hospital proposed, and Morris agreed, that a statue should be erected to him in the hospital, of the same size and of similar material to that of its founder, Thomas Guy. He was now the largest benefactor the hospital had known since Guy. The list included £89,940 for extensions to the nurse's home, a range of various special donations which included X-ray equipment and the purchase of a site for a clinic, and effectively £250,000 towards the rebuilding of the hospital in 1944 after wartime bombing. This was the result of the first repayments of assistance made by the Special Areas Fund. The terms of the fund had provided for any repayments to be given to the King Edward's Hospital Fund for London. This provided for assistance to London hospitals to be allocated in a coordinated way.

Technically, Morris had no say on how it distributed any money which came from the Special Areas Fund. In practice it did not inhibit him at all and he made plain to the Fund that he wished the money to go to Guy's, while conceding he had no right to intervene. A nudge was as good as a wink. Although Sir Edward Peacock for the Fund's management committee claimed that the approach from Morris had raised 'a very delicate question' there appeared little sign of doubt or resistance. 'I know I am speaking for my colleagues,' said Sir Edward, 'when I say it has given us great pleasure and satisfaction to accede to Lord Nuffield's request, first because none of us could refuse Lord Nuffield and secondly because we feel that the money is going to a respectable quarter.'[12]

The arrangements for the other benefactions bore what were by now the characteristic Morris trademarks. There was something for nurses, and those closely involved with him like Thomas or Farrer-Brown all comment on his fondness for nurses. 'He was devoted to them. It was sentimentality, he would do anything for them,' says Farrer-Brown.

But the provision for the donation for the nurses' home extension was precise; it would only be paid when the total balance of the fund – £420,000 – had been subscribed. Morris was anxious that his gifts should not prevent the recipients making efforts to help themselves. He was particularly wary of second time round approaches; occasions when he was told that the original sum had not proved sufficient.

At the same time, the hospital was careful to put the Nuffield name on the new building for paying patients. This was by now an essential way of preserving goodwill. Indeed, the Board of Governors of the United Oxford Hospitals were soon to consider, but vote down, a proposal to change the name of the Radcliffe Infirmary to the Radcliffe-Nuffield. The thinking had been that Morris would then have regarded the hospital as his residuary legatee.[13]

Sir John Stallworthy, a Nuffield professor and President of the BMA and the Royal Society of Medicine, another who had close dealings with Morris, said that he never became big enough to be able to give money without having his name associated with it. In later life he found him obsessed with the fear that he would be forgotten without an heir to carry on his name.[14]

Leslie Farrer-Brown takes a more emollient view.

> I don't think he had to have his name on everything. It was those of us connected with his benefactions who put his name as often as we could on it. He didn't undervalue his place in the world. At the same time he didn't seek a lot of public applause. It did dismay him that he hadn't got a son or family to follow him. He said more than once to me, 'No-one to carry on'.

There can be little doubt however that Morris did luxuriate in the renown his benefactions brought, and there may also have been a feeling that they helped supersede the memory of his unhappy political involvements. But increasingly the sheer weight of requests for assistance were becoming a burden – both to himself, and his friends. 'I will never be pressurised into giving anything for any purpose. I like to make up my own mind, and for that reason I do object to so many people writing to me, asking me to subscribe to this, that or the other,' he said.[15] But his attitude did little to stem the flow.

Sir John Conybeare remembered:

> His daily ration of begging letters was very large, and whenever the press announced a benefaction the number of letters both from private individuals and charities was doubled and redoubled. Those known to be friends are frequently asked to intercede and press the claims of one or other charity. If they are wise they do not do so. Someone once asked him why he had given a large sum to a certain hospital. The reason he gave was that he had never been asked for money although he was on friendly terms with many of the hospital staff.[16]

The pressure of the daily charitable demands, an inclination to tie up the rest of his fortune in a secure and tidy way and the wish to establish another monument to posterity in lieu of the dynasty he could never found, were all to be factors in the creation in 1943 of the crowning pediment on the great edifice of his benefactions, the Nuffield Foundation.

There are differing views about the exact genesis of the foundation. That is scarcely surprising. In retrospect it seems to have been a logical outcome – one which might commend itself as an option to those concerned with the various benefactions. Indeed we know from Morris himself that he had spoken to a secretary of Rockefeller's in New York about charitable giving as early as the mid 1920s,[17] and by the end of the thirties he was openly being compared with the big American philanthropists.

In his history of the Nuffield Foundation,[18] Ronald Clark quotes one story that Morris arrived in his office one morning, announced he was going to found a new trust and settled the details rapidly. Another version had him engaged in intensive discussions with Goodenough at the end of 1942 and beginning of 1943. The first story seems unlikely though it could have marked the culmination of a process. The second may reflect general discussions about the benefactions which certainly went on, although not at first with the idea of a foundation. A detailed and coherent explanation is provided by Leslie Farrer-Brown.

Farrer-Brown, who was to direct the fortunes of the foundation for its first twenty-one years and until after Morris's death, was an experienced administrator. He had been on the administrative staff of the London School of Economics before going on to London University and then into the Civil Service as secretary of the Central Midwives Board, afterwards joining the Ministry of Health to deal with wartime evacuation.

By 1942 he was secretary to the Interdepartmental Committee on Medical Schools whose chairman was Goodenough, who rapidly recognized his qualities.

Farrer-Brown says:

I remember one evening that I was on duty in my office at the top of the building and Goodenough was at the Connaught Hotel. He came to have dinner with me at the Athenaeum. It was all blacked out. Towards the end of the meal he said, 'Nuffield has approached me. He is wanting to make his final series of benefactions. There is a long list of things he might consider and he has said to me, 'What do we do, how do we go about it?'

We talked and I let out the thought – wouldn't it be rather good if he could be persuaded to use all the money to establish a foundation like the Rockefeller Foundation. I had developed great admiration for these international foundations, particularly Rockefeller, because back in 1935 I was asked to go over to America and study what they were doing. Goodenough liked the idea and said he would put it to him. I remember walking back through a blacked-out Pall Mall. A week or ten days later Goodenough phoned me up and said Nuffield likes it, and we are telling Herbert (Morris's lawyer, L.F. Herbert) to get cracking on the deeds.[19]

Discussions followed on the terms with attempts being made to include general areas which would encompass much of the long Morris list which involved the training of dentists, support for industrial and child health and help for the aged poor.

There was legal argument about whether the words 'social well-being' could be classed as a charitable object, and Herbert would write to Hyde, who was naturally closely involved, that 'it is a modern expression not yet construed by the courts and there is just a doubt that, because of its vagueness, it might be construed in a narrow sense.' Similarly there was debate about the phrase the 'aged poor' and whether it would satisfy the charity commissioners. Here Morris was in no doubt. 'It was Lord Nuffield's expressed desire that reference to the care and comfort of the aged poor should be retained in the deed,' said a letter from Hyde to Goodenough on 17 March 1943.[20] Morris was himself now past his sixty-fifth birthday and had always had a concern about old age, but there was also an increasing awareness of the growing needs of the elderly which the Trust would do much to illuminate.

Goodenough was in his element gathering a group of managing trustees together. He picked two from his medical committee, Dame Janet Vaughan, a doctor who was the daughter of his old headmaster, and Sir John Stopford, the dean of the Manchester Medical School. Another acquaintance was Professor Engledow, Draper's Professor of Agriculture at Cambridge. Sir Henry Tizard, a former Government scientific advisor, temporarily out of favour but with wide-ranging contacts was an Oxford acquaintance of Morris. Sir Hector Hetherington was a widely experienced university Vice-Chancellor who had relevant experience as a trustee of the Carnegie UK Trust. The Hon. Geoffrey Gibbs, a banker, was also a relation by marriage of Goodenough. Goodenough naturally became chairman.

The inaugural meeting was held on 1 April 1943 at a round dining table set in an alcove off the main dining-room of the Savoy in London, a place where Morris liked to stay when he could not, as he preferred, return to Oxfordshire. It was a difficult time of the war and the outcome was still uncertain.

Farrer-Brown recalls, 'It was a very cordial kind of lunch. Nuffield was happy. He suggested in part that with these benefactions he was trying to indicate his belief that ultimate victory would come to this country. We had lunch together and then sat around. It was not a formal meeting. It was coffee after lunch, that kind of atmosphere.' Besides Morris and Farrer-Brown, there were five of the managing trustees (Hetherington and Stopford were absent) plus Hobbs and Hyde. It was agreed that Farrer-Brown would become secretary (a title later changed to director) but until he was released from Government service Hyde would stand in.

The objects of the foundation were four. The advancement of health and the relief of sickness, in particular through medical research and by the organization and development of medical and health services; the advancement of social well-being, which included scientific research; the care and comfort of the aged poor, plus a catch-all clause which specified such other charitable purposes as Lord Nuffield or, after his death, the trustees, might declare in writing.

It was a logical progression from the earlier benefactions but a key issue still remained. How far would Morris himself seek to dominate? In legal terms he had a strong measure of control. At the start he was the only ordinary trustee, but then there were three – himself and two he chose to nominate – initially Hobbs and Goodenough. But technically they only held office subject to his 'pleasure' and any decisions had to be unanimous.

Clark argues that the power vested in the ordinary trustees to reject the annual estimates and to block any individual item gave Morris an iron hand on affairs even if well-prepared argument persuaded him to keep the velvet glove on.[21] Farrer-Brown prefers a different emphasis; Morris didn't devise it; it was the lawyers who put it in.

The independence of the trustees was soon to be tested. At their first formal meeting a lengthy list was circulated of subjects to which Morris wanted them to give special attention. It included scientific research, social medicine, medicine, metallurgy, hospital regionalization and health services, Dominion scholarships, rheumatic research, catarrh research, plastic surgery, homes for the aged, opthalmic research, and interestingly, given his difficult relations at the time, Nuffield College. They were in practice broad categories but they could be said to exclude others and to be putting pressure on the trustees.

Janet Vaughan took up the challenge. She wrote to Farrer-Brown to say, 'Nuffield appointed us as trustees. As trustees we are responsible for how that money is spent ... we cannot be directed by him or anybody else ... if he wanted to arrange what was done with it, then he should have appointed a lot of clerks.'[22]

Other trustees were alarmed too. Goodenough however smoothed a delicate compromise. Arguing that they could scarcely ignore Morris's wishes he suggested that it was 'equally clear' that once disposed of, Morris would be anxious to support the trustees' general policy. The stratagem seemed to work. When £180,000, most of the first year's income, went on the special items, Hyde told the trustees that such a large sum was not quite what Morris had had in mind. 'While he very much hoped that the Foundation would give attention to the four items, he wished the trustees to have available at the present stage an adequate sum for their own ideas.'[23]

It was sophisticated footwork and although various requests continued to be passed on by Morris, there were scarcely any lengthy disagreements, a tribute also to skilful handling by Goodenough and Farrer-Brown. The latter regularly visited Morris to talk over the work of the Foundation and succeeded in gaining his confidence. It was the crucial necessity.

'He accepted me and that was one of the important features of Nuffield; his acceptance of a certain number of people whom he trusted. If he once had doubts about you, you were out. You had to be absolutely frank and honest with him. He respected and accepted that.'

The establishment of the Foundation did not only round off the major programme of bequests. It also marked a resolution for the business of Morris Motors which had produced the money for it. The preamble to the Foundation's Trust Deed had stated that 'those individual resources which can only be built up by private enterprise and which are freely given in the service of the community are a vital factor in the growth of the Commonwealth'. It also tried to preserve Morris's particular private enterprise by recording his wish to preserve 'continuity in the management control and administration of Morris Motors' after his death.

The Foundation was now the largest single shareholder. It had 4.8 million shares worth £10 million. With its formation, Morris no longer held a single share in the company, as he pointed out with some satisfaction to a group of city editors of newspapers a few months after its formation. The shares, like those held in the other trusts, were saleable only in his lifetime and with his consent. He told them, 'I can imagine no circumstances in which the sale of any of the shares would become necessary. When I'm dead the sale of any of the shares is totally precluded.'[24]

He had secured the legal future of the business which still held his interest. Unfortunately however he could not allow those who had chosen to run his business the same freedom and trust accorded to the trustees of the Foundation. They remained his creatures, and his interference would continue to drag the business down.

12   Decline

The Second World War marked a watershed both for Morris Motors and its owner. Before it, the company had seemed to have regained something of its old vigour, with good sales and a successful range with a new Wolseley awaiting launch. Under the hard-working Boden it appeared to have reached stability and export prospects seemed to have revived.

After the war, it was a different story. Although the demand for cars was such that British manufacturers could sell all they made and briefly overtook the United States as the world's leading exporters, Morris Motors was limping in the shadows of the brash competitiveness of Leonard Lord at Austin. Faster off the mark into car production and quick to invest, his Longbridge marked a contrast with the Morris empire where the fading of the old man's drive but unfortunately not his wish to interfere sapped both morale and performance. There was little new investment and Morris first held back the production of the exciting new cars developed without him and then started to shuffle his executives again with a series of arbitrary interventions.

For Morris himself the war had been a turning point. Although he had relinquished day-to-day control some time before, he was still energetically, if irritably, driving ahead with his benefactions and the preparations for war – the manufacturer seeking new pastures, still hammering on the doors of Whitehall. Post-war he was an ageing potentate whose empire was obviously ebbing away. Celebrated, still feted, but unmistakably on the downward slope. Yesterday's man.

There had been personal difficulties for the Morris family from the onset of the war. Widespread bombing was expected and Lilian Morris was terrified of German invasion. She was suffering from a goitre and her doctor advised that she should go away if possible. Morris discussed matters with Macintosh and ended by asking if he would take her to the United States.

Macintosh agreed and on 30 September 1939 the Morrises and the Macintoshes travelled down to Southampton accompanied by Kennerley Rumford. Lilian Morris and Macintosh sailed the following day on the American liner *Washington* on the side of which Macintosh remembered a large American flag being painted to discourage U-boat attack.

Lilian Morris recorded in her diary that there was a calm sea which turned rough after the ship left Bordeaux and then a search for apartments in New York. Macintosh arranged for her to be looked after by the American plastic surgeon, Eastman Sheehan, with whom he had worked in Spain. By 22 October Lilian Morris was reviving and recording in her diary, 'had tea at Ritz with Dr Sheehan and enjoyed it very much'. Macintosh returned to Britain by the American Dixie Clipper flying boat via Lisbon in late October.[1]

Later in the war Sheehan offered his services to the British medical authorities, only to be turned down. Morris's furious reaction was to found another medical chair, of plastic surgery, at Oxford. He insisted, once more to the consternation of the university, on choosing the occupant. T.P. Kilner was chosen deliberately because he knew him to be an opponent of the man who had turned Sheehan down, Sir Harold Gillies. War did not impede politics or Morris's determination to have his way.

Lilian Morris was back in England by early 1943 when her diary would record a succession of dull days, interspersed with parcels from Sheehan containing chocolates, hairnets and pins. February 24 was a different sort of occasion. The diary recorded, '*went to Buckingham Palace afternoon At Home. Talked with Queen, King, Two Princesses*'. The motor agent she had married was now a major figure in the defence of the realm.[2]

Morris had thrown himself into war with vigour. At the onset of conscription in May, before hostilities had begun, he had set up yet another trust – the Nuffield Trust for the Forces of the Crown. Backed with a million Morris Motors stock units, it was intended to improve what facilities existed for the recreation and enjoyment of the services.

While originally intended to help conscripts giving up 'the ordinary course of their civil occupations and their home surroundings', its funds provided for capital spending on sports and social clubs on the one hand and individual items like radio sets for the British Expeditionary Force on the other. It also helped to concentrate service minds on the need to consider welfare provisions as the forces swelled.[3]

At the outbreak of war he supplemented this by a typical piece of morale-boosting. On 30 October 1939 *The Times* recorded that he had given the Overseas League Tobacco Fund £1,000 to provide a million cigarettes for the troops and he stood them another million and a half in December.

But with the bruising failure of the shadow factory project and his personal withdrawal from the RAF repair scheme, the flush of enthusiasm started to subside. He was alone, ageing, and the excursions to Australia to which he looked forward for months were impossible. For the first time in years he was forced to spend all his time in England, and an England of rationing and austerity. The Oxford College to bear his name remained unbuilt and in the hands of men he mistrusted, and apparently without a programme of work. The bad news from the front threatened the destruction of everything he had built. It was unsurprising that Miles Thomas should have noted that Morris, sulking in his tent, as he put it, now started to worry excessively about his health.[4]

Thomas had taken over as Vice-Chairman and deputy to Morris after Boden's death in March 1940. Morris told him he would 'leave it all' to him but would like to know what was going on.[5] Thomas was well aware how careful he still had to be to remain attuned to Morris's wishes.[6]

There was no doubt it was Thomas however, who formally ran the operations of what he now renamed The Nuffield Organisation, whether it was the production of armaments, the repair of aircraft or the design work in snatched moments on new cars. What is remarkable in talking to those in quite senior positions is how little they saw of Morris. James Woodcock, who came to Cowley as Director of Aircraft Repair in early 1940 never met Morris during the war, even when he was a key link with Fighter Command during the Battle of Britain. He finally met him in 1947 after being appointed production manager.

The talented designer Alec Issigonis, working on the new cars for the time the war was over, saw little more of Morris, meeting him perhaps two or three times in his life while shaping the car he thought 'Morris should make'.

Morris's interests seemed to lie more with the schemes for special military engineering projects. He was sought out by

Government for the testing of certain bright ideas and a range of futuristic vehicle designs were drawn up.

There was for example the Salamander, an armoured raiding car with demountable flotation and beach landing gear; Nautilus, an 'auto barge' a bit like an open box which packed flat on shipboard and was powered by the rotating wheels of the lorry it carried; Argosy, a freight ferry on the tracked base of a Churchill tank; and the Firefly tank hunter, an anti-tank gun mounted on a car. They were all featured in a folder marked: 'Special Developments for Combined Operations. Most Secret. Personal to Viscount Nuffield'.[7]

The projects remained on the drawing-board but another new development which had occupied him before the war – the cruiser tank – found itself tested in action, with some embarrassing results for the makers. Christened Crusader, it had helped defend Dunkirk, but when it was sent in numbers for the desert fighting it proved appallingly unreliable, leaking its oil supply into the sand when hot, with a quarter out of action at any time. Nuffield engineers had to be sent to Egypt to make modifications, and although Morris blamed the overcomplication of military design, it was an embarrassing reflection on the organization.

Morris spent some time planning cars for the peace, but he seemed less interested in the revolutionary Mosquito on which Issigonis and Thomas were working than in his old dream of the export car – successor to the ill-fated Empire car, which would sweep across the highways of the Commonwealth. It was an idea which took more than Morris's fancy at the time. The war cabinet's reconstruction committee was considering the future of the motor industry and even floated the idea of a high-powered export car, reporting back that it found little enthusiasm for such a project among manufacturers.

Morris however had definite plans. Pictures and a description exist of the Nuffield Imperial Export Model, a saloon bearing some resemblance to the Morris Oxford launched in 1948, and employing the monocoque construction combining chassis and body which the Issigonis team were developing for the Mosquito.

'Expressly designed to meet the requirements of overseas markets, this new model is the outcome of a carefully planned approach to the export problem. The demand for absolute reliability, high performance, attractive appearance, five seater capacity and economy of running costs have in this well-balanced layout been seemingly fulfilled', said a draft sales pitch.[9]

All doors were arranged to open from the rear, welded joints and door seals were to prevent the entry of dust and it had an 'in-built ventilation system'. 'Deep section flared bumpers give protection fore and aft. Although the design gives an impression of low build, ground clearance is actually eight inches.'

The car, like the Government's own plan for an export model designed at the Ministry of Aircraft Production, was never put into production. The Ministry version, which had a rear engine, was brushed aside by manufacturers including Morris, who was violently opposed to rear engines and also to any suggestions that the British industry should combine to build a single export model. 'I do not believe that Great Britain would sell a single additional motor car overseas if the leading British manufacturers were to co-operate in the production of one common model for export,' he wrote in a letter to the *Sunday Times* in June 1946.[10]

But his own plan fared no better, with his own directors, and he resented it. Attached to the description of the car amongst his papers is a used envelope on the back of which is written in pencil, 'The O.K. on the Imperial was given by me in November 1944. It is now Nov. 1947. Three years after. Nuffield.'[11]

When the war ended there was a determined effort to return to the old normality. There was Ascot. Thomas's daughter, Sheila von Bergen, remembers the preparations for the first meeting after the war. Lilian Morris gave her a silk suit and a hat because she feared she would have nothing to wear. 'She was kind like that.' There was the Motor Show at which Morris would break with his usual gin and it to down a pint of Guinness. There were the resumed winter voyages, at the start of which in another ritual he would drink his other Guinness of the year.

Morris resumed the Australian visits even before the war was over – in early 1945. He was soon deep into plans for a new factory. Tellingly the first post-war expansion of the Nuffield Organisation was to be in Australia, while at Longbridge Lord was hastening to update the production facilities worn and disrupted by war. Morris was soon embroiled in a familiar tussle with Government.

Still seized with the desire to export to Australia, the destination of a third of British motor exports before the war, he had been made aware by the managing director of his operation there, George Lloyd ('George bloody Lloyd' the Macintoshes called him because of his habit of interleaving everything he said with swearwords) of growing pressure against imports. There were already heavy duties on imported vehicle bodies and the demands of the war in the Pacific had given the Australians a taste for their own production which American firms were encouraging.

A 'Preliminary Study for the Commencement of Operations in Australia' apparently drawn up by Lloyd in 1945 envisaged the 'ultimate objective' of full manufacture. But it proposed a step by step approach starting with the assembly of imported chassis with subcontracting of bodies locally instead of 'rushing in ... on the basis of complete car manufacture in an attempt to compete for the present pent up demand with a wholly local car'.[12] Privately Morris expected always to ship out parts from Britain.[13]

The first plan was for the Nuffield Organisation to buy an existing company to build bodies for it. But Morris was lobbied by state governments to establish his own plant. He settled on a site on the old Victoria Park racecourse in Sydney but at the last minute the Sydney Turf Club announced that it might use its legal powers to resume control of the site for racing. The club's powers had been specially devised by the New South Wales Government, which was at the same time pressing Morris to set up. Lloyd sought a ruling on the site and the Government vacillated.

By the time Morris returned to Australia at the start of 1946 no answer had been agreed. The old Morris reasserted himself. An alternative plan was rapidly put into action and a contract signed for the bodies to be built in South Australia by a company called Richards which was already manufacturing some bodies for the organization.

A political storm broke in New South Wales over the loss of the business and the employment it would have brought and it was fuelled by Morris's decision to publish his correspondence with the Government. The *Sydney Morning Herald* of 28 March 1946 reported that the state premier had refused an undertaking that the property would not be resumed for a racecourse, and quoted Morris as saying he was disappointed 'and can only describe the existing position as thoroughly bewildering'. The *Sun*, the evening paper, pilloried the Government in a cartoon, accusing it of preferring racecourses to cars and reporting an opposition censure motion attacking disregard of 'the economic well-being ... accruing from such expansion'.

The *Sun* had joked that the reason for the Government's

hesitation had been that horse-racing was the state's second major industry, 'the order of seniority being brewing, betting, bluffing'. Morris sarcastically stirred the pot by remarking that he knew little about horse-racing, 'nor have I any profound understanding of the influence it exerts to the national advantage in the improvement of the horse as an animal'.[14]

There were unsuccessful attempts to get a change of heart but Morris insisted he had signed the contract. Two years later however the factory was built at Victoria Park and the Nuffield Organisation made a handsome profit, selling some of the land for the development of an industrial estate and making £200,000 on the transfer of the site to its Australian subsidiary in 1951.[14]

It was prime Morris, and back at home he asserted himself again in the direction of the business. He had returned from his 1945 visit to Australia, once more praising the qualities of the British small car in overseas markets. It was slightly confusing given his attachment to the concept of the larger imperial export model, but he had no doubts about what was suitable for the British market and proceeded to override Miles Thomas and his team.

They had been working on a car tentatively named the Morris Mosquito. Its monocoque construction combined both body and chassis and its streamlined appearance had been improved by widening the prototype by five inches. The car had been sawn in half and the two halves gradually inched apart until the aspect satisfied Issigonis, the chief designer, Vic Oak, and their team.

This was the car which would appear as the legendary Morris Minor. Thomas was all for production as soon as the stockpiled supplies for the pre-war Morris Eight were exhausted. But Morris would have none of it. He took a dislike to the car, referring to it as a 'poached egg', but he also argued that with orders pouring in for the Eight, it was pointless to change. Thomas, protesting that the demand for cars was such that customers were ordering several at once in the hope of obtaining one of them, was disillusioned. Ford however, took a similar decision, continuing for the time being with pre-war designs. The Minor was eventually launched with a similarly styled larger car, the Oxford, in 1948.

By then it was apparent that the Nuffield Organisation was not what it had been. The conditions for British motor manufacturers, like most of British industry, were particularly difficult after the war. While there was enormous demand for their products at home and abroad, far more than they could satisfy, production was fraught with every kind of problem.

Power supplies were erratic and sometimes failed altogether. Raw materials were scarce and rationed; labour was increasingly militant and so much in demand that men could leave a factory and find another job within a morning. Machinery was worn out, replacements were scarce and the cost of retooling had escalated. All operations were subject to a degree of Government regulation which it had never experienced in peacetime. The new Labour Government, desperate for foreign exchange, tied steel supplies to export levels, eventually decreeing that only firms which exported three-quarters of their output would be allocated any steel at all.

The Nuffield Organisation coped less well than Austins. Pre-war it had produced a third of all the cars made in Britain; in 1947 it had made less than a fifth – about 50,000 compared with 287,000 in total. It had fallen behind Austin while Ford, coupling its reliance on cheaply produced pre-war models with a determination always to undercut the opposition, was catching up fast. At the Nuffield works, productivity had declined by a third from pre-war levels. It was enough to try the patience of men far more equable than Morris.

Thomas noted;

> Gradually we began to realise that in his increasing disenchantment and dislike of the immediate post-war frustrations of shortages of steel, continuing Government controls, and all the trammels and trappings that chafe a man who has sat, however modestly, on the throne of a dictator, he was an unhappy man. He whose implicit wish became translated into a command to the executives of one of the most successful and fast growing businesses in the country, now had to bow to bureaucratic influences in business. Increasingly Viscount Nuffield busied himself with his philanthropies.[16]

Private life was less comfortable too; the reputation of the generous benefactor was increasingly oppressive even though he could claim that most of his great wealth was now administered by trusts. Thomas's daughter Sheila von Bergen watched the embarrassment at close quarters.

> He went to my brother's school at Stowe. He had never been to a school chapel, and said he would like to, and I remember the frightful conversation before 'how much do I have to give

everyone?' My father took him over and immediately the headmaster was there, suggesting what would be nice, what the school could do with.

When I went up to Oxford for an interview, he wrote me a reference very kindly. But they weren't a bit interested in me, asking 'Does your father have the spending of the Nuffield money?' My answer was, 'No, he only makes it'. I suppose it was always like that for him. I remember him saying that everyone wanted something from him.

There was grumbling at Nuffield and Huntercombe that he could have done more for the village and that he was loath to spend money on maintaining the club. Fine indoor tennis courts, added to the club in pre-war years, were reopened with exhibition matches, but Morris refused to spend money on repairing leaks in the roof and they were allowed to decay. Club members complained that they were expected to stand up when Lady Nuffield entered the room. Harold Hester, the Nuffield Place gardener, who had departed for war with a glowing testimonial from Morris, declined to come back, finding new employers in the village. Visitors to the house increasingly found its rooms swathed in dust sheets.

There is a story of Morris on one of his post-war cruises. On a large Orient liner, he had managed to reach the final of a tournament of the deck tennis he so enjoyed. On the day the weather was rough and it was clear there would be no match – yet he appeared on deck in his shorts and singlet all fired up to play. He had to be persuaded to go below.[17] It could stand as a paradigm of Morris at this time; the old man, fiercely determined to continue as if nothing had changed while the world knew a different story.

Morris was a bitterly jealous man. Thomas noticed the way in the thirties that he did not like his executives to take part in the public affairs of the motor industry, even though he did not wish to do so himself.

> He took a particular dislike to those whom he regarded as his employees, even though they were Board members or even his direct Deputy spending their time taking part in the communal activities of the motor industry. He preferred to influence the industry and its policy by, in effect, going his own way, and expecting others to follow, which towards the later years of his life they failed to do.[18]

Morris had broken with Lord when he had tried to demand greater recognition and reward for his crucial role in the organization. It was the old question of sole control to which Morris was committed, but it was also a question of pride. Now Thomas was to feel the impact of the jealousy with which Morris guarded his preserve.

Thomas's efforts in running the Nuffield Organisation and its huge war production and repair programme had been keenly appreciated by the Government. In 1943 he was knighted and became increasingly a public figure in his own right, finding himself on the selection lists of the good and the great for public appointments. He was asked to conduct an industrial survey of Southern Rhodesia and joined the Board of the Colonial Development Corporation. This was a new experience for Morris, to have one of his own people emerging in his own right on the national stage alongside him, and those close to him noticed how it rankled.

Thomas did not last much longer; a coolness had set in between the two men, and in November 1947 Morris suggested he take his 'freedom'. Morris could argue that Thomas's external interests were distracting him, and that objectively the firm was faltering, though this was partly due to his arbitrary interference. Dr von Bergen says that her father was eventually looking to be sacked. Thomas was soon deputy chairman and then chairman of the British Overseas Airways Corporation which ran the long-haul British air services. Morris turned to Reginald Hanks, a much less assertive figure as his deputy, and initiated a final shake-up.

Thomas was followed by Hans Landstad, Morris's early friend who had been greatly responsible for the design of the original Oxford. Then just before Christmas it was announced that six more directors would depart, among them Victor Riley. It was a clear-out on a grand scale and Morris felt it necessary to explain himself.

On 20 December, the London Evening News carried a lead story declaring that;

Lord Nuffield, 70 year old chief of the Nuffield Motors Empire is an angry man. Today it was announced that managing directors of six of the twenty-one companies associated with his concern have resigned.
'For the first time in my 50 years of commercial and

productive activity I have been accused of favouring a policy of higher prices. Anyone who knows me must know that the very reverse is the case.

'I parted with the resigning directors on the most cordial, friendly terms. We had a lunch together and I remarked how lucky they were to be getting some chance for leisure. Now I see someone says they have walked out on me.

'There is one reason and one reason only for the reorganisation that has taken place. We have a fine lot of young men coming along and they deserve their chance.'

And of his own retirement, 'They are lucky who can. But work suits me. I am feeling fine.'

It was the last exertion of the old lion. The bloodbath was spectacular but it did nothing to slow a rationalization of the industry which was becoming increasingly obvious and increasingly encouraged by the Government. The drift of the Nuffield Organisation into merger with its old rival Austin under Leonard Lord was now only a matter of time.

Apart from the sackings, another significant change had occurred in 1946. Wilfred Hobbs had ceased to be Morris's private secretary, becoming instead the official secretary of the organization. Hobbs, the power behind the throne, could and would take an independent line and stand up to Morris. He was replaced by the respected but more pliant figure of Carl Kingerlee. The effect of the changes was that Morris more than ever dominated his organization.

The industry still faced enormous financial and organizational difficulties, and the companies were fiercely competitive. Joe Edwards was Lord's production director at Longbridge. He would produce careful costings for new models and then present them to Lord. Lord would brush them aside, asking instead, 'What's Bill Morris's price? Put it ten pounds under that.' Lord was intent on his purpose of taking Cowley apart 'brick by bloody brick'.

At the same time the industry's lack of standardization and cooperation was increasingly of concern. It did not just have a proliferation of models, there was an extraordinary variation of parts within them. In 1947, the component manufacturer, Oliver Lucas, invited journalists to his Birmingham factory where he laid out on his factory benches 133 head lamp types and 98 variations of windscreen wipers. Even *Autocar* called it 'manufacturing absurdity'.

On 15 October 1948 the magazine reported a Nuffield-Austin agreement. There would, it said, 'be a constant interchange of information on production methods, costs, purchases, design and research'. The objective was a reduction of costs from the pooling of all factory resources. The deal was grossly exaggerated and, given the hostile attitudes on both sides, was effectively still-born. A year later it was formally abandoned and it was also announced that no merger was contemplated.

For all the bitterness however, Morris and Lord retained an enormous personal respect for each other. Perhaps even more so after his change of management, Morris could appreciate Lord's abilities while Lord would have liked to build on Morris's achievements. A link of some kind made sense, but two immensely proud and touchy men kept themselves apart.

It was Lord who made the first move; Kingerlee who painstakingly developed the contact. He recalled:

> I was in my office one day. The phone just rang normally. It was Len. 'Tell me, isn't it the old man's birthday today?' I said yes. 'Well give him my regards.' I said, 'Don't be damn silly, he's in the next office, tell him yourself.' 'Oh he won't talk to me.' 'Don't be damn silly, of course he will.' I went into his office and said 'Len Lord is on the phone.' 'I'm not going to talk to him.' And I said, 'but you must.' Eventually the Old Man got up and in a minute they were back on the old friendly terms.[19]

Kingerlee seized the opportunity. After further discussions with Lord he suggested that on his way to London he should call at Nuffield Place at about four o'clock when Morris normally had tea – a favourite meal. The meeting broke the ice and Kingerlee was soon ferrying Lord through the back door at Cowley for serious discussions.

But once again, jealousies got in the way, this time not from Morris but his managers. The first scheme was blocked by Hanks and his fellow directors. Hanks argued that if the standardization plans being worked on by the committee of the big six motor manufacturers worked, a merger was unnecessary. But a year later in 1952 the merger of the Nuffield Organisation with Austins to form the British Motor Corporation was announced. Morris became honorary president. Lord was chairman. But the bitterness persisted. Hanks, now vice-chairman, but furious with the deal, said, 'We have been in competition with Austins for a long time, and we shall remain in competition'.[20]

It was a momentous point. Morris had at last, at the age of seventy-five, stepped away from the empire he had built. Merged, it had produced the fourth largest motor corporation in the world. Smaller only than the American big three, it surpassed the empires of the pioneers like Daimler-Benz and Peugeot. It was a tremendous achievement yet the seeds of its effective destruction had already been sown by the resistance to change after the war and the bitterness of the split with Lord.

The merger was never properly consummated – Lord continued to damn Cowley and rubbish its management and the necessary rationalizations and standardizations were not put in train. If Morris had at last settled on an heir, he had done so after first queering the pitch for him. Once more it was the double bind, and neither Morris nor Lord were big enough or whole enough men to overcome it.

Morris continued to use his Cowley office. Woodcock, who succeeded Hanks, was given instructions by Lord that 'whatever you do, don't forget to go and see Lord Nuffield and keep him in the picture'. Woodcock would see him every week. 'He used to come in latish and spend most of the morning in his office. Then he used to join us for lunch in the directors' dining room and at that stage his chauffeur used to call for him and he would go home.

'He was still very interested but always in the past. He could tell every nut and bolt on the first car he ever built but he got to the stage where he would say, "James, what did I say five minutes ago?".'

His medical interest and his hypochondria had continued. Ena Berry had had to bring in his Milk of Magnesia on a silver tray promptly at 3.30 in the afternoon and even doctors could find themselves being put right. Sir John Stallworthy bridled when Morris asked him to examine his sister, Mrs Yockney, but told the doctor that there could be no operation as she had a bad heart. He told Morris bluntly that unless the tumour he had found was dealt with, she was far more likely to die.

Morris then told Stallworthy to remove her appendix as well. At this the surgeon could stand no more. He told Morris that he would either run the operation his way or not at all. Morris replied, 'Terms accepted.'[21]

Meanwhile the stream of honours continued to flow – and so did the benefactions. Although most of his fortune was tied up in trusts and he would announce that his pocket was empty he still distributed significant sums. There was £250,000 for a residential college for the Royal College of Surgeons in 1948, and support for a new headquarters for the Institution of Production Engineers.

Farrer-Brown would drive down to Cowley at least once a week to spend a full morning discussing the affairs of the Foundation. 'I used to go down and say, "We've got this idea, what do you think?" Not to ask his permission but to try and involve him. The idea was that what the Trustees did should not give Nuffield great dismay.' It was a crucial role, particularly after the death of Sir William Goodenough, the great fixer, in 1951.

A significant change in the Foundation came in 1951 with the addition of education to its terms. Grants for educational purposes had already been made under the residual powers but the trustees wanted it to become a more dominant interest. Farrer-Brown remembers Nuffield agreeing without difficulty. The resulting programmes made his name a household word among generations of schoolchildren.

There were moments of difficulty. Morris did not like plans for a nurses' school in Cyprus when independence followed a terrorist campaign, but was reluctantly persuaded, while there was a long, but happily resolved saga over support for the Jodrell Bank radio telescope.

For all his technical interest, Morris had been chary of helping, when the Foundation decided to devote a large proportion of its annual resources to the telescope in 1952. He questioned it particularly as the Government was already providing some funds. Farrer-Brown found himself making little progress until, dredging for arguments, he suggested that the telescope might have a strategic role if directed towards Russia. Morris rapidly consented.

In the end he became an enthusiast for the project. As it continued to require extra funds, the Foundation found ways to help and finally in 1956 Morris provided £25,000 for it to be completed. Characteristically he had suggested that the telescope might be called after him although funds had come from a range of sources; the University of Manchester diplomatically suggested that his name be given to the Jodrell Bank laboratories.

Anything like good relations with the university were much longer in coming. As late as 1958, Morris, working closely with Macintosh, forced the university to promulgate a decree reconstituting the Nuffield Committee for the Advancement of Medicine which oversaw his medical school bequest, reducing its numbers from eighteen to eleven and restricting its activities to post-graduate medical training and research.

Behind it lay a long feud. Macintosh believed strongly that the university, once forced reluctantly to accept a Professor of Anaesthetics had found every excuse to deny the department proper facilities, putting him to the back of the queue to such an extent that he still had not been provided with the purpose built accommodation he had expected. He also resented that undergraduate clinical teaching, begun as a wartime expedient had continued after it, taking resources which otherwise might have been used by his department.

Macintosh had the ear of Morris, who backed him implicitly, allowing him to draft letters for him to sign and even providing him with his own notepaper, headed with a coronet, for his correspondence.

On 18 October 1957, Morris wrote to the Regius Professor, Sir George Pickering, speaking of:

> no little uneasiness because of the dilatory way my Department of Anaesthetics has been handled; sometimes it would appear to me that its requirements have been deliberately shelved. I only hope I shall live to see the Department under my Professor of Anaesthetics established in a building worthy of my name. this sort of treatment has cast no little shadow over the Benefactions which I gave with such joy to this University.

In April a letter to the Vice-Chancellor complained that the Nuffield committee had been increased in numbers and made responsible for administering the undergraduate clinical school 'and still plans for undergraduate clinical training to continue while one of my Nuffield professors – appointed over twenty-one years ago – has no permanent accommodation.'

Other dealings with the university were strained, almost to the point of farce. Sir Raymond Streat was present at a lunch at which the warden of Nuffield College, Henry Clay, managed to praise Lindsay, Butler and Cole. Veale whispered to him, 'This is gall and wormwood to Nuffield, all three are betes noirs as far as he is concerned.'[22] Veale himself was no favourite and the college debated whether to invite him to the opening of the college, breathing a sigh of relief that he was unable to attend the main function.[23]

Reconciliation with the college was a long time coming. Morris agreed to attend a tenth anniversary dinner in November 1947, was cheery, pretending to confuse a Fellow called Loveday with a radio comedian called Lovejoy, but it seemed not to effect the stand-off until the laying of the college foundation stone in 1949. Then Morris unexpectedly rose to speak, announcing that, 'it will give me great pleasure to see some of the plans for the College come to fruition in my time.'[24]

It was Norman Chester, later Sir Norman, who was chiefly responsible for reconciling Morris with the college. Chester, an expert in public administration, had been secretary to the Beveridge Committee and was made a Fellow of the college in 1945, becoming warden in 1954. He set as his targets the completion of the building, the securing of both the college's financial and constitutional independence and the improvement of its relations with Morris.

There was still good reason. As late as January 1955, Kingerlee could write to the *Financial Times* that:

probably Lord Nuffield's greatest disappointment is that the College Of Engineering and Technology that he wished to found in Oxford never came into being ... Ancient traditions and conceptions and departmental jealousies of Universities can be equally as dangerous to the country as they are in Government and even more so in industry, because without industry nations cannot survive ... without trained leaders industry is doomed.[25]

Chester lost no time.

I felt the Founder of the College should be proud of it and on the friendliest terms with it. I quickly started to address him formally as Founder. I wanted him to understand that founding an Oxford College was something different from most of the many bequests he had made. He had joined Walter of Merton, William of Wykeham and those others who continued to be honoured by the various Oxford colleges they had founded over the centuries. The building was important but the foundation was eternal.[26]

It was a fresh and ultimately successful approach. Chester then succeeded in the complex and infinitely difficult task of getting Morris to agree to and approve a biography. Morris had had any number of approaches to write his biography, and he had become increasingly paranoid about the idea – anxious that his version of events should obtain – though even that shifted at different points at his life.

Chester, rather mildly, says:

> Just as he did not like sitting for his portrait so he did not like any article or book claiming to reveal to the public the kind of man he was. Several authors thought they might make some money out of writing his biography but he gave them no help or encouragement. He once recollected that one draft biography started something like 'As he lay in his cradle William Morris dreamed of being a great surgeon'. Poppycock, he said.[27]

In fact Morris used every bit of cajolery and legal threat to prevent books about him appearing at all, even challenging a children's book. Friends and colleagues were warned not to speak to would-be authors. One journalist, Robert Jackson, sent the manuscript of his book to Morris for approval, as suggested by his press advisors. The response was an abusive letter threatening libel action if it was published while the newspaper for which Jackson wrote was warned to expect the withdrawal of the company's advertising if the book were to appear. It had to wait until after Morris's death.[28] There was talk too of legal action over Miles Thomas's autobiography which again would appear after the old man's death.

Chester's shrewd politicking however found an author acceptable to Morris in Philip Andrews, an economist who was a Fellow of the college and had a strong philosophical belief in the importance of the contributions of individuals to business success. He made clear his admiration of Morris. He was assisted by Elizabeth Brunner, of the family that helped found one of ICI's constituent parts, Brunner-Mond, to whom Morris took a liking.

There were strong financial reasons for making up with Morris. Costs for the new building were escalating, and in spite of assistance from the Foundation, it was clear that it could not all be completed. One day in 1959, after lunch in the college, Chester showed Morris the model of the building, carefully covering up the parts for which there was no money for completion.

Morris asked the inevitable question to be told that it would cost another £200,000. He took out an old envelope and wrote £250,000. Then he told Chester, 'I haven't got the money. I'm scraping the bottom of the barrel. I will have to ask the Foundation and they will beat me down.' The Foundation found the £200,000.

Chester became a frequent visitor to Nuffield Place but by now the shadows were drawing in. A collision as he drove out of his drive had led to an agreement with the police that the great manufacturer would not drive again. On 1 May 1959 Morris recorded a rare and rather pathetic diary entry. 'Stopped smoking cigs.' Later in the year Lilian Morris, Lady Nuffield, was taken ill. She was taken to a nursing home where she died three days later. Morris himself had a series of operations including a colostomy and a nurse helped look after him at Nuffield Place. There were still some friends left, Macintosh and the Thomas family with whom friendship had been re-established after a difficult two years following the parting. Lady Thomas, once his secretary, visited every week from her home near Henley.

There was some competition for his residuary estate. Visiting one day, Chester relates that he found Morris asking, 'What is going to happen to this when I go?' 'I was moved by his concern and said, quite simply that the College would be very happy to take over and look after his home when he had gone. Subsequently I talked the matter over with Carl Kingerlee. One of the medical royal colleges had expressed an interest in the house but in the end Nuffield decided in favour of the College.'[29]

It is a disingenuous account. Chester was determined to complete his task of securing the college's future. Macintosh remembered Chester's brisk reply when he suggested that Morris's robes went to the Royal College of Surgeons. 'The medical profession have had enough.'

Morris spent a last holiday in Cornwall with the Thomas family, staying at a hotel in St Mawes with Miles Thomas and uncomplainingly enjoying a regular evening drive with Sheila von Bergen, her four children in the back. But his spirit was ebbing.

Carl Kingerlee said, 'He began closing up in a little shell. After Lady Nuffield died ... doctors kept prodding me to try and get him to take more interest. In the end I had his Power of Attorney ... I used to say, "Lord Nuffield, I would like your opinion on this." He would say, "I don't know what you want it for".'[30]

Chester recalled one of his last detailed conversations.

> We talked about a great variety of things. Oxford had been the last town to offer him the Freedom. They were nonplussed when they found he had been born in Worcester. He had the usual moan about the burden of having money – the many begging letters – mainly from women. We also had a little of the usual – things were not what they were. I happened to mention the peacefulness of Ireland where even the hay was scythed. He hadn't seen this done for years. Everything had changed during the last fifty years (impliedly for the worst). At this I said, 'But haven't you caused a great deal of the change?' Very quietly he replied yes but he had tried to do good with the money he had made. (This seemed to be a point he had thought about.)[31]

There was further surgery, limited convalescence, and then on 22 August 1963, William Richard Morris, first and only Viscount Nuffield, died. According to his instructions the hymn 'Abide with me' was sung at his funeral. His ashes were buried in Nuffield parish church.

In his will, the residue of his estate, proved at over £3 million, went to the college and some remaining motor shares to George Harriman who was running the British Motor Corporation. Otherwise he made one family bequest, £4,500 to his niece Mrs Rawlence, and gave two small gifts of £10,000 each to Worcester and Pembroke colleges in Oxford, which had long before made him an honorary Fellow. For his long-serving housekeeper, Kathleen Francis, there was just £1,000 added by codicil, and there were two bequests for his employees. Alfred Keen received £500, 'as a small token of my recognition of his loyalty to me over very many years.' James Woodcock received £5,000 'in recognition of his loyalty to me and the company.' It was indicative enough of his priorities.[32]

It had been a long and staggeringly successful road. In one interview in 1951 Morris was asked whether he thought his achievement in building up a business so personally owned and controlled could ever be repeated. His reply was that although it might still be possible:

I would say it is impossible to expand as we were able to do in the past, with taxation, restrictions as high as at present, so many people doing as little work as possible for the highest pay in the shortest possible time and then grumbling at the high cost of living. If we do not alter our ways, the foreigner will very soon beat us in the world's markets. This will result in large-scale unemployment.[33]

They were prophetic words.

It seemed a fair assessment given the conditions of the time, and the huge investment costs required by the mature motor industry. But it looks more dated from the perspective of the 1990s when one has seen huge privately controlled business empires created with an international range and an access to international money and tax regimes which were not available to Morris.

For a man who started from such limited resources and narrow horizons, his achievement had been remarkable. Almost alone among the enthusiasts of the fumbling early British motor industry he had understood that all the clever ideas in the world would not keep a company going for long unless translated into practically organized, cost-effective, industrial production linked into what the customer wanted.

For an industry in which one motor company chief once put it to me, 'the standard performance for a British car company was to do badly and go out of business', it was a vital corrective. The pity is that its lessons continued to be disregarded by large parts of British industry, which to this day still puzzles about why it failed to make the most of Great British Inventions.

Morris benefited from the fact that he was not a great original inventor. The unspectacular formula of picking out good ideas from the industry, incorporating, developing and continuously improving them in a framework of careful cost control, evident from his early working papers, demonstrated its strength in the shape of satisfied customers. In some ways it was akin to later Japanese practice. Morris seems a man ahead of his time in his concern for the ordinary customer, and the way in which he encouraged a creation of a new market.

He would have liked that assessment. He saw himself very much as a man of the modern age and the way in which he continually introduced new, and often American ideas, into his factories allowed the motor industry to be one of the few British industrial success stories between the wars. There is something immensely

impressive about the small town cycle maker and motor dealer
climbing up the gangway of the transatlantic liner to seek out the
best ideas of Detroit for the enterprise he was about to start.

When he began, the British industry was still heavily dependent
on foreign imports, from the Continent as well as from the United
States, and no one could match Ford's production achievements.
Between the wars, Ford had to confess itself 'licked in England'
and Americans sometimes looked to the Morris factories for
lessons.

It is difficult to judge what would have happened to the British
motor industry without Morris. Tariff restrictions would have
hampered foreign imports and the American giants were for a
while ambivalent about their intentions in the relatively small
European market. But it is likely that they would have become
more firmly established.

The argument that if it had not been Morris, it would have been
someone else, is an obvious but not altogether convincing line. It
might have been Clyno perhaps or Bean or an Austin developing
differently. The skills of the production engineers on which he
depended could have been available to others. But Morris was the
pace-setter for them and apart from his own production, his
example was of vital importance in improving the performance of
his competitors, and of other industries too.

The pity was that the lessons should have been forgotten by his
successors in the rush for production and the admittedly more
difficult conditions after the war – especially the need for reliability
and careful cost-control. It was the lack of these in particular
which brought about the downfall of the British Motor
Corporation into which the Nuffield Organisation had been
subsumed.

In part Morris was responsible. His quarrel with Lord and the
bitter 'beggar my neighbour' price competition which it spawned
after the war reduced the money available for the investment of
which the industry was starved. But more fundamentally it was his
failure to allow the company to change from a grouping round his
autocratic person to a mature and broad-based organization, with
executives who could take initiatives and develop a trained and
organized succession. British business has been particularly bad at
managing the shift from the idiosyncratic impetus of its founding
fathers to effective corporate structures which can manage change
and bring on new executives to preserve their dynamism. Morris's

refusal to relinquish control ensured the downfall of his company as surely as his tight control at the start had contributed to its success.

For all his remarkable business success and the way he was courted by institutions anxious to put his wealth to better use, Morris remained an outsider. He was unhappy in London, uncomfortable in the common rooms of the university and a clumsy political operator, baffled by the way his simplistic and autocratic approach often failed to persuade in either boardroom or political club. In his business he could rule by diktat rather than committee; in politics he had to withdraw from participation, apart from using the necessarily blunt instrument of contributing money to the parties he favoured.

There was something decidedly unpleasant about the way that Morris used his money as a blunderbuss. His benefactions worked best when they were planned and directed by shrewd and sensitive allies who were able to develop mutual trust and respect. It was due to them that the Nuffield Foundation won and maintained a reputation for supporting forward thinking solutions to modern problems, and the fact that its name remains prominent among practical initiatives is a legacy which would have pleased him.

Morris never escaped his origins, however hard he tried. The irony was that he did not need to; his achievement spoke for itself. He was very much a man of his times and his life and activities mirrored them. His horizons were limited, by his own preoccupations, and he was buffeted by the contemporary enthusiasms and prejudices of his time. His lack of wider perspective made him a political dunce.

He has been described as essentially a Victorian, one of the last paternalistic industrialists, and the argument has much to be said for it. I prefer to see him however, as a creature of a slightly later stage, an Edwardian, a product of a more overblown age when much of the Victorian striving had been replaced by a more complacent feeling that Britannia ruled the waves and much of the world by right.

It was a time of full-blown imperialism, which shaped Morris and which he spent much of his energy struggling to recreate. That was never within his power; yet for all his claim to be at the forefront of the modern world, he could not understand it. For all his huge achievement, he died a disappointed man. He could not adjust to the world he had helped to create.

References

1 Early Years

1 Sir Norman Chester. Note of visit to Nuffield Place, 28 July 1962. Chester papers in Nuffield College.
2 Letter from Edgar Duffield, 22 July 1955. Lord Nuffield papers in Nuffield College.
3 *Autocar*, 17 August 1928.
4 Based on interview with Mrs Rawlence, niece of Lord Nuffield.
5 *Autocar*, 17 August 1928.
6 Rawlence interview.
7 Nuffield Papers, 14/5/1.
8 *Oxford Mail*. Nuffield Centenary competition. Oxford Central Library.

2 Cycle Maker

1 G.C. Allen, *Industrial Development of Birmingham and the Black Country*, London 1966, p. 294.
2 Quoted in F. Alderson, *Bicycling. A History*, Newton Abbot, 1972.
3 D.H. Aldcroft (ed), *The Development of British Industry and Foreign Competition*, London 1968, p. 214.
4 Quoted in J. Woodforde, *The Story of the Bicycle*, London 1970.
5 Interview for BBC television programme *The Carmakers*, 12 October 1971.
6 BBC Home Service programme *The Guv'nor*, 30 December 1955.
7 Nuffield Papers, 6/1.
8 *The Guv'nor*.
9 Miles Thomas, *Out on a Wing*, London, 1964.
10 Nuffield Papers, 14/5/1.
11 *Ibid*.
12 *Ibid*, 16/1/4.
13 *Oxford Mail* competition entry from Mrs R. O'Neill. Oxford Central Library collection.
14 *Nuffield Papers, 16/2/1.*
15 *Daily Mail*, 4 May 1896.
16 Nuffield Papers, 14/5/1.
17 *Oxford Mail* competition. Oxford Central Library.
18 Interview with author.

19 *The Guv'nor.*
20 Nuffield Papers, 16/2/2.
21 *Ibid*, 14/5/30.
22 Miles Thomas. Institution of Production Engineers lecture, 1964.
23 Interview for BBC television programme, *The Carmakers.*
24 *The Guv'nor.*

3   The First Car

 1 Nuffield Papers, 14/5/44.
 2 *The Guv'nor.*
 3 *Autocar*, 17 August 1928.
 4 Nuffield papers, 6/5/3.
 5 *Ibid*, 6/5/2.
 6 Radio Oxford interview.
 7 *The Guv'nor.*
 8 *Oxford Mail* competition entry.
 9 *The Guv'nor.*
10 Nuffield Papers (1905 diary).
11 Radio Oxford interview.
12 Maxcy and Silberston, *The Motor Industry*, p. 12, although it understates number of makes.
13 Nuffield Papers, 14/5/36.
14 *Ibid*, 14/3/33.
15 *The Guv'nor.*
16 M. Adeney, *The Motormakers*, pp. 69-70.
17 Nuffield Papers, 14/5/46.
18 *Light car*, October 1913.
19 *System*, Vol XLV No. 2, February 1924.
20 *The Guv'nor.*
21 *Autocar*, 24 August 1928.
22 Nuffield Papers.
23 *The Guv'nor.*
24 *Ibid.*
25 Radio Oxford interview.
26 *The Guv'nor.*
27 Andrews and Brunner, *The Life of Lord Nuffield*, p. 68.
28 *Autocar*, 2 August 1919.
29 *Oxford Chronicle*, 5 December 1923.
30 Nuffield Papers.
31 *Autocar*, 7 September 1928.
32 Nuffield Papers, 4/11/62.
33 For statistics of the Morris business including financial and production figures see Andrews and Brunner, *op.cit.* p. 341; Overy, *William Morris, Viscount Nuffield*, pp. 128-9; and Jarman and Barraclough, *The Bullnose Morris*, pp. 218-236 (detailed early production figures).

4 The Lessons of War

1 See for example James Leasor, *Wheels to Fortune*, p. 49.
2 *Oxford Chronicle*, 5 December 1923.
3 *The Guv'nor*.
4 By her nephew's wife, Margaret Hawes, for example.
5 Personal cash book in Nuffield Papers.
6 Nuffield Papers, 14/5/72.

5 Triumph

1 Edge, *My Motoring Reminiscences*, pp. 270-1.
2 Also see *London Gazette*, 11 April 1919.
3 *System*, Vol XLV No 2, February 1924.
4 Nuffield Papers, 14/5/75.
5 *Daily Mail* and *Oxford Times*, 28 January 1927.
6 Nuffield Papers, 14/5/82.
7 *Autocar*, 17 August 1928.
8 *Ibid*, 31 August 1928.
9 *The Guv'nor*.
10 Institution of Production Engineers. First Viscount Nuffield Memorial Paper, 18 November 1964.
11 Andrews and Brunner, *op.cit.* p. 101.
12 *The Guv'nor*.
13 *Ibid*.
14 *Out on a Wing*, p. 139.
15 Jackson, *The Nuffield Story*, pp. 77-8.
16 IPE lecture.
17 *Oxford Chronicle*, 30 November 1923.
18 Nuffield Papers, 16/12/1A and 1B. *The Times*, 16 May, 2 and 3 June, 31 July 1924.
19 *Ibid*.
20 R.J. Wyatt, *The Austin*, p. 97.

6 Flying the Flag

1 IPE lecture.
2 Challenging America on production, *Autocar*, 6 February 1925.
3 *Autocar*, 20 November 1925.
4 *Out on a Wing*, p. 153.
5 *System*, *op.cit.*
6 Overy, *op.cit.* pp. 28-9.
7 *Morris Owner 14* (1927), pp. 1403-4.
8 *System*, *op.cit.*
9 *William Morris. Viscount Lord Nuffield*. BBC Home Service, 8 September 1963.
10 Interview for BBC television *Carmakers* programme, 12 October 1971.
11 *Daily Express*, 27 June 1927.

12 Quoted in Adeney, *The Motormakers*, pp. 69, 119-20.
13 *Autocar*, 10 July 1925.
14 *Ibid*, 22 April 1927.
15 *Ibid*, 5 March 1927.
16 Nuffield papers, 14/5/107. Andrews and Brunner, p. 159.
17 BBC Radio Oxford interview in Oxford Central Library.
18 *William Morris. Viscount Lord Nuffield* programme.
19 T.C. Barker, *The Glassmakers*, pp. 349-50.
20 *Out on a Wing*, p. 162.
21 Nuffield papers, 14/5/110.
22 Andrews and Brunner, *op.cit*, pp. 162-74.
23 *Ibid*, pp. 173.

7 Pillar of the Establishment

1 IPE lecture.
2 *Autocar*, 7 September 1928.
3 Interview with Mrs D. Silberston.
4 *Out on a Wing*, p. 133.
5 BBC Radio Oxford interview.
6 IPE lecture.
7 *The Guv'nor*.
8 IPE lecture.
9 Andrews and Brunner, *op.cit*. pp. 126-7.
10 *Out on a Wing*, p. 135.
11 Nuffield papers, 6/1.
12 *Out on a Wing*, p. 142.
13 Interview with author.
14 Interview with Mrs Silberston.
15 Interview with author.
16 James Woodcock in interview with author.
17 *Ibid*.
18 *Out on a Wing*, p. 158.
19 For a discussion of Morris Motors' labour policy see particularly R.C. Whiting, *The View from Cowley*.
20 *Daily Mail* reprinted in *Oxford Times*, 28 January 1927.
21 *Daily Express*, 27 June 1927.
22 *Daily Mail*, *op.cit*.
23 *Oxford Mail*, 2 November 1937.
24 IPE lecture.
25 Adams, *Huntercombe Golf Club 1900-1983*, p. 29.
26 Interview for *The Carmakers*.
27 Interview with Mrs Silberston.
28 *Autocar*, 7 January 1927.
29 Nuffield papers, 5/7.
30 *Autocar*, 10 January 1930.

8 The Political Dimension

1 *Out on a Wing*, p. 176.
2 *Daily Express*, *op.cit.*
3 *Daily Mail*, *op.cit.*
4 Nuffield papers, 16/8.
5 Andrews and Brunner, p. 25.
6 Quoted in Skidelsky, *Oswald Mosley*, p. 228.
7 For a description of Mosley's political development see Skidelsky, *op.cit.* and Colin Cross, *The Fascists in Britain*.
8 Skidelsky, *op.cit.* p. 242.
9 Cross, *op.cit.*
10 18 December 1930, Cross, *op.cit.* p. 44.
11 Oswald Mosley, *My Life*.
12 Ibid, p. 345.
13 *Ibid*, p. 282 and see Skidelsky, *op.cit.* p. 264.
14 *Ibid*, p. 283.
15 Cross, *op.cit.* p.48.
16 *The Times*, 21 July 1934.
17 Skidelsky, *op.cit.* p. 386.
18 For a discussion of the diehard movement and 'The Patriot', see Richard Thurlow, *Fascism in Britain. A History*.
19 Nuffield papers, 10/17/2 and 16/17/6.
20 Morris personal cash book in Nuffield papers.
21 Andrews and Brunner, p. 27.
22 *The Times*, 26 October 1938.

9 Reluctant Delegation

1 *Autocar*, 19 April 1923.
2 Maxcy and Silberston, *The Motor Industry*, p. 100.
3 Andrews and Brunner, *op.cit.* p. 194.
4 *The Economist*, 7 December 1935, p. 1152.
5 Birmingham Motor Cycle Club Dinner 1922.
6 Wyatt, *op.cit*, p. 119.
7 *Out on a Wing*, pp. 166-7.
8 IPE lecture.
9 *Out on a Wing*, p. 166.
10 *Autocar*, 6 January 1928.
11 *Ibid*, 27 April 1928.
12 Andrews and Brunner, *op.cit*, p. 170.
13 Interview for *The Carmakers*.
14 Andrews and Brunner, *op.cit*, p. 187.
15 *Out on a Wing*, p. 168.
16 Maxcy and Silberston, *op.cit*, p. 106.
17 IPE speech.
18 *The Economist*, 31 October 1936, p. 196.
19 *Out on a Wing*, p. 180.
20 *Ibid*, pp. 172-3.

21 Nuffield papers, 5/11.
22 Nuffield papers, 44/2.
23 Interview for BBC's *All Our Working Lives*.
24 Quoted in F. Wilson McComb, *The Story of the MG Sportscar*.
25 *The Economist*, 7 December 1935.
26 *The Guv'nor*.
27 Interview for BBC's *The Carmakers*.
28 *Out on a Wing*, p. 181.
29 Nuffield papers, 16/22.
30 *The Economist*, 3 November 1934.
31 Nuffield papers, 16/23.
32 News agency report quoted in *Sydney Morning Herald*. Nuffield papers, 16/20/A.
33 *Ibid*.
34 *Ibid*.
35 *The Economist*, 31 October 1936.
36 Nuffield papers, 16/24.
37 Andrews and Brunner, *op.cit*. pp. 228-30.
38 Nuffield papers.
39 Institution of Production Engineers 14th annual dinner.
40 Nuffield papers, 16/24.
41 *The Economist*, 7 December 1935.
42 *Out on a Wing*, p. 168.
43 Radio Oxford interview.
44 *The Economist*, 13 May 1939. See also *A note on the Policy of His Majesty's Government* in relation to the production of aero-engines. CMD 5295.
45 *Out on a Wing*, p. 204.
46 A.J.P. Taylor, *Beaverbrook*, pp. 422-3.
47 IPE lecture.

10   Town and Gown

 1 *Oxford Magazine*, 5 December 1963. pp. 124-5.
 2 R.C. Whiting, *The view from Cowley*, pp. 5-6ff.
 3 *Daily Express*, 27 June 1927.
 4 Nuffield Papers, 14/5/29.
 5 *Ibid*, 4/4/1-2.
 6 Undergraduate anecdote.
 7 *The Times*, 15 May 1934.
 8 Andrews and Brunner, *op.cit*. pp. 273-4.
 9 Betjeman, *A University Chest*. Jackson, *The Nuffield Story*, pp. 164-5.
10 *The Guv'nor*.
11 Smith, *St Peter's. The founding of an Oxford College*, p. 23.
12 *Ibid*, pp. 49-50.
13 *Ibid*, pp. 178-80, 190, 193 and 235-8.
14 A detailed account is given by Sir Douglas Veale in Dewhurst (ed), *Oxford Medicine*, pp. 143-9 and see also pp. 162-4.
15 Ruprecht, van Lieburg, Lee and Erdmann, *Anaesthetics. Essays on its*

History, pp. 354-5. Springer-Verlag Berlin, 1985.
16 *Dewhurst, op.cit.* p. 145.
17 Chester, *Economics, Politics and Social Studies in Oxford*, p. 73.
18 Scott, *A.D. Lindsay*, p. 229.
19 *Ibid*, p. 232.
20 *Ibid*, p. 231.
21 Chester, *op.cit.* p. 65. Oxford University archives NH/1.
22 *Ibid.*
23 *Oxford Mail*, 13 October 1937.
24 University archives, NH/4f p. 2. Quoted in Chester *op.cit.*
25 Author's interview with Mrs Hawes. Chester, *op.cit.* p. 109.
26 University archive, N/41f, p. 72, quoted in Chester *op.cit.* p. 89.
27 *Ibid.*
28 Chester *op.cit.* p. 99. University archive NH/2/1/1.
29 *Ibid.*
30 Hebdomadal Council papers 185, pp. lxxix-lxxx and xciii.
31 Nuffield papers.
32 University archive, NH 2/1, p. 33.

11 Towards the Foundation

 1 Hobbs' letter to Revd Christopher Chavasse, 27 November 1930.
 2 *Daily Express*, 27 June 1927.
 3 Hobbs' letter, *op.cit.*
 4 *Out on a Wing*, p. 210.
 5 Dewhurst, *Oxford Medicine*, p. 142.
 6 IPE lecture.
 7 *Ibid.*
 8 The Nuffield Provincial Hospitals Trust. A report, 1939-48.
 9 Letter to Mrs Silberston, 27 March 1983.
10 Speech at Guy's Hospital, 3 October 1934.
11 18 January 1944.
12 *Ibid.*
13 Dewhurst, *op.cit.* p. 154.
14 Interview with Mrs Silberston.
15 *The Guv'nor.*
16 Dewhurst, *op.cit.* pp. 140-1. *Oxford Medical School Gazette*, 1958, Vol 10, p. 23.
17 *Daily Express*, 27 June 1927.
18 Clark, *A Biography of the Nuffield Foundation*, pp. 1-15.
19 Interview with author.
20 Clark, *op.cit.* p. 9.
21 *Ibid*, p.10.
22 *Ibid*, p. 21.
23 *Ibid*, pp. 22-3.
24 *Ibid*, p. 7.

12   Decline

1 Nuffield papers, 36/3-11.
2 *Ibid.*
3 Andrews and Brunner, *op.cit.* p. 319.
4 *Out on a Wing*, pp. 205, 209.
5 *Ibid*, p. 204.
6 IPE lecture.
7 Nuffield papers, 5/5.
8 Adeney, *op.cit.* pp. 192-3.
9 Nuffield papers, 5/9/1.
10 Jackson, *op.cit.* p. 237.
11 Nuffield papers, 5/9/1.
12 *Ibid*, 5/8.
13 Adeney, *op.cit.* p. 210.
14 Andrews and Brunner, *op.cit.* p. 246.
15 Nuffield papers, 5/11.
16 IPE lecture.
17 Jackson, *op.cit.* p. 230.
18 IPE lecture.
19 *The Carmakers.*
20 Wyatt, *op.cit.*
21 Interview with Mrs Silberston.
22 M. Dupree, *Lancashire and Whitehall. The Diary of Sir Raymond Streat*, Manchester University Press, 1987.
23 Chester papers, 279. File D. Lord Nuffield. Some personal recollections, p. 6.
24 *Ibid.* p. 3.
25 *Financial Times*, 15 January 1955.
26 Chester papers, *op.cit.* p. 3.
27 *Ibid*, p. 4.
28 Jackson, *op.cit.* p. 23.
29 Chester papers, *op.cit.* p. 9.
30 Radio Oxford interview.
31 Chester papers. Note of a visit to Nuffield Place, 28 July 1962.
32 *The Guv'nor.*
33 BBC radio programme, *Morris; motors and millions*, 1977.

Bibliography

Adams, John. *Huntercombe Golf Club 1900-1983*, Henley, 1984

Adeney, Martin. *The Motormakers*, London, 1988

Aldcroft, D.H. (Ed.) *The Development of British Industry and Foreign Competition 1875-1914*, London, 1968

Alderson, Frederick. *Bicycling: a history*, Newton Abbott, 1972

Allen. G.C., *Industrial development of Birmingham and the Black Country*, London 1966

Andrews, P.W.S. and Brunner, E. *The Life of Lord Nuffield. A Study in Enterprise and Benevolence*, Oxford, 1955 (This book includes tables of financial results of the Nuffield businesses and a list of benefactions over £10,000.)

Barker, T.C. *The Glassmakers*, London, 1977

Barnett, Corelli. *The Audit of War*, London, 1986

Betjeman, John. *An Oxford University Chest*

Bryce-Smith, B. Mitchell, J.V. and Parkhouse, J. *The Nuffield Department of Anaesthetics*, Oxford, 1963

Buist, H. Massac. *W.R. Morris. The Man and the Romance*, *Autocar*, 17, 24, 31 August and 7 September 1928

Clark, R.W. *A Biography of the Nuffield Foundation*, London, 1972

Cross, Colin. *The Fascists in Britain*, London, 1961

Dewhurst, K. (Ed.) *Oxford Medicine*, Oxford, 1970

Dupree, M. *Lancashire and Whitehall. The Diary of Sir Raymond Streat*, Manchester University Press, 1987

Edge, S.F. *My Motoring Reminiscences*, London, 1935

Edwards, H. *The Morris Motor Car. 1913-1983*, Ashbourne, 1983

Foreman-Peck, J. *A History of the World Economy. International Economic Relations since 1850*, London, 1983

Foreman-Peck J. *The American Challenge of the Twenties. Multinationals and the European Motor Industry. Journal of Economic History. Vol 42*, 1982, pp. 865-881

Hull, Peter. *Lord Nuffield*, 1977

Jackson, Robert. *The Nuffield Story*, London, 1964

Jarman, L.P. and Barraclough R. *The Bullnose Morris*, London, 1965 (This book has detailed tables for early Morris production.)

Lacey, Robert. *Ford*, London, 1986

McComb, F. Wilson. *The Story of the MG Sportscar*, London, 1972

Maxcy G. and Silberston A. *The Motor Industry*, London, 1959

Morris, W.R. *Policies that have built the Morris Motor Business, System* Vol XLV, No 2, February 1924

Mosley, Nicholas. *Rules of the Game*, London, 1982

Mosley, Sir Oswald. *My Life*, London, 1968

Nixon, St J. *Wolseley*, London, 1949

Nockolds, H. Lucas. *The First 100 Years*, London, 1976

Overy, R.J. *William Morris, Viscount Nuffield*, London, 1976 (This book collects together tables on production, employment and financial performance of the Morris businesses.)

Pagnamenta P. and Overy, R.J. *All Our Working Lives*, London, 1984

Political and Economic Planning. Motor Vehicles. A report on the Industry, London, 1950

Plowden, W. *The motor car and politics in Britain*, London, 1971

Ponder, W. *Clara Butt. Her Life Story*, London, 1928

Rhys, D.G. *The Motor Industry. An Economic Survey*, London, 1972

Rhys, D.G. *Competition in the Interwar Motor Industry, Journal of Transport History*, Vol III, No 4, September 1976

Richardson, K. *The British Motor Car Industry. A Social and Economic History*, London, 1977

Rupreht, J., van Lieburg, M.J., Lee, J.A. and Erdmann, W. (Eds) *Anaesthesia. Essays on its history*, Berlin, 1985

Saul, S.B. *The Motor Industry in Britain to 1914*, Business History, December 1962

Skidelsky, Robert. *Oswald Mosley*, London, 1975

Smith, Eric, H.F. *St Peter's. The Founding of an Oxford College*, Gerrards Cross, 1978

Stallworthy, Sir John. *Si Monumentum Requiris, Circumspice*, Viscount Nuffield Memorial Paper, Institution of Production Engineers, 1974

Taylor, A.J.P. *English History 1914-45*, Oxford, 1965

Taylor, A.J.P. *Beaverbrook*, London, 1972

Thomas, Miles (Lord Thomas of Remenham). *Out on a Wing*, London, 1964

— *First Viscount Nuffield Memorial Paper*, Institution of Production Engineers, 1964

Whiting, R.C. *The View from Cowley*, Oxford, 1983

Woodforde, J.R. *The Story of the Bicycle*, London, 1970

Woollard, F.G. *Challenging America on Production*, Institution of Automobile Engineers. Reprinted in *Autocar*, 6 February 1925

Wyatt, R.J. *The Austin. 1905-52*, London, 1981

Index